RELIGION

in the

LIVES

of

AFRICAN
AMERICANS

A number of people have been instrumental in shaping
the direction of our personal and professional lives.
Robert Joseph Taylor and Linda Chatters dedicate this book
to the memory of Mrs. Willie H. Taylor, Reverend Walter
R. Murray, Jr., and Mrs. Thelma Murray, who were true
embodiments of the meaning of lived faith. Jeff Levin
dedicates this book, with love, to his wife, Lea.

RELIGION
in the
LIVES
of
AFRICAN
AMERICANS

Social, Psychological, and
Health Perspectives

ROBERT JOSEPH TAYLOR
UNIVERSITY OF MICHIGAN

LINDA M. CHATTERS
UNIVERSITY OF MICHIGAN

JEFF LEVIN

DISCARD
LCCC LIBRARY

SAGE Publications
International Educational and Professional Publisher
Thousand Oaks ■ London ■ New Delhi

For information:

Sage Publications, Inc.
2455 Teller Road
Thousand Oaks, California 91320
E-mail: order@sagepub.com

Sage Publications Ltd.
6 Bonhill Street
London EC2A 4PU
United Kingdom

Sage Publications India Pvt. Ltd.
B-42, Panchsheel Enclave
Post Box 4109
New Delhi 110 017 India

Printed in the United States of America

Library of Congress Cataloging-in-Publication Data

Taylor, Robert Joseph.
Religion in the lives of African Americans: Social, psychological, and health perspectives / Robert Joseph Taylor, Linda M. Chatters, Jeff Levin.
    p. cm.
Includes bibliographical references and index.
ISBN 0–7619–1708–X (cloth)—ISBN 0–7619–1709–8 (pbk.)
    1. African Americans—Religion. I. Chatters, Linda M.
II. Levin, Jeffrey S. III. Title.
BR563.N4T387 2004
200.´89´96073—dc21

                                    2003009117

03   04   05   06   10   9   8   7   6   5   4   3   2   1

Acquisitions Editor:	Jim Brace-Thompson
Editorial Assistant:	Karen Ehrmann
Production Editor:	Melanie Birdsall
Copy Editor:	Kristin Bergstad
Typesetter:	C&M Digitals (P) Ltd.
Proofreader:	Mary Meagher
Indexer:	Teri Greenberg
Cover Designer:	Sandra Ng Sauvajot

Contents

Foreword

The publication of *Religion in the Lives of African Americans: Social, Psychological, and Health Perspectives* reflects the fruition of several areas of inquiry that began close to 20 years ago. Beginning in the mid-1980s, Taylor and Chatters initiated a line of research that investigated issues of church-based social support networks using data from the National Survey of Black Americans (Taylor & Chatters, 1986a, 1986b, 1988). This was followed by other publications that expanded their program of research to examine the antecedents and consequences of religious involvement among diverse segments of this population group. Jeff Levin, a former student of the late Dr. C. Eric Lincoln, the preeminent scholar of black religious life, began his career by investigating the role of the Black Church and pastors for the health and well-being of African Americans (Levin, 1984, 1986). He subsequently went on to author several seminal pieces on religious factors in physical and mental health, effectively establishing the field of "the epidemiology of religion" (Levin & Vanderpool, 1987). As luck would have it, Levin came to the University of Michigan for postdoctoral studies with the Institute of Gerontology in the late 1980s, where Taylor and Chatters were faculty members in the Schools of Social Work and Public Health, respectively. The three began discussing mutual research interests and possible projects, thus initiating a long and productive collaboration and friendship.

This convergence of events could not have occurred at a more opportune time. Despite an established body of literature on African American religion and religious traditions, there had been few, if any, systematic empirical investigations that explored these questions within study samples that adequately represented the black population. In the absence of reliable data, the commonplace assumption within the social and behavioral sciences was that black people, as a group, were uniformly religious in their overall worldviews and that a deeply held religious orientation influenced their perceptions and attitudes on a wide range of issues and concerns. Further, black religious life was typically characterized in a variety of ways that ranged from condescending to overtly pejorative.

Scholarly discourse on the nature, antecedents, and consequences of religious involvement among African Americans was particularly limited, relying heavily on the notion that social deprivations in broader society functioned to motivate and sustain involvement in and attachment to black religious traditions and meaning systems. The implication perhaps being that social advancement and progress would result in significant shifts in religious orientation and preference among African Americans and an abandonment of black religious traditions. As a number of critics observed (see, e.g., Lincoln & Mamiya, 1990), these portrayals of black religious life were deficient in several respects and especially in failing to consider religious expression as a dynamic entity changing with the historical context of black lives. Particularly egregious was the assumption that black religious sentiment and belief was virtually monolithic and devoid of distinctions arising from factors such as social class, region, gender, and socioeconomic status. Coupled with this stereotypical portrayal of black religious expression were equally injurious notions within academic and scientific circles concerning the meaning and use of religion more generally. Levin (1994c) has written extensively about ideological and professional resistance to the serious consideration of religious phenomena by social, behavioral, and health scientists, even in the face of a substantial body of evidence that religion has verifiable effects on health and social behaviors.

Throughout their careers, the coauthors of this volume routinely questioned and critiqued these outmoded perspectives on religion in the lives of African Americans and made important contributions to the systematic and empirical study of the religious experiences of African Americans. Their combined backgrounds and expertise span the disciplines of sociology, psychology, and epidemiology, as well as the fields of gerontology, religious studies, social work, and public health. Their research and approach are firmly positioned within and informed by established theories and models in the social and behavioral sciences. Further, their inquiries have pushed the boundaries of these theories and models in ways that enlarge their scope and depth. Thus their work encompasses both a deeper appreciation of the potential role of religious content and meaning in all aspects of African American life, as well as an understanding of the unique ways that individual and social factors function to pattern and distinguish religious behavior and belief *within* this group.

As these comments suggest, Taylor, Chatters, and Levin bring a unique perspective and focus to their work that has done much to change the face of research on these topics. First, they have argued for conceptual clarity in treatments of religion that embodies an appreciation for a broad and diverse conceptualization of religion. Accordingly, their work has been at the forefront of efforts to understand religious involvement as a multidimensional construct and in exploring both the antecedents and consequences of diverse religious phenomena. So, in addition to the examination of religious beliefs, behaviors, and attitudes among African Americans, they have also explored issues of church-based support networks, religious coping efforts, negative interaction in the church, and the connections and pathways by which religion is linked to physical and mental health outcomes.

Second, they have embraced a standard of methodological rigor in their research that has moved the field beyond a focus on simple bivariate associations to explore the combined and independent effects of a variety of personal, social, and situational factors on religious phenomena. Because much of this work has been conducted using nationally representative samples of African Americans, their results complement and enhance prior efforts that have focused primarily on particular geographic localities and religious communities. This approach has uncovered both important commonalities and differences in religious experience across various segments of the African American population, revealing that while religion and its institutions are indeed important for African Americans, there is significant variability in religious expression on the basis of factors such as age, gender, and region.

Third, they have situated their research questions and the interpretation of study findings within the context of the lived experiences of African Americans. This is most evident in the present volume, which incorporates information from a series of focus group discussions with African American adults ("Appraisals of Religiosity, Coping and Church Support") about issues and concerns that have been the subject of theoretical speculation and survey analysis. In this way, theory and conceptual models of religion and its effects, established survey research findings on religious involvement, and the themes that are identified in the focus group narratives all function to inform and refine one another. This multimethod approach brings several different individual perspectives to bear on these questions, collectively representing the religious lives of African Americans with greater authenticity and nuance.

Finally, over the course of their careers, Taylor, Chatters, and Levin have placed a premium on using their research and writings to engage, encourage, and mentor other scholars and students interested in the empirical investigation of religion and its effects on social, psychological, and health outcomes. Their published work has been cited and read extensively by researchers, students, and clergy who are committed to understanding the nature and meaning of religion for African Americans. The value of the present volume will be evident in its ability to reach a diverse audience of researchers, practitioners, and students in the social and behavioral science disciplines, the health and social welfare professions, graduate seminary programs, and members of the clergy. This book will provide each of these groups with the clear and indisputable message that religion and its effects on social, psychological, and health factors profoundly influences the individual and family lives of African Americans.

—James S. Jackson, PhD
Daniel Katz Distinguished University Professor of Psychology
Director, Program for Research on Black Americans
Research Center for Group Dynamics, Institute for Social Research
Director, Center for Afro-American and African Studies
The University of Michigan, Ann Arbor

Acknowledgments

We have been fortunate to have a number of individuals, groups, and organizations that have been important in supporting the development of this volume. The Program for Research on Black Americans has been a constant source of support and encouragement for our research efforts described in this book. We are especially appreciative of Dr. James S. Jackson, Director of the PRBA, for his constant encouragement and support in this and other scholarly efforts. Special thanks to Dr. Susan Frazier-Kouassi for her friendship and support in our efforts.

We would like to thank James S. Jackson, Belinda Tucker, Phillip Bowman, and Gerald Gurin, who had final authority over the content of the National Survey of Black Americans. Their foresight to include an entire section on religious participation was instrumental in fostering the exponential growth of survey research investigations on the role of religion in the lives of Black Americans. We want to thank Debbie Coral for her help with the analysis of the National Survey of American Life, and Myriam Torres, Julie Sweetman, and Carolyn Pappas for their dedicated work on this survey. Drs. Taylor and Chatters also would like to thank many of the senior scholars who provided advice and assistance during the early stages of their careers, including Drs. Lawrence Gary, Harriette McAdoo, Phillip Bowman, Belinda Tucker, Peggye Dilworth-Anderson, and Vickie Mays.

We thank, also, a number of individuals who were involved in the focus group study, "Appraisals of Religiosity, Coping and Church Support," which forms a portion of the research reported in this book. Thanks to Dr. Karen D. Lincoln, Carol Burrell-Jackson, Phyllis Stillman, and Tamara Middleton, who gave tirelessly to the successful completion of this project. Special thanks to Drs. Harold W. Neighbors and Jacqueline Mattis for their efforts in the development of the focus group protocol, work on the code scheme, and providing critical feedback on research ideas. Additional thanks to Jacquie for her reviews and comments on earlier drafts of portions of the book. Special thanks also to Khari Brown, who assisted in the focus group study, conducted a major portion of the data analysis, commented on earlier drafts of several chapters, and assisted with the bibliographic search and compilation of references.

Several grants from the National Institute on Aging and the National Institute of Mental Health supported the background research on religious involvement conducted by the authors, as well as the overall development and preparation of this volume. The National Institute on Aging funded the grant, "Church-Based Assistance and Older Blacks" (R01 AG18782), Linda Chatters, Principal Investigator, and Robert Joseph Taylor and Christopher G. Ellison, Co-Principal Investigators. Linda Chatters gratefully acknowledges the support provided to her as Co-Investigator on the NIA grant, "Religion, Health and Aging" (R01 AG 14749), Neal Krause, Principal Investigator. Support was also provided to Robert Joseph Taylor as Co-Investigator with the Michigan Center for Urban African American Aging Research (MCUAAAR) (P30 AG15281), James S. Jackson, Principal Investigator. Data collection for the National Survey of American Life was funded by support from the National Institute on Mental Health grant, "National Survey of African American Mental Health" (U01 MH57716), James S. Jackson, Principal Investigator, Robert Joseph Taylor, Co-Principal Investigator. The development, data collection, and analysis of the focus group study, "Religiosity, Coping and Church Support," was conducted under the auspices of the program project grant "African American Mental Health Research Program" (PO1 MH58565), James Jackson, Principal Investigator. Robert Joseph Taylor was the Principal Investigator of the focus group study, and Linda Chatters, Jacqueline Mattis, and Harold Neighbors were Co-Principal Investigators. We especially appreciate the encouragement and support of Dr. Emeline Otey of the National Institute of Mental Health for her work with the African American Mental Health Research Program and Dr. Sid Stahl of the National Institute on Aging and his work with the Michigan Center for Urban African American Research (MCUAAR) at the University of Michigan and Wayne State University.

Robert Joseph Taylor and Linda Chatters give special thanks to their children, Harry Owen Chatters Taylor and Mary Louise Chatters Taylor, for graciously accepting the fact that for several very intense months, all of life seemed to revolve around "the book." Preserving the appropriate balance between family and work life has required that we constantly review our priorities and values and our sense of what is really important in life. We hope that we have shown, by example, that love and conscious and committed involvement in family life enrich and give meaning to work. Jeff Levin wishes to thank his wife and partner, Lea Steele Levin, for all of her love and support as he focused his energies on completing this project.

We would like to thank the women and men who comprised the corps of interviewers and who worked diligently to collect the data that have provided the basis for this research. Interviewing is an extremely difficult profession that requires perseverance and methodological rigor. Interviewers spend a considerable amount of time in the home of a person whom they have never met, and interview respondents under sometimes less-than-ideal circumstances. Finally, we are especially indebted to the African American men and women who participated as respondents in the various data collection efforts that form the basis of this book. Respondents in the National Survey of Black Americans, the subsequent waves of data collection from the initial study, and the new National Survey of American Lives have made an immense contribution to social science knowledge on religion among this population group. Similarly, the participants in the focus group study, "Appraisals of Religiosity, Coping and Church Support," provided a unique and unparalleled portrait of the ways in which religion influences various aspects of life for African Americans. In participating in the study, they entrusted us with their innermost thoughts and feelings about the role of religion in their lives. We felt it was our personal and professional duty and responsibility to relate their stories with honesty, integrity, and dignity. We hope that we have done so. To all of our respondents and interviewers we extend our deep and sincere appreciation.

Chapter 1

Introduction

Since the early 1900s, there has been ongoing academic interest in the nature, patterns, and functions of religion in the lives of African Americans (see, e.g., Du Bois, 1903) that is reflected in the scholarly traditions of fields as diverse as African American studies, African American history, religious studies, and the sociology of religion. The topic of religion in the lives of African Americans has an enduring fascination, partly because of the apparent pervasiveness and persistence of the religious context for this population group. Black religious traditions have persisted over time, geographic location, and social context and circumstance. Although their distinguishing characteristics and features have changed and adapted in response to external forces and diverse social contexts, the black religious tradition and the Black Church have remained pervasive and central features in the lives of individuals, families, and communities.

Close to 20 years ago, sociologist Jacquelyne J. Jackson (1983) commented on the myths and generalizations surrounding black religion and the lack of systematic research on this topic. We agree with this assessment and further posit that the relative lack of systematic information about religion and religious participation among black Americans is attributed to several factors. For the most part, there was very little survey research on this topic. On the whole, survey researchers were not concerned with investigating religious matters, or had only a cursory interest in behaviorally focused topics like denominational affiliation and church attendance. Individuals who were fully versed in black religion tended to be either theologians (i.e., Cone, 1985) or social historians (Lincoln & Mamiya, 1990) who were concerned with exploring the development and growth of black religious expression (e.g., growth and expansion of particular denominations, development of black theology). These scholars contributed importantly to our historical understanding of black religion and its development but did not possess the skills, expertise, or inclination to conduct survey research. In addition, this impressive body of research investigated the church as the unit of analysis (e.g., role of the Black Church in contemporary society), whereas the work presented in this volume examines the individual as the unit of analysis (e.g., frequency of prayer [Chapter 3], frequency of church attendance [Chapter 2], the role of prayer in coping with a stressful life event [Chapter 4], religious participation and life expectancy [Chapter 8], religious participation and mental well-being [Chapter 9]).

Those survey efforts that did assess religious involvement typically contained no more than two or three religious items, usually those related to church attendance and denomination. One exception to this was the General Social Surveys, which often included several questions about religion but, like most national surveys of the population, contained a small number of black respondents, thus limiting the generalizability of study findings. The National Survey of Black Americans (NSBA) was clearly a turning point in survey research efforts to assess religious involvement. Its incorporation of a full complement of items on religious involvement (i.e., organizational, non-organizational, and subjective religiosity) represented a marked improvement over prior efforts. In addition, the NSBA's use of a nationally representative sample of adult blacks offered the opportunity to explore how religious involvement varied across important social and demographic groups and generated findings that could be applied to the broader African American population.

When we began our investigations of church support among African Americans using survey data from the NSBA, we were surprised to discover that the topic had not been previously addressed in the literature. Furthermore, when researching the topic of religious participation among blacks, we were similarly surprised that there were few prior survey-based studies in this area (one notable exception being Nelsen & Nelsen, 1975). This was despite the fact that numerous scholars had written about the historic importance of the supportive functions of the Black Church in the face of a frequently hostile social and economic environment and the role of the church as a focal point of community life. The state-of-the-literature at that time was characterized by several informative social histories and narratives on religion and the role of the Black Church, as well as ethnographic studies of individual religious communities.

To a large extent, the field of gerontology has been at the forefront of efforts to explore the role of religion in the lives of Americans. A number of professional journals in gerontology (e.g., *Journal of Gerontology: Psychological Sciences* and *Journal of Gerontology: Social Sciences, The Gerontologist, Journal of Aging and Health*) have published research examining the nature and extent of religious involvement and its association with a variety of social indicators and quality-of-life outcomes, such as measures of health and well-being. Further, the National Institute on Aging, a branch of the National Institutes of Health, has provided significant federal funding for empirical research on religion among the African American population. Despite significant increases in the volume of research focusing on the role of religion in American life, however, relatively few efforts have rigorously and systematically explored these questions within the African American population.

Over the past 30 years, only a handful of books have used survey research methods to explore the role of religion in African American life. The most prominent is Lincoln and Mayima's (1990) *The Black Church in the African American Experience,* a very useful and thorough investigation of the historical and contemporary role of churches in African American communities. Similarly, Nelsen, Yokley, and Nelsen's 1971 book, *The Black Church in America,* provided important insights into the nature of the Black Church. Andrew Billingsley's 1999 volume, *Mighty Like a River: The Black Church and Social Reform,* provides an in-depth, socio-historical study of two Southern black congregations as part of his overall classification scheme for black churches. These and other efforts that involve historical, ethnographic, or theological accounts of black religion and the Black Church constitute an important foundation of leading scholarship on these concerns. To date, however, there has been no volume that specifically explores the role of religion as it relates to the behaviors, attitudes, and perceptions of African Americans. The perspective represented in this book is an important departure from and extension of past efforts.

As authors of the present volume, we have conducted research on the role of religion in African American life for more than 20 years, both as members of a collaborative research team and as individual investigators. Collectively, we have conducted research that has (a) explored the structure and sociodemographic correlates of religious involvement, (b) examined the role of religion with respect to health and well-being outcomes, (c) investigated issues of church support and use of ministers in response to personal difficulties, and (d) explored the role of religion within specific subgroups (i.e., older adults, women) of the African American population. This book and our collaborations as a research team reflect our interdisciplinary academic and professional backgrounds, which include sociology, psychology, social work, public health, epidemiology, and religious studies. We bring these combined perspectives and experiences to bear in addressing the topics that are explored in this book.

Goals for the Book

We have several goals in writing this book that are reflected in our approach to the subject matter and the overall format of the book. First, the approach taken in the book is to review recent theoretical and empirical literature in the social, behavioral, and health sciences on selected topics related to the role of religion in the lives of African Americans. Previous books, because they have typically focused on black churches, did not examine the impact of religion on individual processes and outcomes (e.g., religious participation, religion and physical health, religion and mental health). Further, only a few earlier efforts have examined the role of religion for African Americans within an explicit research framework. We feel that this volume makes an important contribution by providing a profile of empirical research on religious involvement of various types among African Americans and by exploring the impact of religion on individual attitudes, behaviors, and statuses.

Second, in keeping with our own training and perspective on research, we wanted the reviews of the literature to reflect research findings that are largely based on nationally representative samples of African Americans. Previous research was often based on small and unrepresentative samples that were not generalizable to the broader population of African Americans. The existence of research based on nationally representative samples allows the investigation of broader geographic or place-of-residence effects (e.g., regional and urbanicity effects) in the relationships under study, as well as overall greater diversity with respect to other important sociodemographic factors such as income and education. Further, as an examination of religion in the lives of African Americans, the book is primarily focused on data sources that address these questions within the African American population. Race-comparative research is presented in a number of chapters throughout the book, but such comparisons are not the focus or intent of the volume. This is the case for a number of reasons.

In prior research and writing (Ellison & Levin, 1998; Jackson, Chatters, & Taylor, 1993; Taylor, Jackson, & Chatters, 1997), we have long argued that the use of simple race-comparative approaches in examining social and behavioral phenomena carries with it significant conceptual and methodological limitations (see Dilworth-Anderson & Burton, 1996; Jackson, 1991; Jackson, Tucker, & Bowman, 1982). These include issues related to the basic conceptualization and the substantive meaning of social and psychological constructs across racial and ethnic groups, difficulties in understanding the essential nature of any race differences that are observed, and analyses that are fundamentally and profoundly acontextual. Research that focuses exclusively on simple race differences in religion typically provides little information beyond the fact that differences can be documented, leaving us with no clear insight about the underlying processes involved.

Further, a focus on simple race comparisons diverts attention from the investigation of within-group variability in religious involvement—that is to say, how religious involvement within the African American population varies on the basis of factors such as socioeconomic status, gender, or region. The investigation of contingent or interactive relationships involving race, ethnicity, and other sociodemographic factors has been especially ignored in research on religion (Ellison & Levin, 1998). Finally, the ability to critically and methodically examine religious involvement within the African American population and to position black religious expression within appropriate social, political, historical, and cultural contexts, is a useful and powerful corrective to characterizations of black religious behavior that are naïve, misinformed, and/or blatantly pejorative. Ultimately, a rigorous and systematic approach to the study of black religious involvement best serves the overall goal of developing more meaningful comparisons across race, ethnicity, and culture.

Third, we wanted to write a book that would address a variety of topic areas in such a way that it would have intrinsic interest and appeal to a fairly broad cross-section of readers. Our approach in presenting the topics included in the book is to synthesize diverse findings from several research traditions and present them in a manner that reflects their scientific merit and rigor and yet remains both interesting and accessible. In keeping with this, we focused on particular topics (e.g., religion and physical and mental health, the use of prayer as a form of coping, informal social support among church members) that we felt had high intrinsic interest, as well as substantial theoretical importance and empirical validation. These are topics that reflect our own research interests and expertise and that have an established research literature. Further, in compiling and synthesizing study findings on these topics, we attempted to provide a broad assessment and profile of major conclusions from this research. Readers seeking more detailed treatments of particular research questions can refer to the original articles that are cited at the end of the book. We anticipate that these topic areas, and the approach that we have adopted in presenting them, will have broad appeal to students and practitioners in the health and social sciences, as well as to members of the clergy and students in graduate seminary programs. Accordingly, the book concludes with a chapter that addresses the implications of this research for practitioners in these fields.

Fourth, in addition to the discussion of survey research investigations that employ various quantitative approaches to data, we also felt it was important to include information from qualitative studies of the role of religion in the lives of African Americans. Consequently, the literature reviews that are included in each chapter include a number of studies that are based on qualitative data (e.g., in-depth interviews, focus groups). Chapters 2 through 7 of the book also include qualitative data from a focus group study of adult African American men and women that was conducted by the authors and members of the Program for Research on Black Americans. The focus group study, "Appraisals of Religiosity, Coping and Church Support," was funded by the National Institute of Mental Health as part of a larger research project examining African American mental health. The procedures, format, and composition of the focus groups are discussed in Appendix A.

The emphasis on both quantitative and qualitative approaches to selected topic areas provides different and valuable perspectives for understanding the nature and functions of religion. As will be illustrated in the following substantive chapters, information from the focus group participants provides a greater sense of context, nuance, and process in understanding many of the research questions that are oftentimes only cursorily assessed in survey research efforts. The focus group data, used in conjunction with prior theory and research on these issues, have been an unexpected and astonishing source of insight into the meaning and significance of religion in the lives of individuals.

Lastly, we wanted the book to be useful to readers in several ways and potentially to serve as a catalyst for their own reading and investigations of these topics. In addition to the references cited at the end of the book, we have included a Resource Guide that highlights a number of pivotal readings on these issues, along with a brief description of the types of information that each provides.

Data Sources

The structure of each chapter of the book includes a review of relevant research findings for the particular topic area examined. The reviewed literature includes our own research and writing on these topics—work that is based primarily, but not exclusively, on data from the National Survey of Black Americans (NSBA)—as well as the theoretical and empirical work of other investigators examining these questions. Several chapters also include a basic descriptive profile of selected variables that are taken from data sources such as the 1998 General Social Survey (GSS), the Three Generation Family Survey, the recently completed National Survey of American Life, and the Monitoring the Future Survey. For example, Chapter 7, "Negative Interaction Among Church Members," presents descriptive data from the 1998 GSS on problems with congregation members. Overall, data from eight national surveys and one focus group study are used for this book. A detailed description of these studies is provided in Appendix A, "Data Sources."

Further, as mentioned earlier, Chapters 2 through 7 contain complementary information from African American men and women who participated in the focus group study, "Appraisals of Religiosity, Coping and Church Support." This study was conducted by the Program for Research on Black Americans at the Institute for Social Research in 1999. The focus group study used a semi-structured protocol that assessed the major topic areas that form the basis of Chapters 2 through 7 of this volume. A total of 13 focus groups of African American adults were conducted that were stratified by age (young participants were 18 years to 54 years of age and older participants were 55 years and above) and gender. A complete description of the focus group study procedures is also provided in Appendix A.

Format and Scope of the Volume

The book is organized around three main parts. Part I considers the patterns of religion, Part II considers the functions of religion, and Part III discusses the effects of religion. Further, each of the chapters in Parts I and II includes a section that discusses relevant information from the focus group narratives from the study, "Appraisals of Religiosity, Coping and Church Support."

Part I: Patterns of Religion, consists of two chapters that focus on profiles of overall religious involvement and prayer. Specifically, Chapter 2, "African American Religious Participation," provides a basic profile of religious involvement and activities. This includes a discussion of survey research findings on the sociodemographic correlates of religious activities such as denominational affiliation, church attendance, and use of religious media. Chapter 3, "The Frequency and Importance of Prayer," examines the issue of prayer as a distinct form of religious activity, again focusing on the personal and social correlates of this behavior. Focus group information on this topic provides a description of specific types of prayer.

Part II: Functions of Religion, begins with Chapter 4, "Prayer as a Source of Coping," which explores in greater depth the ways individuals use prayer to cope with personal problems. Complementary information from the focus group study provides additional insights regarding the use of prayer to cope with problems. Chapter 5, "Use of Ministers for Personal Problems," examines the circumstances under which individuals turn to clergy for assistance in dealing with problems and the types of problems that respondents bring to ministers. The focus group data discuss the availability of clergy and the reasons why individuals both use and decline assistance from clergy. Chapter 6, "Church Members as a Source of Social Support," examines the extent to which church members exchange informal social support in the form of advice, companionship, and financial assistance with one another. Again, the focus group study provides additional insight regarding these exchanges and information about the benefits that accrue to both recipient and provider. Finally, Chapter 7, "Negative Interaction Among Church Members," discusses issues of problematic social interactions involving other members of the church (e.g., gossip, interpersonal conflict). Theory regarding the significance of negative interaction for well-being is described, and survey data analysis examines reports of negative interaction involving fellow church members. Information from the focus group study discusses the types of negative interactions that occur and their impact on interpersonal dynamics within the church.

Part III: Effects of Religion, consists of two major substantive reviews of research on the connections between religion and physical and mental health. Chapter 8, "Impact of Religion on Physical Health," surveys scientific writing on the potential health effects of religious participation among African Americans. Chapter 9, "Impact of Religion on Mental Health and Well-Being," examines studies of religion's impact on mental health and dimensions of psychological well-being among African Americans. Both chapters include overviews of existing research findings and of efforts to address just what it is about religion that makes it beneficial for health. Finally, Chapter 10, "Conclusions and Implications," briefly reviews the research presented in previous chapters and discusses their implications for clergy and health and social welfare practitioners.

Having described the goals of the book and the approach taken in writing this volume, it is important to clearly delineate other boundaries in perspective and scope. The book is geared to explicitly examine empirical research on the role of religion in the lives of African Americans. As such, it does not incorporate a distinctly historical perspective nor does it consider religion within a theological framework (e.g., black theology). As noted previously, a number of esteemed religious scholars and historical researchers have produced excellent treatments of these topics. Further, although several of the comments generated within the focus groups provide cogent and compelling evidence of personal faith, this book does not attempt to address religious practices with respect to personal devotion nor is it meant to provide a resource for religious inspiration. There is a sizable religious devotion literature based in the African American experience that ably accomplishes this mission. This book's aim and focus is to examine the role of religion in the lives of African Americans as represented in research literatures from the social, behavioral, and health sciences. Stated another way, we are interested in the personal and social correlates of various forms of religious behaviors, attitudes, and beliefs and their consequences for different types of social and health behaviors and statuses.

For the most part, the book mirrors the predominant religious preferences of African Americans and thus describes theory and research pertaining specifically to Christian traditions. Information concerning other faiths is discussed, typically with respect to overall profiles of denominational preference. Further, unless otherwise noted, the literature and research reviewed here focuses on African Americans holding U.S. citizenship (native born or naturalized); ethnicity and immigrant status are not explored as major stratifying variables in the present discussion. Although these are significant and important factors in their own right for understanding religious involvement, the status of current research literature prevents a comprehensive assessment of their influences on the form and function of religious expression.

Finally, we view this book as part of broader efforts undertaken by a number of individuals to enhance scholarship and research on religion in the social, behavioral, and health sciences, specifically as this research relates to African Americans. This book provides social scientists, health researchers, and individuals in the helping professions (especially medicine, nursing, public health, social work, clinical psychology, and counseling) with an enhanced view of the intricate and complex functions of religion for African Americans. We also feel that the book will be of value to members of religious professions (e.g., ministry, pastoral care, religious education) who seek a greater understanding of social and behavioral processes as they relate to religious involvement of various types. Ultimately, we hope that this book will encourage constructive dialogue and reflection within and between these diverse groups for the purpose of improving our scientific and practical understanding of the role of religion in the lives of African Americans.

Part I

Patterns of Religion

The religious faith of African Americans has many avenues of expression, and, accordingly, research on religious involvement has focused on different forms of public and private behaviors, attitudes, and beliefs. Formal participation in church services and related activities, and prayer and other types of devotional activities all contribute to the overall portrait of African American religious life as being multifaceted and complex. African American religious life, in all its forms, is a vibrant, creative, and resourceful testament to the power of faith to uplift and sustain in the face of prejudice, discrimination, and exclusion. Perhaps the most striking characteristic of religion in the African diaspora is its diversity. Religious historians and social scientists still too often paint a stereotyped portrait of black churchgoing and worship, and its presumed motivations, as psychological accommodations to a presumed common sociocultural experience. This misclassifies African Americans as a monolithic social entity and fails to do justice to the sweeping breadth of religious expression even, and especially, in black churches.

In Part I, we explore overall patterns of religious expression among African Americans, both generally and within particular subgroups of the population. Chapter 2 includes discussions of the socio-historical role of the church in African American life, as well as the many ways that African Americans affiliate with religion and participate in churches. We especially highlight the numerous sociodemographic correlates of religious involvement indicating the heterogeneity of black religious life. In addition, Part I also includes a more extended and focused discussion of prayer (Chapter 3) as a particularly important religious activity. Both chapters explore material derived from focus groups of African American adults to elaborate on the basic themes described in the research literature.

Chapter 2

African American
Religious Participation

Religion and religious institutions of African Americans have had a profound impact on individuals and broader black communities. This influence is documented in the historical experiences of blacks within American society, as well as the role of religion and black churches in the development of independent black institutions and communities (Lincoln & Mamiya, 1990; Nelsen & Nelsen, 1975). Black religious institutions are cohesive spiritual and social communities that foster the religious and social well-being and integration of individuals and families. Their important and central position within black communities is demonstrated by the variety of secular activities and functions they perform. These include facilitating linkages to community health resources (Levin, 1984, 1986) and providing various forms of instrumental, social, and psychological support (see Chapter 4, "Prayer as a Source of Coping"; Chapter 5, "Use of Ministers for Personal Problems"; and Chapter 6, "Church Members as a Source of Social Support"). In addition, black churches have historically served as a base for political mobilization and social movements (Billingsley, 1999; Lincoln & Mamiya, 1990).

Any discussion of the form and functions of religion and religious involvement among African Americans must be grounded in an understanding of the historical origins of these traditions and the social, cultural, economic, and political experiences that served to define individual and collective religious expression for this group. Lincoln and Mamiya (1990) and others (e.g., Frazier, 1974) argue that African American theological orientations and religious practices emanated from the unique and dynamic social, political, and historical contexts that characterized their position within American society. In common with all religious traditions, black religious expression addressed itself to questions of ultimate concern and existential meaning (e.g., illness, personal suffering, death). However, because black religious expression also occurred within the context a hostile larger society, the aims and purposes of religious belief and expression were uniquely oriented and adapted toward addressing life conditions that were deleterious to the well-being of African Americans.

Historically, African American religious traditions have also necessarily reflected the salient issues of emancipation, individual and community enfranchisement, civil and human rights, and social and economic justice (Lincoln & Mamiya, 1990). Further, theological understandings and questions of ultimate concern were framed within the context of the unique conditions and life circumstances affecting African Americans. The enduring emphasis on the improvement of the tangible life circumstances of African Americans suggests that spiritual matters, per se, were but one of the purposes of black religious traditions. To varying degrees and across different faith traditions, the conditions of the immediate physical existence, as well as the spiritual life, have exerted powerful and complementary influences on the nature and functions of black religious expression.

Overview of the Chapter

This chapter provides a general summation of our research conducted over the past 20 years on the correlates of religious participation among black Americans. Collectively, our research team (Taylor, Chatters, and Levin) has published more than 40 journal articles and book chapters on the topic of religious participation among black Americans. Although this body of work forms the core of the chapter, other research in this area is discussed as well. In addition, new analyses based on survey data and focus group information is provided. The chapter begins with a discussion of the interface of spirituality and religiosity. Next, a discussion of theoretical models of the Black Church and religious involvement is presented, followed by a discussion of research on blacks' attitudes regarding whether the church has had a beneficial or detrimental impact on blacks in America. Next, data are presented on the denominational affiliation of African Americans, including research on denominational switching and a profile of denominational affiliation among members of three-generation black families.

Subsequent sections of the chapter focus specifically on various dimensions of religious involvement and a discussion of advances in measurement. This is followed by a review of research on the demographic correlates of religious participation, with a specific focus on race (i.e., black-white), gender, age, marital status, region, urbanicity, income, education, health status, and religious denomination differences in participation. The next section summarizes information on religious involvement among elderly blacks, a group for which there is a sizable body of research in the gerontological literature. This is followed by a discussion of religious participation among black adolescents, a group for which there is extremely little research. We then turn to a discussion of research findings for a group for which we have relatively little systematic information—persons who are not involved in formal religious organizations (i.e., unaffiliated or unchurched). A section of new analysis explores the correlates of religious identity and the presence of religious artifacts (e.g., paintings, symbols) in the home. Data from the focus group study "Appraisals of Religiosity, Coping and Church Support" are then presented that explore a variety of daily and weekly religious practices. The chapter concludes with a summary of these areas of research and a discussion of the range and diversity of religious participation within the African American population.

The Interface Between Religiosity and Spirituality

The distinction between religiosity and spirituality is one of the most fundamental issues facing researchers and scholars of the sociology and psychology of religion. Often, one of the first questions that we are asked by audiences when we are lecturing on African American religious participation is, "What is the role of spirituality?" or "Have you done any research on spirituality?" When we ask members of the audience to talk about the differences between religion and spirituality and how they are related to one another, we are likely to get as many different answers as there are people in attendance. Typically, what emerges from the discussion is a fairly polarized debate in which one group indicates that, in general, people are more spiritual than they are religious, while the other group argues the opposite point. These debates occur, in both popular and scientific circles, because there is no agreed-upon common understanding or definition of religion and spirituality and their distinctions. Part of the confusion also results from the fact that, among social scientists and the general public alike, there is a tendency to use these terms interchangeably. For example, researchers may use spirituality in the title of their article, but the focus is really on fairly standard indicators of religious participation (e.g., church attendance).

One of the best and most concise discussions of religiosity and spirituality is provided in Koenig, McCullough, and Larson's (2001) *Handbook of Religion and Health*. They present a schematic diagram of the interface between spirituality and religion and note the characteristics that distinguish these two concepts. Religion is more community focused, formal, organized, and behaviorally oriented, whereas spirituality is more individualistic, less visible, more subjective, less formal, less systematic, and more emotionally oriented. The authors define religion as an organized system of beliefs, practices, and rituals designed to facilitate closeness to God, whereas spirituality is seen as a personal quest for understanding answers to ultimate questions about life, meaning, and relationships to the sacred (see Koenig et al., 2001, for a more thorough definition of religiosity and spirituality and a more in-depth discussion of these issues).

One further example of the ambiguity surrounding the constructs of religiosity and spirituality is provided by a recent survey by the Gallup Organization titled "The Spiritual State of the Union." This survey found that 72% of Americans said that their lives have meaning and purpose because of their faith, and 60% that their faith is involved in every aspect of their life. Although these measures are discussed as indicators of spirituality, it is debatable whether they more accurately represent spirituality or subjective religiosity (i.e., attitudes and beliefs about the role of religion in daily life).

Historically, the major goal of organized religion was to assist individuals in becoming more spiritual in their orientation and, thus, to prepare them for the afterlife. In recent years, however, some individuals experience a disconnect between religion and spirituality, whereby organized religion and religious participation in general are not viewed as being necessary to achieve a high level of spirituality. Further, for some individuals who are often disaffected with formal, organized religion, individual spirituality is believed to be superior in terms of its personal benefits and outcomes. Pargament (1997, p. 38), however, notes that the popular characterization of spirituality-as-good and organized religion-as-bad does not hold up to empirical scrutiny. As will be seen in later chapters, religion and explicitly religious behaviors have proven to be advantageous to physical and mental health and well-being. In addition, some research shows that most Americans do not view religious participation and spirituality as being diametrically opposed to one another. Given the large percentage of Americans in general and black Americans, in particular, who are members of a religious denomination and who participate in religious activities, the most accurate characterization of Americans is that most identify as being both religious and spiritual.

Zinnbauer and colleagues (Zinnbauer, Pargament, Cowell, Rye, & Scott, 1997) conducted one of the few studies that directly examined the question of how individuals define themselves—religious, spiritual, or both. Using a occupationally and religiously diverse sample (i.e., hospice nurses, mental health professionals, nursing home residents, New Age church members, conservative and mainline Christians), they investigated the degree to which respondents categorized themselves as being: (a) both religious and spiritual, (b) religious and not spiritual, (c) spiritual and not religious, or (d) neither spiritual nor religious. Three out of four respondents categorized themselves as both religious and spiritual. Nineteen percent of respondents indicated that they were spiritual and not religious. One of the interesting findings was that mental health professions were more likely to categorize themselves as spiritual and not religious. Using the same categories, Shahabi and colleagues (2002) investigated the correlates of religiosity and spirituality using a national probability sample. Half of the respondents (52%) indicated that they were both religious and spiritual, 10% said that they were spiritual and not religious, 9% were religious and not spiritual, and 29% were neither religious nor spiritual. Unfortunately, African Americans, Hispanics, Asians, and Native Americans were combined into one nonwhite category for analysis, making it impossible to ascertain racial and ethnic differences in religious/spiritual self-descriptions.

Based upon findings from our previous research on black-white differences in religious participation (Taylor, Chatters, Jayakody, & Levin, 1996), we anticipate that the percentage of respondents who are neither religious nor spiritual would be much lower than that reported by Shahabi and colleagues (2002). We examined this issue using the same data (1998 General Social Survey) and identical coding scheme as Shahabi et al. Profiles by race show that 69.9% of black Americans state that they were both spiritual and religious, 3.1% were spiritual only, 6.7% were religious only, and 20.6% reported that they were neither religious nor spiritual. These percentages are somewhat different from those for white Americans. Among whites, only 50.2% indicated that they were both spiritual and religious, 11.2% reported spiritual only, 9.4% were religious only, and 29.2% reported that they were neither religious nor spiritual. Moreover, an examination of the National Survey of American Life reveals that 8 out of 10 black respondents report that religion is very important in their lives, and 8 out of 10 also say that spirituality is very important in their lives.

Although empirical research on spirituality in black Americans is virtually nonexistent (Armstrong & Crowther, 2002), a few isolated treatments of this issue can be found in the literature. The topics of religion and spirituality have garnered significant attention from Afrocentric theorists and practitioners who are interested in the philosophical foundations, ritual practices, and psychotherapeutic treatment implications of black religiosity and spirituality (Myers, 1987; Nobles, 1991; Potts, 1991; Wheeler, Ampadu, & Wangari, 2002). McKay's (1989) historical analysis of the spiritual narratives written by black women in the 19th century suggests that women during this era used spiritual narratives to present "a radical revision of prevailing White myths and ideals of Black life" (p. 141). For these women, Biblical texts and/or their own personal spiritual convictions provided the framework for reinterpreting their roles and identities within slave societies. The work of feminist theologian Jacquelyn Grant (1989) suggests that contemporary black women continue the use of spirituality and religion for purposes of personal and group liberation.

Probably the best empirical work on spirituality among blacks has been conducted by Mattis and associates (Mattis, 2000; Mattis, Murray et al., 2001). In an analysis among black men, Mattis and colleagues (Mattis, Murray et al., 2001) found that subjective religiosity (i.e., consisting of three items: self-assessed religiosity, importance of religion, importance of religion for children) and subjective spirituality (i.e., self-assessed spirituality) were moderately correlated. In addition, age was significantly associated with subjective religiosity but not subjective spirituality. Collectively, these findings show that religiosity and spirituality are related but distinct constructs. In another article examining how black women define spirituality and religiosity, Mattis (2000) found that respondents view spirituality and religiosity as intertwined but conceptually distinct experiences. In particular, analysis of in-depth interviews revealed that respondents made three conceptual distinctions between spirituality and religiosity. Similar to traditional theological writings, the first distinction emphasized that religious participation was a conduit for achieving spirituality. The second distinction focused on religiosity as adherence to predefined rituals and beliefs, whereas spirituality was the internalization and consistent expression of positive values and the effort to manifest goodness in daily life. Lastly, the third distinction defined spirituality in terms of relationships with God, with self, and with transcendent forces, including nature (Mattis, 2000). Interestingly, even though there were three different perspectives on spirituality, respondents were in general agreement about the definition of religion.

Models of Religious Involvement in Black Churches

Over the years, several models of the Black Church and religious involvement have been developed that attempt to characterize the form and function of black religious expression. Critiques of these models note that they are limited in a number of respects. So-called *traditional models* of black religious involvement have been criticized for being, for the most part, static and ahistorical (Stump, 1987) and for a tendency to focus on a limited set of characteristics in defining black religious expression. Overall, traditional models exhibit an inadequate appreciation for the impact of social and historical contexts for understanding religious involvement, insufficient attention to the processes of change, and an overemphasis on individual and discrete manifestations of black religious expression. In reviewing traditional models of black religious expression, Lincoln and Mamiya (1990) suggest that, because the Black Church (and its roles and functions in black communities) is viewed primarily as a product of lower-status black culture, it is depicted in a largely negative manner. Among the prominent themes articulated in this literature are that black religious traditions have served to isolate black communities, impeded the assimilation of blacks into broader society, promoted "other-worldly" religious orientations, and function primarily in order to compensate for deprivations experienced within American society (e.g., Marx, 1967).

The *deprivation compensation perspective* is one of the more conventional and popular notions concerning black religious expression. That is, African Americans are motivated to engage in religious expression as a means to compensate for deprivations (e.g., social, economic, political, personal) in other areas of life (Glock, Ringer, & Babbie, 1967). However, data bearing on this question (e.g., Taylor, 1988a, 1988b) do not support the contention that mere "deprivation" with respect to various social statuses motivates black religious involvement. The family surrogate model (Glock et al., 1967) is a variant of the deprivation-compensation perspective that suggests that unmarried persons and childless couples compensate for the absence of spouse and/or family through religious involvement. Similarly, the available data do not support the view that persons who are unmarried and couples who are childless demonstrate higher levels of religiosity. In contrast, the relationships between social status factors and religious involvement among African Americans are more complex than previously thought (Stump, 1987).

In contrast to the traditional models of black religious involvement, Lincoln and Mamiya (1990) propose a *dialectical model of the Black Church*.

The model includes an appreciation for: (a) the historical origins of the institutional structures in black religion, (b) a dynamic orientation emphasizing change and adaptation to both immediate circumstances and conditions and to larger societal forces, and (c) a conceptualization of the Black Church that reflects its position along a number of dimensions that are organized as polar opposites (dialectical tensions). These dialectical tensions are identified as reflecting the polarities of: (a) priestly versus prophetic function, (b) other-worldly versus this-worldly orientation, (c) universalism versus particularism, (d) communal versus privatistic tradition, (e) charismatic versus bureaucratic form, and (f) resistance versus accommodation. These dimensions of the Black Church, because they have received only isolated treatment in previous research, provided a limited and incomplete understanding of the nature of black religious expression. The incorporation of all of these dimensions in the dialectical model provides a more comprehensive treatment of the Black Church, including notions of dynamic interaction with historical forces, ongoing change and adaptation in response to contemporary factors and conditions, and an inherent multidimensional character.

Lincoln and Mamiya's (1990) work provides a useful conceptual framework for understanding several features of black churches and religious involvement and, in particular, the central and pivotal role of the church in many communities and the diversity of functions and objectives it fulfills. The authors argue that specific features of African American culture, in dynamic relationship with the larger American context, have given rise to a tradition in which religious and secular concerns are only partially differentiated. Black religious traditions have historically defined their mission as being one of transforming the social and political conditions that impact on the lives of African Americans as a group, whether this involved direct political action, civic projects, health ministries, or educational endeavors. As a consequence, religious pursuits have not become fully differentiated (i.e., privatized) from secular concerns. As evidence of this, among other things, black churches are viewed as being instrumental in the development of the black self-help tradition (i.e., mutual aid societies) and in providing the institutional foundations for educational, civic, and commercial endeavors within black communities. Historical and ethnographic research on the nature of black religious involvement verifies its multidimensional character (Cone, 1985). With respect to black churches, they are noted for their role in social welfare, political, and civic and community functions (Frazier, 1974; Taylor, Thornton, & Chatters, 1987). The apparent diversity of function within black churches, and black religious involvement more generally, suggests a number of means by which the spiritual, emotional, social, and political strivings of African Americans might be achieved. As will be discussed later, multidimensional characterizations of black religious involvement have been empirically validated in recent studies. Further, models emphasizing the multifarious nature of religious involvement provide a useful framework for understanding the possible mechanisms whereby religious factors impact on a number of outcomes of interest (Ellison, 1994; Ellison, Gay, & Glass, 1989; Levin & Vanderpool, 1989, 1992).

Socio-Historical Role of the Church

Scholars have debated whether the functions and activities of black churches have been a benefit or detriment to the African American community. We examined this issue directly by exploring African Americans' attitudes regarding the role of black churches (Taylor et al., 1987) using data from the National Survey of Black Americans. An item from the NSBA asked, "In general, do you think the church has helped the condition of black people in America, hurt, or made no difference?" We found that the majority of respondents (82.2%) stated that the church had had a beneficial influence on the circumstances of blacks in America, 4.9% reported that the church had hurt the status of blacks, and 12.1% reported that the church had made no difference. Positive assessments of the church's socio-historical role tended to be voiced by older persons, women, persons who lived in the South (vs. Northeast), and those with more years of formal education. This is similar to other findings on religious participation, in which women, older persons, and Southerners generally evidence greater investment in religious concerns.

Responses to the follow-up question—"Why do you feel that way?"—indicated that persons who felt that the church has helped reported that the Black church has (a) provided spiritual assistance, (b) had a sustaining and strengthening influence for communities and individuals, (c) provided personal support and aid, (d) promoted a set of guidelines for moral behavior, (e) functioned as a source of ideological unity, (f) provided an organizational infrastructure by serving as a community gathering place, and (g) actively encouraged social progress for black Americans. In contrast, those with a negative opinion of the church stated that (a) churches and clergy were motivated by money, (b) organized religion did not reflect a true sense of personal religiosity and spirituality, and (c) Christianity, as a product of white culture, was inherently detrimental to the condition of black Americans. Overall, this analysis revealed extensive support for the perception that the church has a beneficial impact on the lives of black Americans (see Taylor et al., 1987 for a more in-depth discussion).

Religious Denomination

Table 2.1 presents a profile of religious denomination among black Americans that is based upon data from six national surveys (a detailed description of these surveys is provided in Appendix A: "Data Sources"). More than 40 different religious denominations are reported, demonstrating the breadth and diversity of religious preference among black Americans. The three denominations that blacks are most likely to be affiliated with are Baptist, Methodist, and Catholic. Half of all blacks report they are Baptists, and this percentage is consistent across all of the surveys. About 1 out of 10 blacks is Methodist. Among the high school seniors in the Monitoring the Future Survey, this number drops to 4.9% or 1 in 20. About 5% to 6% of blacks are Roman Catholic. Lastly, about 5% to 10% of black Americans indicate that they do not have a current religious denomination. Beyond these broad characterizations, we are less confident about the accuracy of the percentages reported for the religious groups with smaller percentages of blacks. For instance, we suspect that the percentage of respondents who say that they are African Methodist Episcopal (AME) is larger than what is reported in these surveys. The reasons for these discrepancies are discussed below.

This percentage distribution of religious affiliations is one the most basic profiles of African American religious denominations possible. However, there are several caveats to these distributions that are worth noting. First, while black and white Americans can typically identify their basic denominational affiliation, many do not know the specific intra-denomination organization that their church is affiliated with. For instance, analysis of the General Social Survey shows that more than half of both black and white Baptists do not know with which specific church organization or convention (e.g., National Baptist Convention of America, National Baptist Convention, U.S.A., Inc., Southern Baptist Convention) their church is affiliated (this observation also holds for Methodists, Lutherans, and Presbyterians). This lack of knowledge is quite understandable.

Americans know the name of the individual church that they attend (e.g., 15th Avenue Baptist Church, Zion Baptist Church). However, because the specific intra-denomination affiliation of the church is not important for their everyday life or spiritual well-being, that information may not be particularly important for them to know. Identification of intra-denominational distinctions and affiliations may be more salient for members if there are important historical schisms (e.g., over doctrine, theology, political and social activism) that are reflected in the appellation of individual congregations such as St. Mark Lutheran Church–ELCA (e.g., distinctions between

Table 2.1   Religious Denominations of Black Americans[a]

Religious Denomination	NSBA 1979–1980 Percentage	NBES 1984 Percentage	ACL 1986 Percentage	MTF 1996 Percentage	GSS 1972–1998 Percentage	NSAL 2001–2003 Percentage
Congregational	0.2	0.3	0.1	—	—	0.1
Episcopalian	1.2	0.9	1.5	0.8	1.3	0.5
Lutheran	0.4	0.9	0.5	0.2	0.6	0.2
Presbyterian	0.9	1.3	0.8	0.6	0.8	0.6
United Church of Christ	0.1	0.2	—	0.6	—	0.1
African Methodist Episcopal	1.2	0.9	1.4	—	2.2	—
African Methodist Episcopal Zion	—	—	—	—	0.8	—
United Methodist	—	—	—	—	—	—
Methodist	10.4	7.5	10.6	4.9	7.8	6.1
CME (Methodist)	0.1	—	—	—	—	—
Baptist	52.1	58.4	59.8	55.0	55.8	51.9
Disciples of Christ	0.3	0.3	0.8	0.4	—	0.6
Apostolic	0.5	—	0.5	—	—	0.6
Church of Christ	1.2	1.2	3.1	7.8	—	0.3
Church of God	0.3	2.8	0.8	—	—	0.8
Church of God in Christ	1.2	—	0.9	—	—	0.2
Fundamentalist Baptist	1.4	—	0.9	—	—	—
Nazarene/Free Methodist	0.0	—	—	—	—	—
Pentecostal/Assembly of God	1.5	2.0	2.8	—	—	—
Pentecostal	—	—	—	—	—	4.6
Assembly of God	—	—	—	—	—	0.1
Salvation Army	0.0	0.1	0.1	—	—	—
Sanctified	0.6	0.3	0.3	—	—	0.4

NOTE: a. A line indicates that either there are no cases in this category or that this denomination is not a valid category for this dataset. A percentage of 0.0 indicates at least 1 case in this category. Percentages may not sum to 100 due to rounding error.

Table 2.1 (Continued)

	NSBA 1979–1980	NBES 1984	ACL 1986	MTF 1996	GSS 1972–1998	NSAL 2001–2003
Seventh-day Adventist	0.4	1.1	0.9	—	—	0.6
Southern Baptist	0.1	0.8	0.1	—	—	—
Other Baptist	0.0	—		—	—	0.1
Other Fundamentalist	0.0	0.1		—	—	—
Christian	0.7	1.2	0.1	—	0.2	1.8
Protestant (no denomination specified)	0.8	1.5	0.9	—	—	2.8
Nondenominational/ Interdenominational Protestant	0.5	1.2	0.4	—	1.9	0.5
Community Church	0.1	0.3	0.3	—	—	—
Other Protestant	0.0	0.7	0.6	2.0	12.7	0.2
Catholic	6.3	6.0	5.4	4.4	7.7	5.8
Holiness	3.2	—	—	—	—	2.5
Jehovah's Witness	2.1	1.9	1.5	—	—	1.8
Latter-day Saints, Mormons	0.1	—	—	0.0	—	0.1
Spiritualist	0.2	0.2	0.1	—	—	0.2
Unity	0.1	0.1	—	—	—	0.1
Islam	0.7	—	0.5	1.6	—	—
Muslim, Moslem	0.2	0.4	—	—	0.0	1.0
Nation of Islam	0.0	—	—	—	—	—
Jewish	0.1	—	0.1	0.1	0.2	0.1
Buddhist	0.0	—	—	0.4	0.0	0.2
Bahai	0.0	0.1	—	—	—	0.0
Hindu	—	0.1	—	—	0.0	0.0

(Continued)

Table 2.1   (Continued)

	NSBA 1979–1980	NBES 1984	ACL 1986	MTF 1996	GSS 1972–1998	NSAL 2001–2003
Other non-Christian	—	—	0.2	—	0.1	—
Mennonite, Amish	—	0.1	0.1	—	—	0.1
Evangelical and Reformed	—	0.1	—	—	—	2.4
Primitive, Free Will, Missionary	—	0.4	—	—	—	—
Rastafarian	—	—	—	—	—	0.1
Christian Orthodox	—	—	—	—	—	0.1
Nondenominational, religion not specified	—	—	—	—	—	—
None	10.1	4.9	4.0	10.9	5.9	0.9
Atheist, Agnostic	0.5	0.8	0.1	—	—	10.2
Born Again Christian	—	—	—	—	—	0.1
Other	0.2	0.7	—	10.2	2.0	0.7
TOTAL	100.0	100.0	100.0	100.0	100.0	100.0
N	2,094	1,121	1,168	2,137	4,359	3,579

Lutheran congregations as Evangelical Lutheran Church in America–ELCA, Lutheran Church Missouri Synod–LCMS, and Wisconsin Evangelical Lutheran Synod–WELS, and between Presbyterians as the Presbyterian Church in America–PCA and the Presbyterian Church in the United Status–PCUS). These circumstances notwithstanding, questions of within-denominational affiliation and differences are generally more salient for theologians, divinity students, ministers, and religious researchers than they are for the average black or white American.

Second, many surveys of the population do not report information on the full diversity of denominations and, in particular, the variety of nonaffiliated churches and storefront churches that black Americans attend. Third, anecdotal evidence indicates that there is major variation across black Baptist congregations within the same convention, with some churches exhibiting more conservative "Pentecostal-style" services and theology, while others display more liberal and progressive orientations. Given that more than half of black Americans report Baptist affiliation, it is likely that there are important within-denomination differences along these and other relevant dimensions (e.g., region, socioeconomic status). In sum, broad denominational classifications that are taken at face value may conceal important within-group variability in beliefs, practices, and institutional structures (Ellison, 1999; Woodberry & Smith, 1998).

Denominational Switching

Ellison and Sherkat's (1990) analysis of patterns of religious affiliation among African Americans examined change in religious preference between 1972 and 1988 using data from the General Social Survey (1972–1988) and the National Survey of Black Americans. Overall, their findings showed that religious affiliation or denominational preference was relatively stable over the period of time studied, with only small declines in the percentage of persons who identified as either Baptist, Methodist, or Catholic, or were affiliated with predominantly white organizations. For those who did change affiliations, Baptists were more likely to switch to small Conservative Protestant groups, and Methodists were more likely to become Baptist. Catholics, on the other hand, were more likely both to *indicate* no current religious preference and, similar to persons raised without formal religious ties, to affiliate with nontraditional religions. Sherkat's (2002) analysis of data from the 1973–1998 General Social Survey found similar trends in denominational switching among this group.

Sherkat and Ellison (1991) examined demographic and racial group identity correlates of individuals who: (a) had remained members of black mainline denominations (i.e., Baptists, Methodists), (b) changed from a black mainline denomination to another affiliation (i.e., religious switchers), and (c) were previously members of black mainline denominations but were currently unaffiliated (i.e., apostates). In comparison to persons who remained in black mainline religious denominations, religious apostates were more likely to be male, younger, and reside outside of the South. Further, they tended to hold negative attitudes about black churches, had lower levels of racial group identification, less frequent contact with family members, and were less likely to be a member of a national or neighborhood organization. In contrast, religious switchers (persons raised in a black mainline denomination but with a different current religious affiliation) were more likely than persons remaining in mainline denominations to be married, reside in urban areas, and to support political protest to gain equal rights. However, religious switchers had lower levels of racial group identity than their religious mainline counterparts.

Generational Differences in Religious Denomination

In one of the few studies of its kind, Taylor (1993) examined older black adults' current religious affiliation in conjunction with reports of their childhood (i.e., religion when growing up) and parents' (mother and father) affiliations. The overwhelming majority of elderly black adults identified their own current affiliation, as well as that of their parents', as being either Baptist or Methodist. However, important differences were revealed when comparing respondents' current religious affiliation with: (a) their own childhood affiliation and (b) parents' affiliation. With respect to their current affiliation, respondents were slightly less likely (as compared with childhood and parent affiliation) to report being Baptist or Methodist and were slightly more likely to indicate that they held another religious affiliation. Further, although current religious affiliation and both childhood and parents' religious affiliation were strongly associated, mothers' religious affiliation were a somewhat stronger correlate of respondents' current religious affiliation than were fathers'.

Table 2.2 presents a frequency distribution of religious affiliations using data from the Three Generation Family Study. All respondents in this study are black and members of a three-generation family (see Appendix A for a description of this study). Similar to the other studies of denominational

Table 2.2   Current Religious Affiliation Across Three Generations of Black Families

Religious Affiliation	Grandparent Generation	Parent Generation	Child Generation
Congregational	0.0	0.0	0.2
Episcopalian/Anglican	0.4	1.5	1.1
Lutheran	0.1	0.1	0.7
Presbyterian	0.7	0.8	0.6
Reformed Dutch	0.0	0.1	0.0
United Church of Christ	0.0	0.1	0.0
Methodist/CME	1.0	0.5	0.0
African Methodist	2.8	1.0	0.6
Baptist	59.0	54.0	50.1
Disciples of Christ	0.0	0.2	0.2
Methodist	13.4	10.3	8.1
Apostolic	0.3	1.0	0.7
Church of Christ	1.0	1.5	0.9
Church of God	0.1	0.5	0.1
Church of God in Christ	1.4	1.3	0.9
Fundamentalist	4.4	1.2	0.2
Pentecostal/Assembly of God	1.7	1.5	1.3
Salvation Army	0.0	0.1	0.0
Sanctified	0.7	0.2	0.5
Seventh-day Adventist	0.4	0.8	0.7
Other Fundamentalist	0.0	0.1	0.0
Southern Baptist	0.0	0.0	0.1
Christian	0.0	0.4	1.3
Protestant (no denomination)	0.4	1.0	0.6
Nondenominational Protestant	0.0	0.5	0.5
Other Protestant	0.4	0.2	0.2
Roman Catholic	4.2	6.9	7.7
Holiness	3.5	4.0	3.2
Jehovah's Witness	1.8	2.4	2.2
Latter-day Saints	0.0	0.1	0.1
Spiritualist	0.1	0.2	0.3
Unity	0.1	0.2	0.1
Islam	0.0	0.2	1.3
Muslim	0.0	0.1	0.6
World Community	0.0	0.0	0.1
Jewish	0.0	0.0	0.1
Bahai	0.0	0.0	0.1
Other non-Christian	0.0	0.0	0.1
None/No Preference	2.1	6.2	14.3
Atheist, Agnostic	0.0	0.2	0.3
Other	0.3	0.4	0.1
TOTAL	100.0	100.0	100.0
N	723	866	897

affiliation among blacks, the majority of respondents are either Baptist or Methodist. Further, there are important generational differences in denominational switching (Ellison & Sherkat, 1990; Sherkat, 2002) across three family generations. The Grandparent Generation had the highest percentage of respondents who were Baptist or Methodist and reported the fewest number of denominations, followed by the Parent Generation and the Child Generation. Members of the Child Generation reported almost twice the number of denominations as those in the Grandparent Generation and were much more likely to report that they were currently unaffiliated. The data in Table 2.2 reflect the trends found by Ellison and Sherkat (1990) and Sherkat (2002) on declines in the percentage of blacks affiliated with Baptist and Methodist denominations. These data are particularly noteworthy because they show that although most of the adults and young adults of the Child Generation (ages 14–34) have the same religious affiliation as their parents and grandparents, they clearly are less likely to be Baptist or Methodist, have a greater diversity of denominational affiliations, and are more likely to indicate that they do not have a current religious affiliation.

Conceptualization and Measurement of Religious Involvement

The conceptualization and measurement of religion and religious involvement is one of the most fundamental and difficult issues in this field. Interest in the conceptualization and measurement of religious involvement is long-standing (Mindel & Vaughan, 1978). Currently, no single index or scale is recognized as the gold standard that adequately represents the construct of religiosity. Given the variety of religious and spiritual phenomena and the recognized complexity of their diverse relationships to physical and mental health outcomes, a meaningful scale of this sort is not feasible (Fetzer Institute/National Institute on Aging, 1999). Despite these challenges, significant progress has been made with respect to the conceptual meanings, methods, and analytic approaches that are best suited to study these relationships. Given recent interest in religion's associations with health and other outcomes, systematic programs of research are involved in developing conceptually based and empirically validated measures of religious involvement for use in research (Chatters, 2000; Fetzer Institute/National Institute on Aging, 1999; Ellison & Levin, 1998; Idler & George, 1998). Current programmatic efforts in this area demonstrate greater clarity in defining the nature and boundaries of relevant content areas (e.g., conceptual definitions, multidimensionality) and careful consideration of the research methodologies and procedures (e.g., measurement, sampling, study design) that are appropriate to these questions.

For well over 20 years, researchers in the social and behavioral sciences have defined religious involvement as comprising multiple dimensions that reflect behavioral (i.e., public and private) and subjective (i.e., attitude, belief, and experience) dimensions (Chatters, Levin, & Taylor, 1992; Ellison, 1994; Idler & George, 1998; Krause, 1993; Levin, Chatters, & Taylor, 1995; Pargament, 1997; Schiller & Levin, 1988; Williams, 1994). The behavioral component refers to activities that involve organizational or public religious expression (e.g., denominational affiliation, religious service attendance), as well as private activities or non-organizational practices that are performed independently of formal religious institutions (e.g., private prayer, devotional reading). On the other hand, attitudes, experiences, self-perceptions, and attributions that involve religious or spiritual content (e.g., religious identity, feelings of closeness to God) are designated as subjective dimensions of religious involvement (Levin, Taylor, & Chatters, 1995; Williams, 1994).

Despite advances in the conceptualization and measurement of religious involvement (Ainlay & Smith, 1984; Chatters et al., 1992; Chatters & Taylor, 1989a; Matthews et al., 1998; Mindel & Vaughan, 1978), some research continues to use church attendance as the only indicator of religious involvement (see Kennedy, Kelman, Thomas, & Chen, 1996, and editorial response by Packer, 1997). Research in the health and medical professions (e.g., psychiatry, social epidemiology, clinical medicine), in particular, often defines religious involvement with respect to behavioral measures of a single dimension (e.g., church attendance or denominational affiliation) and is based on samples from community and national probability surveys. This is particularly the case in studies investigating the independent effects of church attendance on mental health outcomes such as depression, anxiety, suicide, drug and alcohol abuse, and psychiatric care utilization (Gartner, Larson, & Allen, 1991). This practice disregards efforts to define and measure religious involvement comprehensively (i.e., as a multidimensional construct) and precludes the investigation of the distinct mechanisms through which religious effects influence diverse health outcomes (Ellison & Levin, 1998; Levin, Taylor, & Chatters, 1995; Levin & Vanderpool, 1987; Schiller & Levin, 1988; Williams, 1994).

Research in the psychology and sociology of religion, which is typically based on samples of college students or members of a single religious denomination (e.g., Presbyterians: King & Hunt, 1972; Mormons: Cornwall, 1989), examines religious involvement as a dependent variable. In this line of research, religiosity is defined in a very broad manner and may embody

10 or more dimensions and include up to 70 individual items (e.g., King & Hunt, 1969, 1972). Further, many of these scales (King & Hunt, 1972) include items that are not measures of religiosity (e.g., "my life is full of joy and satisfaction," "my life is often empty and filled with despair") and are more appropriately classified as indicators of subjective well-being or quality of life. Given the specialized samples on which the majority of this research is based and the arduous task demands of these scales, there are valid concerns as to the representativeness and validity of findings. For example, there may be selection factors operating whereby only extremely religious persons or those required to participate in the study (e.g., psychology undergraduate students) would complete a battery of 50 to 70 items. Finally, in terms of understanding religion-health relationships, this practice obscures how social factors pattern religious involvement and, in turn, how discrete aspects of religiosity (e.g., attitudes, public vs. private behaviors) operate with respect to health and well-being outcomes.

A number of recent investigations have examined various dimensions of religious involvement and their association with discrete health outcomes. Research in social gerontology has focused on the development of multidimensional, yet parsimonious measures of religious involvement. A three-dimensional model of religious involvement, consisting of organizational, non-organizational, and subjective religiosity, has been verified in several LISREL-based analyses on black adults (Levin, Taylor, & Chatters, 1995) and older blacks (Chatters et al., 1992) and in analyses of older whites (Ainlay & Smith, 1984). Several programs of research on the conceptualization and measurement of religious involvement are currently under way that it is hoped will yield conceptually based, empirically validated measures of religious involvement that are consequential for health and permit the investigation of the proximate causes and mechanisms that link religion and health (Ellison & Levin, 1998; Fetzer Institute/National Institute on Aging, 1999; Idler & George, 1998).

Measurement development efforts by the Fetzer Institute/National Institute on Aging Working Group resulted in the development of a brief, multidimensional measure of religion/spirituality for use in health research (Fetzer Institute/National Institute on Aging, 1999). Initially, this work identified 12 domains of religious involvement that were thought to be significant for health outcomes; these domains were later used to develop the Brief Multidimensional Measure of Religiousness/Spirituality: 1999 (BMMRS). Several of these domains are well represented in existing research (e.g., religious preference, organizational religiousness, private religious practices, daily spiritual experiences, religious/spiritual coping, religious support). However, other domains have been identified as potentially important but have not been extensively examined in research on religion and health (e.g., meaning, values, beliefs, forgiveness, religious/spiritual history, commitment). The BMMRS was included in the 1998 General Social Survey (analysis of the black subsample of this data is presented in several chapters), and initial information on the psychometric properties of the measure verifies the value of the multidimensional approach. Further, the items formed reliable indices that were only moderately correlated with one another (Idler et al., 2000). With continued use and wider application in diverse samples, the BMMRS holds real promise for generating useful information on religion-health relationships.

Our own research on religious involvement among African Americans has led us to conceptualize a three-dimensional model of religious involvement (i.e., organizational, non-organizational, and subjective religiosity). Organizational religious participation refers to behaviors that occur within the context of a church, mosque, or other religious setting (e.g., church attendance, membership, participation in auxiliary groups). Non-organizational religious participation refers to behaviors that may occur outside of a religious setting (e.g., private prayer, reading religious materials, watching or listening to religious television and radio programs). Subjective religiosity refers to perceptions and attitudes regarding religion. This dimension is measured by questions on such topics as perceived importance of religion, the role of religious beliefs in daily life, and individual perceptions of being religious (Chatters et al., 1992). An investigation of the three-dimensional model of religious participation among older blacks (Chatters et al., 1992) indicated that the proposed measurement model provided a good fit to the data, was preferable to alternative models of these relationships, and was convergently valid. The findings were subsequently confirmed within the entire adult age range of the NSBA sample (Levin, Taylor, & Chatters, 1995). In addition, the study by Levin, Chatters, and Taylor (1995) extends the work on the measurement model of religious participation by investigating the role of religion on health status and life satisfaction among black Americans.

Structural Determinants of Religious Involvement

Recognizing a general lack of basic information concerning the structural antecedents of religiosity among African Americans, research studies in this category document the nature and extent of sociodemographic differences (i.e., race, age, gender, marital status, health, urbanicity, socioeconomic status, and region) in religious involvement. The religious indicators of interest include organizational, non-organizational, and subjective religiosity. The findings presented in this section are from a series of studies conducted by the authors on the demographic correlates of religious participation (e.g., Chatters & Taylor, 1989a; Chatters, Taylor, & Lincoln, 1999; Levin & Taylor, 1993, 1997; Levin, Taylor, & Chatters, 1994, 1995; Mattis, Taylor, & Chatters, 2001; Taylor, 1986, 1988a, 1988b; Taylor, Mattis, & Chatters, 1999; Taylor et al., 1996). This research primarily utilized the National Survey of Black Americans (NSBA), but data from several other national probability samples, including Americans' Changing Lives, the General Social Survey, Monitoring the Future, the National Black Election Survey, and the Quality of American Life, were also analyzed.

Profile of Religious Participation

Data from a variety of surveys indicate that black Americans demonstrate a high degree of religious involvement. Analyses using the NSBA show that fewer than 10% of black Americans report that they have not attended religious services as an adult except for weddings and funerals. Of those respondents who have attended, roughly 70% state that they attended religious services at least a few times a month, and two thirds report that they are church members. With respect to non-organizational religious participation, close to 80% of black Americans report that they pray nearly every day, 27% report that they read religious books, and 21% watch or listen to religious programming on television or radio almost daily. With regard to subjective religiosity, 80% of respondents considered themselves to be either very or fairly religious.

The profile of religious participation from the National Three Generation Family Study data (Table 2.3) shows generally high levels of religious participation among black adults. Consistent with age differences in religious participation (see sections on Age Differences and Religious Participation Among Elderly Blacks later in this chapter), respondents in the Grandparent Generation had the highest levels of religious participation, and those in the Child Generation had the lowest. This is particularly evident for indicators of non-organizational religious participation (e.g., frequency of prayer, reading religious materials, and watching/listening to religious programs) and subjective religiosity. For instance, 67.3% of persons in the Grandparent Generation report that they are very religious, compared to 38.2% of the Parent Generation, and 15.7% of the Child Generation.

The elevated levels of religious involvement among black adults are very much consistent with other findings across a variety of national surveys, including a recent survey of the population, the National Survey of

Table 2.3   Frequency of Religious Activities Across Three Generations

Religion Activities	Grandparent Generation Percentage	Parent Generation Percentage	Child Generation Percentage
Attend Church Since 18			
Yes	97.3	94.3	83.0
No	2.7	5.7	17.0
TOTAL	100.0	100.0	100.0
N	221	423	477
Church Attendance			
Nearly every day	5.2	5.5	3.4
At least once a week	48.2	40.3	27.8
Few times a month	32.1	26.4	31.9
Few times a year	8.6	18.0	24.7
Less than once a year	6.0	9.9	12.2
TOTAL	100.0	100.0	100.0
N	717	841	821
Importance of Church			
Very important	93.7	82.8	59.7
Fairly important	5.1	12.6	30.2
Not too important	0.9	4.0	7.4
Not important at all	0.4	0.7	2.7
TOTAL	100.0	100.0	100.0
N	534	629	407
Frequency of Participating in Church Activities Other Than Worship Service			
Nearly every day	5.6	2.8	4.1
At least once a week	28.5	29.6	16.5
Few times a month	31.3	29.6	27.6
Few times a year	18.6	23.3	29.7
Never	16.0	14.6	22.1
TOTAL	100.0	100.0	100.0
N	462	493	290
Frequency of Reading Religious Books			
Nearly every day	44.3	44.3	11.6
At least once a week	27.0	27.0	20.6
A few times a month	15.0	15.0	30.6
A few times a year	4.8	4.8	27.8
Never	8.9	8.9	9.4
TOTAL	100.0	100.0	100.0
N	582	734	543
Frequency of Watching/ Listening to Religious Television/Radio			
Nearly every day	39.1	22.5	10.3
At least once a week	47.3	50.5	41.7

(Continued)

Table 2.3   (Continued)

Religion Activities	Grandparent Generation Percentage	Parent Generation Percentage	Child Generation Percentage
A few times a month	7.4	12.7	18.8
A few times a year	3.1	9.1	16.0
Never	3.1	5.3	13.3
TOTAL	100.0	100.0	100.0
N	581	735	543
Frequency of Prayer			
Nearly every day	95.3	83.0	59.3
At least once a week	2.2	7.3	15.9
A few times a month	1.5	4.4	11.4
A few times a year	0.3	2.9	7.5
Never	0.7	2.4	5.9
TOTAL	100.0	100.0	100.0
N	724	865	902
Frequency of Asking Others to Pray for You			
Nearly every day	20.4	15.0	10.4
At least once a week	21.7	20.3	12.2
A few times a month	21.6	19.1	17.0
A few times a year	13.7	23.3	23.9
Never	22.6	22.3	36.7
TOTAL	100.0	100.0	100.0
N	575	734	539
Important for Black Parents to Send Their Children to Religious Services?			
Very important	95.2	86.7	68.1
Fairly important	4.4	9.9	24.8
Not too important	0.2	2.5	5.9
Not important at all	0.2	1.0	1.1
TOTAL	100.0	100.0	100.0
N	586	736	790
Subjective Religiosity			
Very religious	67.3	38.2	15.7
Fairly religious	29.1	51.7	57.4
Not too religious	3.0	9.0	22.0
Not religious at all	0.7	1.6	5.3
TOTAL	100.0	100.0	100.0
N	587	733	796
Attend Church More, Less, or About the Same as You Did 10 Years Ago?			
More	34.7	38.4	21.7
Less	12.2	18.5	44.4
Same	53.1	43.1	33.9
TOTAL	100.0	100.0	100.0
N	501	601	419

American Life (NSAL). Slightly more than half of the black respondents in the NSAL study report that they read religious materials, watch/listen to religious programming, and listen to religious music at least once a week. In addition, even higher levels of participation are noted for other religious indicators. Roughly 8 out of 10 black Americans in that survey indicate that: (a) they pray nearly every day, (b) religion is very important in their life, (c) spirituality is very important in their life, and (d) it is very important to take children to religious services.

Black-White Differences

Only a few studies focus on racial differences in religious participation. The majority of existing studies do not use multivariate analysis techniques, and, in the few instances in which they were applied, important intervening variables such as region and religious affiliation were not included. Taylor and colleagues (1996) investigated racial differences in religious involvement using data from seven national probability samples, each of which had a substantial number of black respondents and, at a minimum, a measure of church attendance and religious denominational affiliation. Except for one (Monitoring the Future), all of the studies were based on adult samples, and six of the data sets were collected under the auspices of the same social science organization (the Institute for Social Research). Data from the General Social Surveys were collected by the National Opinion Research Center (the University of Chicago). As compared to whites, black respondents demonstrated higher levels of both public (e.g., religious attendance) and private (e.g., reading religious materials) religious behaviors and were more likely to endorse positive statements or attitudes that reflected the strength of personal religious commitment (e.g., religious minded, importance of religion, religious comfort). These differences persisted despite controls for demographic (e.g., socioeconomic status, region) and religious (i.e., religious affiliation) factors that are differentially distributed within black and white populations and are known to be of consequence for religious involvement. These findings verified the presence of consistent racial differences in religious involvement across seven national data sets that were conducted at different points in time. A similar analysis investigating black-white differences in religiosity among elderly adults also found that blacks had significantly higher levels of religious participation than whites (Levin et al., 1994).

Gender Differences

Consistent gender differences in religious involvement indicate that across subjective, organizational, and non-organizational measures of religious participation, black women are more religiously involved than are men (see Chatters & Taylor, 1992; Chatters et al., 1999; Levin & Taylor, 1993; Levin, Taylor, & Chatters, 1995; Taylor, 1988b). These findings should not be interpreted to mean that black men are not religious, but that black women report higher levels of religious involvement. For instance, analysis from the National Survey of Black Americans indicates that 68% of black men pray nearly every day. This is significantly lower than the 84% of black women who pray nearly every day but refutes the notion that black men are not religious. In addition, only 6% of black men say that they never pray, compared to 1.5% of black women. These significant gender differences among blacks are consistent with previous research among white adults (Argyle & Beit-Hallahmi, 1975; Blazer & Palmore, 1976; Cornwall, 1989; de Vaus & McAllister, 1987; Koenig, Kvale, & Ferrel, 1988). The critical point of these studies is that, in analyses using multivariate procedures across several surveys of African Americans, women demonstrate significantly higher levels of religiosity than men.

Theorizing as to the nature of gender differences in religiosity highlights the nature of the social roles performed by women and men. In particular, gender-based differences in family and work roles and labor force participation are thought to facilitate women's involvement in religious pursuits (de Vaus & McAllister, 1987). Women's social and family roles have been suggested as one source of the gender difference in religious involvement. Specifically, various aspects of religious teachings, beliefs, and practices (e.g., care of the sick and elderly) are compatible with women's roles and normative expectations as caregivers (e.g., nurturing and supportive). Further, the position of women as the primary agents of socialization for young children customarily involves them in moral instruction and the inculcation of religious values.

Gender differences in religious involvement could also be associated with the stressful character of family and social obligations and roles. The constellation of women's multiple roles (i.e., wife, mother, worker, caregiver) may expose women to greater levels of overall stress than men, and women may employ religious coping strategies in response to these stressors. Religious coping strategies that emphasize problem reappraisal and mood regulation may be effective in coping with the stresses associated with these roles (Ellison & Taylor, 1996).

The caregiving role, in particular, involves substantial physical, emotional, and psychological demands on the caregiver. Often, caregiving situations involve struggling with the nature of human experience (e.g., human suffering, pain, grief) and questions of ultimate meaning. These and other issues of ultimate concern are the foundation of all religious traditions and are reflective of the ongoing human efforts to understand and come to terms with life exigencies. Religious teachings often employ stories of exemplary individuals who triumph over personal adversity (e.g., sickness, grief, poverty, personal peril) through the use of religious strategies. A recent review of research on coping with caregiving (Dilworth-Anderson, Williams, & Gibson, 2002) indicates that religious resources and coping strategies were frequently identified by African American caregivers. African American caregivers were more likely than whites to report that they were religious, to use prayer and religion to cope with the demands of caregiving, and to report greater spiritual meaning in the caregiving experience. Religiosity was important in reframing the caregiving experience and in perceptions of the rewards of caregiving.

Other possible explanations for gender differences in religious participation involve differences between women and men in relation to psychological traits (e.g., locus of control, social desirability) that may be related to religious orientations. Alternatively, women may be more prominent members of the social networks that comprise religious settings, thus availing themselves of more opportunities to be involved in religious pursuits. These and other explanations suggest several interesting mechanisms that deserve further investigation.

Age Differences

Collectively, findings from our research demonstrate that age has strong, positive effects on religious involvement across numerous indicators (Chatters & Taylor, 1989a; Ellison & Sherkat, 1995; Levin & Taylor, 1993; Taylor, 1988b), such that older black Americans report higher levels of religious participation than younger blacks (Nelsen & Nelsen, 1975; Welch, 1978). Across several data sets, age was a uniformly positive predictor of religious service attendance and non-organizational and subjective religious involvement. This is in contrast to prior evidence in which age differences are less straightforward. Specifically, declines in formal organizational activities have been noted with advanced age (Blazer & Palmore, 1976; Markides, 1983a; Mindel & Vaughan, 1978; Moberg, 1965), while non-organizational behaviors and subjective religiosity have been described as being either stable or increasing with age (Hunsberger, 1985; Levin, 1989; Moberg, 1971; Young & Dowling, 1987).

Chatters and Taylor (1989a) examined the specific effects of age on seven indicators of organizational, non-organizational, and attitudinal forms of religious involvement among adults across the entire age range. Among women, age was positively associated with each of the religiosity measures, while for men, "requests for prayer from others" was the only indicator for which age was not a significant predictor. Current models of age and religious involvement were evaluated, along with a discussion of possible age, period, and cohort differences. Together with other empirical data on religiosity among black Americans, these findings suggest that the religious experiences of African Americans are characterized by both relatively high levels of overall religious involvement and, further, a general linear and positive age trend whereby religious involvement increases with advanced age. Continuing research should investigate possible age differences in discrete aspects of religious involvement, as well as understanding the contribution of aging versus age cohort membership in observed age disparities.

Marital Status Differences

Previous research on marital status effects on religious involvement describes two patterns of relationships. The family surrogate model (Glock et al., 1967), a variant of the deprivation-compensation perspective, suggests that unmarried persons and childless couples compensate for the absence of spouse and/or family through religious involvement. In contrast, other work suggests that the institutions of church and marriage share a common core of values that foster integration within social contexts (Cornwall, 1989; Mueller & Johnson, 1975) and continuity in social and personal relationships (Levin & Vanderpool, 1989). In other words, the fundamental values that underlie marriage and religious commitment are mutually reinforcing and facilitate involvement in both spheres. Further, religious institutions sponsor a number of programmatic initiatives that specifically focus on marriage and family life. As a consequence, religious involvement is expected to be higher among married persons.

Previous findings, however, are equivocal, and being married is related to both higher (Beeghley, Van Velsor, & Bock, 1981; Cornwall, 1989; Mueller & Johnson, 1975; Taylor, 1986, 1988b) and lower (Berardo, 1967; Glock et al., 1967) levels of religious involvement. Although marital status is related to religious service attendance (marriage is associated with higher levels of attendance), the overall pattern for marital status effects is not entirely consistent. Research based on the NSBA consistently demonstrates that married black adults are more religious with respect to organization, non-organizational, and subjective religious participation (Chatters & Taylor, 1994; Ellison & Sherkat, 1995; Levin, Taylor, & Chatters, 1995; Taylor, 1988b). Conceivably the presence of a spouse provides a link or facilitates the involvement in religious pursuits.

Conversely, being divorced is a status that may not be condoned by the church and engenders a certain amount of stigma. This may result in negative sanctions from church members, including social isolation, ostracism, and an inordinate amount of gossip (Taylor & Chatters, 1988) (see Chapter 7 in this volume, Negative Interactions Among Church Members). These sanctions may over time result in lower levels of service attendance (Taylor, 1988b), lower levels of requesting prayers from others (Taylor & Chatters, 1991a), and less support received from church member networks (Taylor & Chatters, 1988).

Education and Income Differences

When we began conducting research in this area 20 years ago, we expected to find fairly large socioeconomic status differences in religious participation. Based upon traditional theoretical approaches to black religious behavior, we expected that respondents with lower levels of income and education would have significantly higher levels of religious participation. Much to our surprise, we found only a few significant income and education differences and, in some cases, the relationships were the reverse of what was expected.

As discussed previously (see section on Models of Religious Involvement in Black Churches), traditional models of black religious experience viewed the Black Church as a product of lower status black culture and, consequently, depicted this institution in a largely negative manner. Black religious traditions were thought to have isolated black communities from the mainstream, impeded the assimilation of blacks within broader society, promoted "other-worldly" religious orientations, and merely functioned as compensatory mechanisms for social and economic deprivations experienced within broader American society. Given this perspective, persons of lower social status were thought to demonstrate higher levels of religious involvement because it functioned to compensate for deprivations (e.g., social, economic, political, personal) in other areas of life (Glock et al., 1967). The contention that mere "deprivation" with respect to various social statuses motivates black religious involvement is not supported by our research (Taylor, 1988b; Chatters et al., 1999), as well as other previous work (Jacobson, Heaton, & Dennis, 1990; Nelsen & Nelsen, 1975).

Findings investigating the relationship between socioeconomic status (income and education) and religious participation help to shed light on these issues and many of the assumptions underlying traditional models of black religious expression. For example, in contrast to a deprivation-compensation explanation, individuals who occupied the devalued status position (i.e., lower education levels) were less likely to attend religious services and less likely to be church members (Chatters et al., 1999; Taylor, 1988b). The positive impact of education on these two measures of organizational religiosity may reflect generally higher levels of social integration and greater social resources among more educationally advantaged persons (Lenski, 1961). Educational attainment was important with respect to two types of private religious activities. Those with fewer years of education were less likely to read religious materials but were more likely to watch or listen to religious programming on television or radio (Chatters et al., 1999; Taylor & Chatters, 1991a). Research on religious television broadcasting suggests that viewers of religious programs tend to be of lower income and education levels. In our analyses, the findings suggest that persons with fewer years of formal education (and who presumably have lower levels of literacy) may use religious radio and television as an alternative or supplement to reading religious materials.

Our research has found that there were no significant income differences in religious service attendance, church membership, frequency of prayer, frequency of reading religious materials, and frequency of watching/listening to religious programming (Chatters et al., 1999; Taylor, 1988b). In one instance (Chatters et al., 1999), significant income differences were found for several measures of subjective religiosity—seeking spiritual comfort and support and intensity of denominational identification. Black adults with lower incomes were more likely than those with higher incomes to seek spiritual comfort and support and to consider themselves strong members of their denomination. Theoretical work on black religious orientations (Lincoln & Mamiya, 1990) and empirical investigations of religiosity among this group (e.g., Ellison & Gay, 1990) indicate that more complex models of black religiosity are necessary to reexamine and clarify the relationships of social status factors to religious involvement.

Regional and Urban-Rural Differences

Our research has found that Southern blacks had significantly higher levels of religious participation than blacks from other regions of the country. The regional difference is noted in higher levels of religious participation in terms of service attendance, non-organizational participation, and subjective religiosity (Chatters et al., 1999; Taylor, 1988b). These findings are consistent with other research that shows higher levels of religiosity among Southerners generally (Fichter & Maddox, 1965; Glenn, Gotard, & Simmons, 1977).

The impact of place of residence (i.e., region, urbanicity) on religious involvement is thought to reflect features of the personal relationships and broader social environments that ensue in these settings (Cornwall, 1989; Ellison & Gay, 1990; Roof, 1978; Stump, 1987). Lincoln and Mamiya (1990) describe socio-historical forces (e.g., migration patterns, residential segregation, Jim Crow laws, economic decline) as well as contemporary dynamics that influence social conditions that, in turn, fashion the character of black religious expression in differing contexts. Historically, black churches in the South exercised a pivotal role in responding to the oppressive social, political, and economic circumstances that characterized this region. As a result of widespread segregation and discrimination in other sectors and institutions in society, black churches were virtually unrivaled in that role. As a consequence, churches often assumed a variety of social welfare, educational, and political functions within black communities. The church and its related structures and mechanisms permeated the social and cultural environment of the South. Although only briefly sketched here, these and other social and historical factors combine to make the non-metropolitan South, or the traditional rural black belt, a uniquely distinctive setting with respect to the depth of religious commitment and involvement (for additional discussions of this issue see Ellison & Sherkat, 1995, 1999; Hunt, 1998; Hunt & Hunt, 1999, 2001; Nelsen, Yokley, & Nelsen, 1971; Sherkat, 1998).

In a comprehensive analysis of urban-rural differences (using 6 different national surveys and 16 measures of religious participation), Chatters et al. (1999) did not find any significant urban-rural disparities for organizational, non-organizational, or subjective religiosity. In contrast to this, other work using the National Survey of Black Americans found that in comparison to their urban counterparts, African Americans who resided in rural settings were more likely to be church members (Taylor, 1988b) and be involved in organizational religious activities (Ellison & Sherkat, 1995; Levin, Taylor, & Chatters, 1995). Religious services in rural churches are typically held on an occasional basis because they are served by circuit ministers who maintain several pastorates simultaneously (Jackson, 1983). Lincoln and Mamiya (1990) suggest that churches that are served by absentee pastors tend to develop congregations that function relatively independently of clerical leadership and are characterized by high levels of organizational activity. In a related vein, Taylor's (1988b) analysis demonstrated that urban-rural differences in church attendance are clarified when controls for frequency of religious services are taken into account. Whereas, previously, urban-rural differences in church attendance were nonexistent, the application of controls for frequency of religious services revealed that rural residents attended services more frequently than their urban counterparts.

Denominational Differences in Religious Participation

Only a limited amount of research has examined denominational differences in religious participation among black Americans. This may be due to the large number of different religious denominations, intra-denominational distinctions, and independent churches, which makes it extremely difficult for researchers to recode this variable into a few theoretically justifiable categories for complex statistical analysis. Chatters and colleagues (1999) found that black Catholics, as compared to Baptists, reported significantly lower levels of reading religious materials, watching or listening to religious programming, seeking spiritual comfort and support, and frequency of prayer. Research on older blacks (Taylor & Chatters, 1991a) also found that black Catholics had a significantly lower frequency of reading religious materials and watching religious programming than black Baptists, although there were no significant differences between Catholics and Baptists in the frequency of prayer. Chatters et al. (1999) found an interesting pattern with respect to non-organizational religious pursuits among blacks who are members of non-Christian denominations. Persons of non-Christian denominations are more likely than Baptists to read religious materials but less likely to watch or listen to religious programming. The lower frequency of watching/listening to religious programming almost certainly reflects the predominantly Christian focus of most black religious radio and television broadcasts.

Physical Health Differences

The majority of research on physical health and religious participation investigates the protective factors of religious participation on health. That is, particular types of religious participation may foster adaptive and protective behaviors (such as less risky health behaviors and positive coping strategies) that may have a positive impact (e.g., decreasing health problems or increasing longevity) on individual health status (this issue is explored in detail in Chapter 8). Considerably less research has focused on the impact of health on religious participation. That is, do health problems increase or decrease levels of religious participation of various types (e.g., church attendance, private devotional activities) among black Americans?

Taylor (1986) found that health impairment was not significantly associated with church attendance among older blacks adults, while Chatters and Taylor's (1989a) more detailed examination of age differences in religious participation found that there was a decrease in church attendance among blacks who were 75 and older. However, this age group still attended religious services more frequently than blacks who were between the ages of 18 and 45. Taylor and Chatters (1991a) found that among older blacks (55 years of age and older), health impairment was positively associated with watching or listening to religious programs but unrelated to frequency of prayer, reading religious materials, and requests of prayer from others. Collectively, these findings suggest that persons in poor health do not substitute non-organizational religious activities for church attendance but instead engage in both of these activities simultaneously. In addition to offering the ability to participate vicariously in religious services, religious television and radio programs, in particular, may contain elements that are particularly attractive to older persons who are in poor health. Common features of religious programs, such as special regard for persons who are experiencing a disability and an emphasis on the use of religion for healing and as a means of coping with physical ailments, have particular significance for persons who are ill.

A similar analysis (Hays, Landerman, Blazer, Koenig, Carroll, & Musick, 1998) among elderly blacks and whites found that overall health problems were associated with a decrease in service attendance, while frequency of watching or listening to religious programs was unaffected. Separate subgroup findings indicated that African American elderly had higher levels of watching/listening to religious programming than whites and, over time, increased their engagement with religious media. Musick and colleagues (Musick, Koenig, Hays, & Cohen, 1998) conducted a longitudinal analysis of religious participation among elderly adults with and without cancer. In the first wave of the study there were no differences in religious participation among elderly blacks with cancer and those without cancer. In the second wave of the study (3 years later) elderly blacks with cancer reported increases in private devotional activities (prayer, reading the Bible) but a decrease in church attendance.

Religious Participation Among Elderly Blacks

A previous section of the chapter that addressed age differences in religious involvement (see Age Differences) found that age is positively associated with a range of religious activities and sentiments. In this section, we review research findings that specifically explore variation in religious participation among older adults. First, Levin et al. (1994) found that elderly blacks had significantly higher levels of religious participation than elderly whites. This black-white difference in religious participation was consistent across several different measures and across four national surveys. Subsequent analysis of other data sets have also revealed the higher levels of religious participation among elderly blacks (e.g., Hays et al., 1998). Second, findings indicate that even though older blacks show overall elevated rates of church attendance, church membership, and identifying oneself as "religious," there are, nevertheless, significant differences in religious involvement within this group (Taylor, 1986). With respect to age, the oldest of this older group of respondents were more likely than their younger counterparts to describe themselves as "religious." Men demonstrated lower levels religious involvement on all three measures (i.e., attendance, membership, subjective religiosity) than women. With regard to marital status differences, persons who were divorced from their spouses had lower levels of all three indicators of religious involvement as compared with married persons; those who were widowed attended church less frequently and had lower levels of subjective religiosity as compared with married persons. Third, focusing only on non-organizational religious participation, Taylor and Chatters (1991b) found that the majority of older persons engaged in daily prayer, read religious materials, and watched or listened to religious programs on a weekly basis, and requested prayer on their own behalf several times a month (see Chapter 3 for a more detailed discussion of research on prayer and requests for prayer). Fourth, Chatters et al. (1992) proposed and tested a multidimensional model of religious participation among elderly black adults. Taken together with previous work, an emerging profile of religiosity among older black adults emphasizes a high degree of organized religious participation such as church attendance and church membership coupled with extensive involvement in private religious activities. In addition, research on elderly blacks has found that religion has a major impact on mental (see Chapter 9) and physical health (see Chapter 8), including significant differences in mortality rates.

Levin and Taylor's (1993) study of religiosity, gender, and aging among black Americans found that throughout the life cycle, both black men and women reported high levels of organizational, non-organizational, and subjective religiosity. Women, however, exhibited higher levels of religiosity than men for each of 12 religiosity indicators and across seven age strata. These findings persisted despite controlling for several established sociodemographic predictors of religious involvement. Interestingly, for certain organizational indicators, this gender gap narrowed somewhat or even reversed in the very oldest age groups, not unlike the famous "crossover" of black and white mortality rates. This gender crossover in religiosity may be a function of a progressive selecting-out of men due to declining health. In other words, older men may evidence lower levels of organizational religious indicators because poor health prohibits their participation.

Religious Participation Among Black Adolescents

Research examining religious participation among black adolescents (13–17 years of age) is virtually nonexistent. A search of the literature using several journal article search engines (i.e., Wilson Index, PsycINFO, and Sociofile) and using the keywords *black, adolescent,* and *religion,* produced only a handful of articles. The majority of research on religion within adolescent samples investigates the preventive role of religious beliefs on a wide range of negative behavioral and health outcomes such as criminal behavior, drug usage, binge drinking, drunk driving, cigarette smoking, sexual activity, and dietary patterns (see Wallace & Forman, 1998; Wallace & Williams, 1998; also see Chapter 8 in this volume, "Impact of Religion on Physical Health"). Overall, this research finds that adolescents who report higher levels of religious involvement are less likely to engage in risky behaviors.

Despite the emergence in the past few years of a body of research on religious participation among adolescents (Gunnoe & Moore, 2002; Smith, Denton, Faris, & Regnerus, 2002), almost no research focuses specifically on black adolescents. Overall, this research finds that 9 out of 10 adolescents have a religious affiliation and about half of all adolescents regularly participate in religious organizations in the form of service attendance and participation in religious youth groups (Smith et al., 2002). Consistent with research on adults and the elderly, black adolescents have significantly higher levels of religious participation than do white adolescents (Gunnoe & Moore, 2002; Smith et al., 2002; Taylor et al., 1996). As noted earlier in the chapter, denominational affiliation patterns of black adolescents are similar to those of black adults, with half stating that they are Baptist, 5% reporting Methodist, 7.8% indicating Church of Christ, and 10.9% stating that they do not have a denomination. Chatters et al. (1999) found that among black adolescents, girls had higher levels of religiosity than boys, and Southerners had higher levels of religiosity than adolescents in other regions.

Religious Noninvolvement

The evidence reviewed here indicates that affiliation with a religious tradition, in some manner or form, is a relatively common circumstance among African Americans (Nelsen, 1988; Welch, 1978). However, we know relatively little about a minority of persons who are seemingly disengaged from a religious framework (i.e., apostates). Data from the NSBA (Taylor, 1988a) suggest that relatively few people (10%) are religiously noninvolved (i.e., no current religious affiliation and have not attended religious services as an adult). Persons who were not involved with religious pursuits were generally male, younger, never married, had low levels of income and education, and resided outside of the South. Interestingly, a substantial number of those who identified themselves as religiously noninvolved said that they prayed on a frequent basis and characterized themselves as being fairly religious. This seemingly paradoxical pattern of an absence of overt religious involvement, coupled with private religious behaviors and religious self-characterizations, clearly underscores the multidimensional nature of religious behavior and sentiment.

Mattis, Taylor, and Chatters (2001) conducted a follow-up study of religious noninvolvement using the women's subsample of the NSBA along with data from several women's focus groups. Black women who report that they do not have a religious affiliation and never attend church, nonetheless pray on a fairly frequent basis and state that they are religious. For instance, among women who do not have a current religious affiliation, almost half (48.4%) report that they pray *nearly every day*. Further, two thirds of women who attend religious services less than once a year, and 56.8% of those who never attend religious services, indicate that they pray *nearly every day*. Similarly, half of the black women who report no religious affiliation, and 60% of those who never attend church or attend less than once a year, characterize themselves as either very or fairly religious.

Collectively, these findings suggest that black women who are seemingly detached from organized religion may not be irreligious. The lack of involvement in formal religious activities could conceivably reflect dissatisfaction with organized religion, as opposed to a lack of religious belief or doubt about the importance and efficacy of private prayer. Further, low levels of church attendance may also be due to the presence of severe health problems that prevent attendance. Complementary information from the focus groups amply demonstrated that religious experiences were important to African American women and were both a source of comfort when confronted with problems and facilitated a closer relationship with God. Finally, although the focus group participants varied in the degree to which they thought of themselves as "religious people," they uniformly indicated that their religious experiences were an integral part of their lives. Even women who characterized themselves as being "only a little religious" provided narratives indicating a deep personal commitment to religious concerns (Mattis et al., 2001).

In a recent qualitative study of patterns of religious noninvolvement among African American men, Mattis and colleagues found that men attributed their noninvolvement in organized religion to a number of factors. Twenty-nine percent attributed their noninvolvement to logistical problems and concerns (e.g., lack of transportation, health concerns, conflicts in time). Nineteen percent cited ideological clashes with churches, church leaders, or members; 16% identified moral or ethical concerns (e.g., corruption and hypocrisy of churches, church leaders, or church members) as the reason for their nonattendance; while 17% reported motivational issues (lack of interest). Finally, 11% reported a general belief that group worship was neither useful nor necessary, and 9% said their noninvolvement was because of dissatisfaction with the selection of local religious institutions (Mattis, Eubanks et al., in press).

Consistent with other work on religious participation among African Americans, it is important to note that, for most of these men, noninvolvement in organized religion does not reflect a lack of religious devoutness. Indeed, only 17% of the men who did not attend religious services identified themselves as "not at all religious," and only 12% reported that they "never pray." Men who were not involved in organized religious life were more likely than those who attended religious services to report that their fathers had low levels of service attendance. However, both religiously involved and uninvolved men were comparable with respect to their reports of how frequently they or their mothers attended church. It appears, then, that patterns of noninvolvement may be learned and that fathers play an important role in influencing religious involvement as well as noninvolvement. Similarly, men may learn a range of ways of expressing their faith (e.g., through prayer and other non-organizational strategies) that do not require them to be involved in organized religious life. Collectively, these findings corroborate other research indicating that, historically and contemporaneously, religion and religious institutions play a significant role in the lives of African Americans (Lincoln & Mamiya, 1990; Taylor et al., 1987).

Religious Artifacts

The presence of religious paintings, sculptures, and other religious items in the home is an important indicator of the salience of religion to the individual. The National Survey of Black Americans questionnaire contained a section in which the interviewer could record specific observations about the home environment. After the completion of the interview, interviewers indicated whether the following items were in the household: (a) black literature–like books, magazines, newspapers, (b) black art–like paintings of blacks, African artifacts, weavings, sculpture, etc., (c) religious paintings or other religious items, and (d) African- or non-European-style clothing like dashikis, headdress, robes, etc. Religious items (31.2%) were noted in the home most often, followed by black literature (21.8%), black art (17.2%), and African clothing (1.9%). These percentages likely underestimate the presence of these objects in the household, as interviewers may have had access to only one or two rooms in the home.

We conducted a multivariate analysis to determine who was more likely to have religious items in their homes. Consistent with other information on demographic correlates of religious participation, women and persons who were older, married, and resided in rural areas and the South were more likely than their counterparts to have religious items in their homes (see Table B.1 in Appendix B). Further, similar to other findings on religious involvement, neither income nor education level predicted ownership of religious artifacts.

Religious Identity

Group identity is a core aspect of an individual's life. For black Americans, group and personal identity is developed within an environment that is characterized by the presence of racism and discrimination, prejudice, and pejorative images of their racial group. The topic of group identity has become a major area of study in the behavioral and social sciences, encompassing a vast literature on issues of racial socialization (Demo & Hughes, 1990; Thornton, Chatters, Taylor, & Allen, 1990), developmental stages of racial identity (Cross, 1991), preferences for particular racial labels (i.e., black vs. African American; Thornton, Taylor, & Brown, 1999), and attitudes toward out-groups (Thornton & Taylor, 1988). Current conceptualizations of racial group identity (Sellers, Smith, Shelton, Rowley, & Chavous, 1998; Thornton, Tran, & Taylor, 1997) suggest that it is a complex, multidimensional construct that encompasses attitudes and beliefs about a wide range of identity groups (e.g., see work by Marx, 1967, on black Americans' attitudes toward black militants). However, very little research focuses on black Americans' identification with discrete subgroups of the black population (e.g., elderly blacks, poor blacks). Further, despite the high levels of religiosity among black Americans and the centrality of religious institutions, only a few research studies examine perceptions of closeness to "religious blacks" and their relation to questions of racial group identity.

A series of questions from the NSBA data set assesses respondents' perceptions of "closeness" to 11 subgroups of the black population (i.e., black people who are poor, religious/churchgoing black people, young black people, middle-class black people, working-class black people, older black people, black elected officials, black doctors/lawyers and other professionals, black people who rioted in the cities, black Americans who take African names, and black people who have made it by getting around the law). Respondents reported feeling closest to poor blacks, followed by working-class blacks, older blacks, and religious blacks. The groups that respondents felt least close to were "blacks who made it by getting around the law," followed by "black people who rioted in the city" (analysis of the NSBA panel data shows that these percentages are extremely stable across all waves of the survey). Focusing only on the category of religious blacks, 62% of respondents reported that they felt very close to religious, churchgoing black people, 26% stated that they felt fairly close, 10% said not too close, and only 2% reported not close at all.

We conducted a multivariate analysis to determine whether particular demographic factors were related to perceptions of closeness to religious, churchgoing blacks. Again, the results of this analysis were consistent with the general demographic differences in religious participation (see Table B.2 in Appendix B): women, older, married, rural, and Southern blacks were more likely than their counterparts to report feeling close to religious, churchgoing blacks. Interestingly, persons with fewer years of formal education were more likely to report feeling closer to religious blacks than their better-educated counterparts (in contrast to previous analyses in which socioeconomic status factors were unrelated to religious involvement).

Focus Group Findings

The survey research findings provide a broad profile of religious participation and information about how social status factors (e.g., age, gender, region) pattern religious activities and perceptions. In addition, we have qualitative data from the focus group study, "Appraisals of Religiosity, Coping and Church Support," that provide complementary information on the nature and meaning of the daily religious activities and observances of black Americans. These focus group narratives reveal a number of themes that speak to both the prominence and patterns of particular forms of religious activities and their functional significance in the lives of individual participants.

Prayer

Among focus group participants, one of the most frequently noted religious activities was prayer. Not only do individuals in the focus groups report that they make use of prayer as a daily religious activity (see Chapter 3 for a more in-depth discussion of prayer and Chapter 4 for a discussion of the use of prayer as a coping strategy), but many emphasized the importance of starting one's day with prayer. This first set of statements is by women:

> I pray at various times during the day. I do try to make sure I pray every morning 'cause I think it's good to start in the morning really talking with God.

> When I rise, you know, I have to have my devotional time. And that is seeking the face of God in prayer and praise and in the Word. I believe in acknowledging him in everything that I do.

> For me, my day usually starts about 5:30 in the morning because I do not like to rush you know. So as soon as I get out of bed I am on my knees praying just to set my mind for the day, just thanking God that it was by his grace and mercy you know that I saw another day.

> There was a time that I wouldn't say them in the morning, but I've learned that when I sacrifice and make sure that when I open my eyes and say, Thank you Lord for a beautiful day, regardless of what the weather looks like to anybody else, it makes my whole day, sets the tone for my whole day.

Two other women said that they pray at night:

> I say my prayers every night. I don't say them in the morning. I don't really have time in the morning. I get up kind of running, but I do say, Thank God. Thank you God for waking me up this morning. Thanks for the day. Whether it's snowing or raining or whatever and I'm moving. So I say my prayers at night and sometimes I go to bed and I forget to say them and I make myself get up. If I'm really exhausted, I'll lay there. I'll say, you understand Lord. I'm going to say my prayers lying right here like this. But most of the time I get up here on my knees. I feel like that's really important for some reason.

> I just say my prayers every night and I say prayers for other people. Every day I include somebody in my prayers. I'm a nurse. I work in a hospital and if I can't think of their name, I just say, help all the sick people.

It is important to note that these responses do more than highlight the role that the timing of prayer plays in the lives of these women. Indeed, these narratives reveal that prayer is a relational enterprise in which women are actively and dynamically engaged with God, and in which they establish or maintain systems of social support by seeking intercession on behalf of others (Mattis, 2002). The timing and circumstances in which women pray may reveal much to us about the role (e.g., reflective, protective, supportive) that the relationship with God plays in the lives of individual women.

Reading Religious Materials

Reading the Bible and other religious and devotional materials was another religious activity that was frequently mentioned. The overall tenor of these comments suggests that participants feel that reading religious materials is an integral part of their daily lives and is critical to their religious and spiritual development.

> I am reading the Daily Word and the Bible pieces that go along with that and then meditating on that and prayer. That is how I start my day.

> I do Daily Word that's put out by Unity Church and I read that. I try to each day, and if I don't, I try to go back and get current. I also pray at night. Daily, throughout the day I do affirmations in terms of God's evidence in my life.

> Well, the very first thing in the morning when I open my eyes, I thank the Lord for waking me up and then I go through this routine of reading my Bible every day. I have a daily bread that I go through. I have about three or four different books that I read every day and when I don't do this, it seems like my day does not go right. I usually do this before I even leave the house, you know, get up, wash my face, brush my teeth and go through my routine.

> I begin my day, as soon as I am aware of being alive, I give thanks. Sometimes I fall back to sleep because the conversation gets good. But, then when I get up, I have devotional books that I have one's that I do especially, and I try to depending upon my time, do 5 books from the Psalms each morning, one book of Proverbs, John 17, 23 Psalms.

> The other thing that would be a daily event or as often as possible was reading the Bible. It's like you get bits and pieces of it, so that's

something that I try to do on a daily basis. I'm not going to lie and say I do it on a daily basis, but as often as I can.

These narratives highlight the integrative and complementary roles that religious reading materials play. The act of reading, for some women, is fairly routinized, and the ritualistic nature of the activity may serve important palliative functions. However, it is also clear that the materials and perhaps their content are complements to women's active prayer lives.

Religious Programming

Survey data from both the National Survey of Black Americans and the American Changing Lives Survey indicate that more than half of the black population watches or listens to religious programming at least once a week. Underscoring the importance of religious broadcast media, several of the focus group participants mentioned that they watched religious television programs and listened to religious music as important aspects of their daily religious activities.

Every morning when I'm waking, I watch it the Christian station with [Television Minister A].

I usually like to start, as she was saying, [Television Minister A] a lot of mornings is my person I listen to sometime [Television Minister B], depends on what the subjects are that they are doing.

These points are consistent with research that suggests that televangelism and the electronic media now play increasingly important roles in the religious and spiritual lives of adults, especially black adults (see Hays et al., 1998).

Meditation

Focus group participants also reported that spending quiet time in reflection or meditation were important religious activities. These types of activities are not generally included in most major surveys. Fortunately, the 1998 General Social Survey has a measure assessing frequency of meditation. Overall, two out of three black Americans engage in meditation. Slightly more than half of all black Americans meditate at least once a week, and one out of three meditates at least once a day. Clearly, meditation is an important activity for a large portion of the African American adult population.

I don't have any strict tradition or anything in the morning. I have three children and a husband and a lot of work, so um…I'm always mindful of him [God], and I always greet Him in the mornings and sometimes I get my kids out and then I have some quiet time with Him.

Well for me I try to read a daily scripture every day and pray. But, more importantly, I think I just try to reflect. I have the tendency to get like over anxious or very impatient and so when I feel like kind of overwhelmed I'll try to reflect on times in my life where I know that He's kind of guided me and supported me and just shown me the way. And just to remember that I can't do everything by myself. And so, it may not actually be prayer but just like quiet time to try to soothe things out.

First thing in the morning, I would get on the bus around 6:30, so I would use that as some quiet time. Sometimes I don't pray. I kind of just sit there and try to listen, you know, sit down and the Holy Spirit, how I respond to that will be how my day goes.

I start my day by praying and before I get my husband up then I have my quiet time to kind of meditate and get myself ready for the rest of the day, cause once the day starts…

I also maintain a regular, daily form of meditation along with my workout schedule that I have. I found out that prayer and meditation and working out works for me and that's at least, and I say at least, every day that I am working out so that's minimum of 4 days a week. There are other times when I am not working out where I do meditate, I do pray.

These narratives are consistent with Mattis's (2002) finding that "waiting," "being still," and "going inside" are important aspects of one's religious experience that reveal the dynamic, relational nature of religious life. That is, they demonstrate the importance of not just talking with God (i.e., praying) but crafting ways to listen to and discern God's will. These moments of reflection also provide opportunities for emotional self-regulation. In one of the focus groups, two men also mentioned the importance of daily meditation as a type of religious activity. The second statement directly followed the first comment:

Meditate. It is something I do in the morning and sometimes during the day, later during the day and it relieves the stress. You just really

just let go of whatever it is you have, you let this other, you let the
spirit in, you know, like, it is like reading really.

I would have to agree with that. But it is not just at a specific time of
day, whenever, you know, at every opportunity or whenever something
comes up . . . but prayer and meditating would be a daily occurrence
throughout the day for me.

Religious Participation in the Context of Work

In contrast to comments about discrete religious activities, a number of
focus group participants talked about the tangible ways in which they practiced their religion in their daily lives. Several noted that they practiced their
religious beliefs within the context of their work and jobs. It is important
to note that all of the individuals quoted in these passages indicated that
they had jobs in social welfare agencies.

I think that when I go to work every day, that's me tapping into the
things of God. My job is working with like a social service type
agency—working with indigent seniors, finding ways to enable them to
remain in their homes, finding ways to make sure that they can have
lights and water and gas and making sure that they are able to have
three squares in some kind of way. To me, that's doing it unto God.
The Bible says that when you do it to the least of them, that you've
done it unto me.

And then I also work at a Christian agency and I think that's important
because I look at that as being a part of the ministry to other people.

Once I get to work, I am constantly praying and witnessing because of
the type of job I am doing. I work with battered and abused women
and children and I know the Lord has called me there for that reason
and constantly just sharing the Lord with them, you know, given the
situation that they are in and that's like all of the time. It's like a
constant thing so it's keeping me abreast and I believe I have
something to share with them which is Christ you know.

These statements highlight the role that religion and spirituality play in
imbuing work with meaning. Work, when seen as a part of a divine mission
or as a way of giving honor to God, is interpreted as an extension of Christian
ministry. In this regard, the workplace becomes a context in which individuals can witness directly or indirectly (e.g., by personal example) to others.

Living in a Christ-Like Manner

Focus group participants also mentioned that their daily religious activity involved consciously living in a Christ-like manner and treating others with dignity and respect. These narratives also underscore the importance of conducting oneself in a manner that embodies an authentic religious life (i.e., giving witness to Christ through one's actions).

> I also think it's important that your life is an example of Christ too. I mean, so everything you do should be in his likeness. You know you should be trying to do stuff, everything you do should be I guess spiritual if that's the word you want to use.

> Me, I don't attend church regularly, so I just use everyday life as far as respect towards elders and what one should do. You know, I think that's important.

> I'm a member of [X] Baptist Church. I don't attend like I'm supposed to attend, you know what I'm saying? But I have religious preferences in my heart towards people.

> I try to deal with my coworkers in a Christ-like manner. Sometimes they'll come to me and we'll talk over problems. We've had opportunities from time to time to start Bible studies there at work. I work with seniors every day all day long, and sometimes I may be the only person that they see in the course of their day, and I let them know that I love God and all the things that I do and I'm here to help you in any kind of way, to reassure them along those lines.

Volunteerism as a Form of Religious Participation

Focus group participants also noted that pro-social activities, such as volunteering in prisons and soup kitchens, were part of their religious activities. One man characterized these activities as an example of living in a Christ-like fashion as a form of religious participation.

> I also visit, maybe twice, three times a month I'll go to visit the elderly at the home for the aged if I have time during the week or if I ever have spare time I'll go and visit people in the hospital or that's confined to home.

This articulated link between religion and volunteerism is consistent with the civic orientation of the Black Church (see Lincoln & Mamiya, 1990) and highlights the point that, for many African Americans, civic and charitable involvement may be seen as essential aspects of devotional life. Further, this link between religion and volunteerism is consistent with recent findings that suggest that religiosity is potent predictor of volunteerism among African Americans (see Mattis et al., 2000; Mattis, Beckham et al., in press; Musick, Wilson, & Bynum, 2000).

Organized Religious Activities

With respect to more formal, organizational activities, focus group participants also discussed the weekly religious practices they are involved in at their churches. There was a considerable variability in both the amount and level of participation; some went to church on Sundays only, while others attended twice a week or more. For some participants, attending church on Sunday could involve activities for most of the day (i.e., Sunday school class, the regular service, dinner at church, and evening service). The following statements reflect different types and levels of participation in organized religious activities.

> Well about the last three weeks, I have been running to the church with pastor. He calls a prayer at seven o'clock every morning. So, we have been going to church at seven o'clock and have our prayer for an hour.

> With me, it's regular church attendance, definitely Sundays. I grew up where you didn't miss church on Sunday. That was an absolute no-no. So, I was kind of ingrained in the church so I knew Sunday was God's day.

> And so basically I am in Bible class on Wednesday and Sunday all day. We are basically at church from about 9 probably until 2, 2:30 and then we break and go back to 4:30 services and finish by about 7:30 or 8 o'clock on Sundays.

> For me it's structured church services twice a week, Sunday and Thursday. Thursday is our midweek service. Also structured daily, reading of the bible, trying to read a couple of chapters, at least a chapter, every morning as well as spending some time in prayer and praise of God. Unstructured would probably be as I am driving or going to take care of some business or even in work settings as I think about something that bothers me I tend to try to pray about the issue.

These statements reveal that the type, level, and schedule of religious practice are determined by a number of factors, including institutional practice (e.g., whether or not there is a Bible study and when Bible study is scheduled), institutional demands (e.g., requests made by religious leaders), as well as by early socialization experiences (e.g., growing up in a household where church attendance was expected and reinforced). In addition, one man noted that even though there are occasions when he travels on weekends, he finds other means of observing religious services on Sunday mornings.

> Other than getting to church as much as possible with my busy schedule, which includes not only working for [Company X], but also running a business, so it takes me away sometimes on weekends out of town. So in those times because they created mediums that will allow you to still kind of continue religious practices, I watch several of the ministers on TV during those times.

Religious media play a supplementary role in the worship experiences of men such as this. The increasing popularity of these venues of worship offers a direct challenge to those who uncritically insist that churches and religion are declining in significance and that the numbers of people who are physically present for worship services can be used as the sole indicator of the fate of the church or religion.

Finally, the following description of daily and weekly religious practices by a woman focus group member provides a sense of both the diverse forms of religious observance that she engages in and their personal significance for her life.

> I usually get up in the morning. I have two very lively kids and I get up very early for work...and morning time, that's my time, peaceful time for God. I pray before I go to work and then I pray out loud also in the car so my kids can hear and because I choose to bring them up knowing God, knowing the spirit of God and so they won't be ashamed of who God is and it's okay to for them to have faith in God. And I read my Bible every chance I get. I work in a factory so sometimes I work harder at two jobs sometimes I don't. Definitely when I get onto an easy job I read my Bible and study my Sunday School and on breaks and things like that, I try to read my Bible and pray and meditate. That's the most important is meditate on God, his Word mostly because when you get that word in your spirit and in your heart and that just, that helps you, through different trials and tribulations you might be going through or just to get through the day. And I go to Bible class on Wednesdays and prayer meetings and that helps because you need to be social with different sisters and brothers in the Lord and that, that gives you encouragement to go through,

keep walking in God and, and to grow in God and that helps others too. Church on Sundays and I pray. I don't feel like praying is a schedule. It is something that God bring to you any time of the night, any time of the day as far as movement, you know, you might feel more spiritual through praying more than other times praying. I pray at night and I pray with my children. They say their little prayers at night.

Throughout the week she uses a variety of strategies (e.g., private readings of the Bible, attending Bible class) to help her to internalize certain ideas, beliefs, and understandings and to facilitate her own religious growth. However, we once again see the relational focus of religiosity, for she is concerned about and responsible for both her own religious development and the religious lives of her children. She explicitly uses publicly voiced prayers as a way of socializing her children into a particular understanding about God and about the value of prayer (i.e., she shapes their prayer lives, in part, by exposing them to hers).

Focus Group Summary

The focus group information provides an additional lens through which to view African Americans' religious participation. The analysis of survey data provides a general profile of religious involvement and an appreciation of status group differences in these behaviors. The focus group information, on the other hand, develops a broader sense of context within which to situate these experiences and the personal meaning that individuals attach to these activities. Of special note were references to specific private activities (e.g., religious reading, use of broadcast media) that are not adequately assessed in general surveys. Particularly prominent in these discussions were references to the functional aspects of specific religious activities, such as prayer (e.g., stress reduction) and meditation. We will turn to more in-depth considerations of what prayer is, how individuals define prayer, and the functions that it serves in Chapters 3 and 4. Finally, the focus groups provided important information about how religious activities reinforced specific role identities (particularly those involving work) and standards of interpersonal behavior and conduct (Ellison, 1991b). Focus group members commented on their attempts to give witness to their faith by embodying and enacting specific behaviors and attitudes that were reflective of an authentic religious life.

Chapter Summary and Conclusion

The nature and determinants of spirituality and religious participation among African Americans has been a topic of systematic research interest for well over 50 years. Research shows that the majority of African Americans report that they are both spiritual and religious and that spirituality and religiosity are intertwined but conceptually distinct experiences. Theoretical models of the Black Church and religious expression often viewed these manifestations and religious practices in isolation from the unique and dynamic social, political, and historical contexts that characterized the position of blacks within American society. As a result, characterizations of black religious behavior and attitudes (e.g., otherworldly, cultural isolation, and stagnation) often emphasized its deleterious influence on the development and advancement of black communities. In contrast, Lincoln and Mamiya's Dialectical Model emphasized the adaptive nature of black religious institutions and expression and presented a more nuanced understanding of the Black Church. In addition, research efforts involving large and representative samples of the black population began systematically to assess and evaluate hypotheses regarding black religious expression suggested by theory.

This chapter reviewed published research documenting the nature and extent of sociodemographic variation in religious involvement within samples of African Americans across the entire adult age range, as well as investigations focusing solely on older persons. In addition, other work reviewed advances in the conceptualization and measurement of religious involvement, investigated race differences in religious participation, and explored religious involvement within discrete groups of the black population. Several conclusions can be drawn from this body of research.

African Americans hold a positive attitude about churches and the diverse functions (e.g., social, religious, material support) that they fulfill for individuals, families, and communities (Taylor et al., 1987). African Americans exhibit fairly high levels of religious involvement and report more than 40 different religious affiliations; half identify with the Baptist tradition, about 1 out of 10 report being Methodist, and 6% to 8% state that they are Catholics. Religious affiliation among black Americans is relatively stable over time (Ellison & Sherkat, 1990), but among those who changed affiliations, Baptists were more likely to switch to small conservative Protestant groups, and Methodists were more likely to become Baptist. Individuals who relinquished their affiliation with black mainline denominations (i.e., apostates) were more likely to be male, younger, reside outside the South (i.e., in the Northeast, North Central, and West), hold negative attitudes about black churches, and have infrequent contact with family members.

Research efforts using NSBA data have confirmed that religious involvement can be effectively measured (among elderly and non-elderly groups) in terms of organizational, non-organizational, and subjective religiosity dimensions. Sociodemographic factors (e.g., age, gender, marital status, income, education, urbanicity, and region) performed largely as expected as predictors of religious involvement and were differentially predictive of the three dimensions, suggesting that the constructs are distinct. Overall, black Americans attend religious services on a frequent basis, have high rates of church membership, characterize themselves as being religious, and are extensively involved in private religious activities (e.g., prayer, reading religious materials, viewing/listening to religious programming). However, there is considerable heterogeneity in religious involvement despite overall high levels of religiosity, as reflected in significant age (Chatters & Taylor, 1989a), gender (Levin & Taylor, 1993), and regional (Ellison & Sherkat, 1995; Taylor, 1988b) differences. Although less consistent, marital status and urbanicity differences in religious involvement are also found. The direction and pattern of empirical findings for sociodemographic correlates (e.g., age, gender, socioeconomic status, region) of religious involvement are consistent with current explanatory models of religious involvement (e.g., social roles, social networks, and place-of-residence effects).

Race comparative analyses involving both elderly (Levin et al., 1994) and adults in general (Taylor et al., 1996) find that blacks exhibit significantly higher levels of religious participation than whites. Levin et al.'s (1994) analysis of four national surveys and Taylor et al.'s (1996) analysis of seven national data sets found that, compared with whites, blacks demonstrated higher levels of public (e.g., religious attendance), private (e.g., reading religious materials), and subjective (e.g., importance of religion, religious comfort) religious involvement. These differences persisted despite controls for demographic (e.g., socioeconomic status, region) and religious (i.e., religious affiliation) factors that are differentially distributed within black and white populations and are known to be of consequence for religious involvement.

Our analyses suggest that the small minority of persons who report a complete absence of all overt religious involvement (i.e., no affiliation or church attendance) are distinctive in several ways: They tend to be male, younger, never married, have low levels of income and education, and live outside of the South. Interestingly, a substantial number of persons who are not involved in formal religious activities nonetheless say that they pray on a frequent basis and characterize themselves as being fairly religious

(Taylor, 1988a). This apparent paradox highlights the distinction between formal and private religious activities. With regard to issues of group identity, when asked how close they are in their feelings towards various groups, we find that almost 9 out of 10 black adults indicate that they are either very close or fairly close in their feelings toward religious, church-going blacks. Approximately 30% of black Americans have religious paintings or other religious items in their homes. Similar to other measures of religious involvement, women, older persons, married persons, and rural and Southern residents were more likely to have religious artifacts in the home. Finally, the findings from the focus group study provided important information on the ways in which individuals enact their faith in their everyday lives (i.e., embodying religious principles) and a variety of religious activities (e.g., prayer and meditation, reading religious materials, attending religious services) that are integral components in the daily lives of African Americans.

Chapter 3

The Frequency and Importance of Prayer

Prayer, in one form or another, is the most widely recognized and universally practiced religious behavior (Castelli, 1994; Levin & Taylor, 1997). As distinct from other types of religious involvement, prayer is an activity that can be done any time of day or night and engaged in by anyone regardless of their income level or health status. Prayer figures prominently in anecdotal and personal narratives of religious experiences and is identified as one of the most fundamental and important forms of religious participation (Patillo-McCoy, 1998). Despite the prevalence and apparent significance of this religious behavior, prayer as a religious phenomenon has been largely ignored by social scientists. Investigations of prayer are typically restricted to overall assessments of its frequency within the population or, at best, cursory treatments of the use of prayer as a coping strategy (a topic that is discussed in greater depth in Chapter 4). Prayer is undoubtedly the most personal and immediate of religious activities and holds particular interest in terms of the distinctive and individual meanings that are attached to this practice and the particular forms that prayer may take. Investigating the nature and meaning of prayer, however, does not lend itself easily to survey research formats. Other types of research (e.g., qualitative studies, in-depth interviews) and sources of information (e.g., personal religious narratives) about prayer provide an important resource both for developing items suitable for survey administration and in the interpretation of survey results (Krause, Chatters, Meltzer, & Morgan, 2000b).

The present chapter examines available research on the use of prayer among black Americans. It begins with a brief literature review of survey research estimates on the overall frequency of prayer, followed by a review of findings on the correlates of prayer among black Americans. National estimates of prayer frequency among African Americans from the 1998 General Social Survey are included in this section. Following this, findings on the importance and meaning of prayer from the focus group study, "Appraisals of Religiosity, Coping and Church Support," are discussed. Lastly, the chapter ends with a summary and conclusion on the nature and meaning of prayer for African Americans.

Research on Prayer

National surveys of the American population demonstrate that prayer is an important religious activity and that the vast majority of Americans pray on a frequent basis (Poloma & Gallup, 1991). Survey data indicate that, overall, roughly 9 out of 10 Americans report that they engage in prayer. Data from the 1998 General Social Survey indicate that half of all Americans engage in private prayer at least once a day, while a quarter of Americans engage in private prayer more than once a day. One of the limitations of most survey research investigations is that only one or two questions about the frequency of prayer are typically asked, and it is rare that more detailed questions are asked regarding the type of prayer or the personal meaning of prayer.

The most extensive survey research work on prayer was conducted by Margaret Poloma and George Gallup and reported in their book *Varieties of Prayer* (Poloma & Gallup, 1991). The book describes the results of a national survey involving in-depth inquiries about the nature of prayer, including interest in prayer activities (what people do when praying) and prayer experiences. Four types of prayer were identified: ritualist or ritual prayer, colloquial or conversational prayer, petitionary prayer, and meditative prayer. *Ritual* prayer includes reading from a book of prayers or reciting memorized prayers, such as those appearing in daily devotionals. *Conversational* prayer is a broad category that is characterized as an informal conversation with God. *Petitionary* prayer is requesting spiritual or material things in response to perceived needs. Lastly, *meditative* prayer includes quietly thinking about, experiencing, or worshipping God or listening for God's voice.

Poloma and Gallup (1991) found that 95% of Americans engaged in conversational prayer, 22% read from a book of prayers, 50% recited prayers that they had memorized, 42% indicated that they prayed for material things (i.e., petitionary prayer), and 52% engaged in some form of meditative prayer.

Blacks were significantly more likely than whites to engage in ritual prayer and petitionary prayer. The black-white difference in petitionary prayer is especially pronounced, with 38% of whites engaging in petitionary prayer as compared with 66% of blacks. The four types of prayer identified by Poloma and Gallup are not mutually exclusive. Rather, particular individuals seem to have a preference for more than one type of prayer, and multiple forms of prayer are typically manifested within a single worship experience, such as a church service (Levin & Taylor, 1997, p. 85).

Krause and colleagues examined beliefs about how prayer works among a sample of older black and white adults (Krause et al., 2000b). Their examination of focus group narratives uncovered three major themes regarding prayer. The first concerned various ways in which prayer operates, with particular attention given to issues of the timing of prayer (e.g., length of time for prayers to be answered) and how prayers are answered (e.g., discontinuities between what was requested and what was received). The second theme discussed by focus group participants involved perceived differences between group prayer and private prayer with respect to their purpose, efficacy, and benefits to participants. The third identified theme, how prayer is helpful when coping with a personal problem, touched upon issues of personal control and the role of God in responding to life problems (i.e., "Turning the problem over to God," Krause et al., 2000b, p. 210). Importantly, this study revealed that perceptions and beliefs about prayer and how it operates are extremely complex and subjective and deserving of additional study.

Research on Prayer Among Black Americans

To date, very little research has examined prayer among black Americans. The majority of the research on blacks and religion has centered on the institution of the Black Church and, as such, has not focused on the public and private religious behaviors of individuals. In large part, research on African American religion has been concerned with social-historical treatments of the church or in-depth ethnographies of individual congregations. For instance, Lincoln and Mamiya's (1990) classic social history of the Black Church does not address the issue of prayer, and the term itself is not included in the index to the book.

An exploration of prayer as a personal religious behavior can provide us with a greater understanding of black Americans' beliefs and perceptions regarding prayer and the particular uses for which it is relevant and appropriate. Table 3.1 provides the percentage distribution for frequency of prayer among black Americans from the 1998 General Social Survey. According to the table, about 3 out of 10 black Americans pray at least once a day, and

Table 3.1   Prayer Frequency from the 1998 General Social Survey

How Often Do You Pray? (10 Category Response)	*Percentage*
Several times a day	36.4
Once a day	31.8
Several times a week	8.4
Every week	3.9
Nearly every week	3.9
2–3 times a month	3.2
About once a month	2.6
Several times a year	4.5
Less than once a year	0.6
Never	4.5
TOTAL	100.0
N	154

How Often Do You Pray? (5 Category Response)	*Percentage*
Several times a day	38.9
Once a day	35.9
Several times a week	12.1
Once a week	3.0
Less than once a week	10.1
TOTAL	100.0
N	198

How Often Do You Pray Privately?	*Percentage*
More than once a day	41.3
Once a day	31.1
A few times a week	9.2
Once a week	3.6
A few times a month	4.1
Once a month	1.0
Less than once a month	3.6
Never	6.1
TOTAL	100.0
N	196

4 out of 10 report that they pray more than once a day. Overall, 80% of respondents state that they pray several times a week. These percentages are consistent with recent findings from the National Survey of American Life, which reports that 8 out of 10 black adults say that they pray nearly every day, and less than 2% indicate that they never pray. These percentages are also consistent with findings from other surveys, including various Gallup polls and the National Survey of Black Americans.

Our research team has conducted initial work on the correlates of the frequency of prayer among black Americans. First, in an analysis of black-white differences in religious participation, Taylor and colleagues (Taylor,

Chatters, Jayakody, & Levin, 1996) found that, consistent with other types of religious participation, blacks prayed more frequently than whites. This finding was upheld when controlling for socioeconomic status, region, religious affiliation, and other variables that are known to be associated with race and religious participation. Gallup Poll data also indicate blacks (23%) are more likely than whites (19%) to report that they pray three or more times a day (Poloma & Gallup, 1991).

An analysis based on the National Opinion Research Center's General Social Survey (Levin & Taylor, 1997) found that prayer is practiced at all ages but is more frequent among the elderly, women, and African Americans than their counterparts (i.e., younger adults, men, and whites). Several reasons were identified for why some people pray more often than others. Those who pray more frequently (a) tended to be more religious, overall; (b) have religious beliefs or worldviews that approved of and encouraged frequent prayer; (c) are motivated to pray frequently because of their perceived connectedness to God or the spiritual world; and/or (d) they belong to social groups that involve common life experiences that foster more frequent prayer (i.e., distinctive age cohorts).

Research on black Americans indicates that age and gender are particularly strong correlates of prayer (Chatters & Taylor, 1989a; Chatters, Taylor, & Lincoln, 1999). Chatters and Taylor (1989a) found that successively older age groups reported a higher frequency of prayer, with the oldest age group (75 years and older) reporting the most frequent rates of prayer. Women also prayed more frequently than men, although both groups reported high levels of prayer. In addition, Chatters and colleagues (1999) found denominational differences indicating that Catholics prayed less frequently than Baptists. Analysis of frequency of prayer using the National Survey of Black Americans revealed several significant demographic differences. In particular, women, older respondents, and Southern residents reported that they prayed more frequently than their counterparts (see Table B.3 in Appendix B). These findings are consistent with other work on demographic differences in religious participation (see Chapter 2).

A separate line of research examining black Americans who are not formally associated with religion (i.e., persons who are unaffiliated and don't attend church) provides further confirmation of the importance of prayer in this group (Taylor, 1988a). Four out of 10 blacks (40.9%) who are not affiliated with a religious denomination and almost half (48.2%) of blacks who have not attended church since the age of 18 report that they pray nearly every day. An investigation of religious noninvolvement among black women also revealed fairly high levels of prayer in this group (Mattis, Taylor, & Chatters, 2001). For instance, almost half of the black women (48.4%) who do not have a current religious denomination, 66.3% of women who attend religious services less than once a year, and 56.8% of women who never attend religious services say that they, nonetheless, pray every day. Similar findings emerged from a study of noninvolved African American men. Fifty-six percent of men who report that they do not attend religious services indicate that they pray "sometimes," and an additional 32% report that they pray "very often" (Mattis, Eubanks et al., in press). This pattern of findings suggests that, while formal religious participation may not be essential for these individuals, prayer remains an important element of their lives.

Requests for Prayer

The practice or act of requesting prayer from others is another important dimension of prayer that has been investigated among black Americans. In the National Survey of Black Americans, requests for prayer was measured in the following manner: "How often do you ask someone to pray for you?" Thirteen percent (13.6%) of respondents reported that they asked someone to pray for them nearly every day; 17.9% at least once a week; 19.1% a few times a month; 20.8% a few times a year; and 28.6% reported that they never requested prayer from others. The same question was asked in the National Survey of American Life. In this recent survey the frequency of requesting prayer was substantially higher, with almost one out of four respondents indicating that they asked someone to pray for them nearly every day and roughly 20% indicating that they never requested prayer from others. In contrast to private prayer, requests for prayer from others were reported less frequently. This is likely due to the fact that requests for prayer involve a social exchange between individuals (and may be constrained by time and opportunity), whereas private prayer can be independently initiated at any time.

Analysis of the National Survey of Black Americans (Chatters & Taylor, 1989a) shows that similar to private prayer, age and gender were also strong correlates of requesting prayer from others, with black women and older blacks requesting prayer from others more frequently than their counterparts. Across age groups, there was a modest decline in the percentage of respondents who requested prayers from others among the oldest age group (75 years of age and older). Again, this likely reflects the more social nature of this religious activity and the fact that, as compared with younger persons, older adults of advanced age may have serious health problems that restrict their ability to interact with their family and church members. Finally, an additional study among older blacks (Taylor & Chatters,

1991a) underscored the social nature of requesting prayer from others. In this analysis, divorced respondents were less likely than married persons to request prayer from others. This finding is consistent with other work indicating that divorced blacks were less involved in church support networks (see Chapter 6) and attend religious services less frequently than their married counterparts (see Chapter 2).

Focus Group Findings

The focus group study, "Appraisals of Religiosity, Coping and Church Support," devoted a portion of the protocol to the investigation of the nature and meaning of prayer. In particular, we asked focus group participants why they prayed and what they prayed for. Their responses are discussed below.

Communication and Relationship With God

Several of the major themes that emerged from the focus group discussions centered around the idea that prayer was a form of communication with God that often served the purpose of maintaining one's relationship with God. In some instances, the focus group responses mentioned communication and relationship as separate ideas. In several cases, however, they were discussed together. In these instances, the notion of a relationship with God appeared to follow from the ability to use prayer to communicate with God. For example, many of the participants said that through prayer they had a direct link to God.

> Sometimes you just want to sit back and say, "What's up?" Just chill with him. I don't think that you have to have any type of ritual or any specific way that you have to go to him. I think that just be yourself and just tap into him and he hears you. He's a loving kind of God.

> Communicating on a consistent, regular basis to, you know, get through what we need to get through.

> I guess, we think of prayer as certain designated times like a blessing at the table or at night when you go to bed as a child, but I also think of like when people are in trouble, suddenly they find religion or they turn to prayer when they need it. You see athletes on the field all the time. And, you know, I thought about how I have perhaps or am

maturing as a Christian and now there are times when I use prayer as
communication and not so much asking for something, just even
expressing thanks, but it's communication. So I do think that prayer is
a big part, but not only when, you know, at times of stress, but when
times, things are going well.

To me, like I say, prayer, praying to me is like your personal time with
God. It's like you away from everybody and you can just talk to God,
communicate with him and then, you know, I pray about things like, I
mean to help me. I go ask God to help me show me the right way, lead
me in the right direction because some things I know I ain't doing
right, so I pray, and I know prayer changes things, so, that's what
prayer is to me.

These narratives reveal a range of important points about the significance of prayer as a mode of communication between God and believers.
The first of these narratives points to the fact that for some believers, prayer
is not an act that is steeped in formality. This focus group member reveals
that for her, prayer involves a particular kind of comfortable familiarity
and intimate communication with God. This comfortable familiarity is consistent with scholarly arguments that African American believers experience
God as the ultimate ally, brother, father, and friend. Further, the act of
praying adds another layer of intimacy by carving out a private space that
grants a certain kind of intimate exclusivity to the relationship and the communication. Prayer, from the perspective of these narratives, is a form of
communication that requires no particular structure. There are no rituals,
or times of day, or conditions that are necessary for accessing or communicating with God. Prayer requires only that the person have an interest in
connecting, a need that drives the connection, a commitment to honesty
(e.g., being yourself), and consistency of communication.

Other references to prayer as communication were linked to the idea of
building relationship, as illustrated in the following responses:

I sincerely believe that Christ is able to talk to you through prayer. And
for me, I know, prayer is sometimes difficult because and when it's
just you alone, there is no lies to anybody, it's just you and Christ, it's
like if you talk to someone who really knows you really well, who really
cares about you, they see right through you, and you don't even want
to talk to them, you don't even want to be around them because you
know as soon as you start talking, they be like, Man please. Going to
Christ is building that relationship, but Christ requires all honesty, you
know, so being in prayer, so prayer helps to get you to that point and

whether people understand it or not, Christ can be a little more revealing than your family or friends because your family and friends, they always have their skepticism or their doubt, but Christ knows you inward and outward.

For me, the ability to just communicate with God is the primary reason for prayer. I grew up in foster care, in foster homes so I really never had anybody that I could particularly depend on, and when I discovered Christianity, unlike other religions I had looked at it was the only religion that offered me a relationship with God instead of an organized system of rituals, so that really attracted me.

These statements by focus group participants clearly reveal the importance of prayer, not only as a means of communicating with God but also as a process of building a relationship with God. Focus group participants also made a distinction between this type of personal communication with God versus prayer that is more formal, ritualistic prayer. In particular, although focus group participants felt that ritualistic prayer was important, engaging in prayer as a form of communication reflected a more mature aspect of prayer that was critical for developing a close relationship with God. This type of communication with God is consistent with Poloma and Gallup's (1991) category of conversational prayer. However, Poloma and Gallup note that conversational prayer may, in fact, be more of a monologue than a dialogue with God. In contrast, the focus group participants clearly indicated that they felt that through their prayer they were in true dialogue with God, in which they not only spoke with God but also one in which God spoke with them.

Other themes expressed by participants had a relatively stronger emphasis on the relational aspects of prayer and its significance as a means by which to establish connection with God.

Prayer is very instrumental, you can't have a relationship with someone that you don't talk to, just flat out.

Yeah, you know, like God's a friend, he's a peer and he's an employer, I mean he's a physician, he's a lawyer, he's whatever you need him to be and so you go to him correctly for those different reasons for those circumstances.

Prayer, prayer is the same question why you would have communication with your wife or your girlfriend. It develops your relationship and as Christians that's one thing that we or I believe that we need to do.

I have to elaborate on prayer. I can't leave that alone, I can't leave that alone, I can't leave that thing alone. It's like the brother said, it is a relationship, a relationship. This intimacy with him, ah, just like that brother said, it's a privacy that you can go to him anytime. His line ain't never busy. And I think about coming up as a kid that my mother used to say, "Son, pray."

God as Best Friend

As a further elaboration on the themes of communication and relationship, some focus group participants characterized their prayer relations with God as possessing ever-increasing levels of intimacy and specificity—from communication, to relationship, to a specific kind of intimate relationship, such as a best friend.

> Prayer for me is just so many things for me because God is like, my best friend, you know, he is with me all the time.

Consistent with the expectations of close friendships, one focus group participant emphasized the point that the relationship that is constructed with God is one of mutual care. She states:

> I just talk with him and sometimes I just talk with him just to get an update. So, sometimes I am in class—I am a student—and I'm in class and we're in break and I am like, "Hey God, how are you today? I know you are doing great 'cause you're God," you know, stuff like that, and then we just talk about stuff. I say, "You know the craziest thing happened today," and then I say, "Oh, I gotta go because break is over and the teacher is starting to teach again gotta pay attention in class because you did have me here to be a student right." And stuff like that, and sometimes we just talk 'cause, he's our friend.

> When I was thinking about prayer, I was thinking, there are so many different levels of prayer. Some people, they think of prayer when we sit down at the dinner table and we all pray together and we just ask God's blessing over our food. And then, and then there is people, you know, that this is their daily life, this is their communication, this is my ultimate friend that is with me at all times. I can tell him everything. I can sit, you know, I can drive up the expressway just me and him alone and I have my praise and my prayer. To me it's almost like my friend just stays with me, you know, that never leaves me, always protects me in any situation or even when I'm in trouble, he is there.

> Prayer has to do with maintaining a communication, a relationship
> with the Lord. I have to concur with all those that said in the beginning
> because prayer, study and meditation is what brings you into a
> relationship and is what maintains the relationship and what enables
> you to be able to continue to move on. So, with me personally, ah, I
> seek to commune with God on a daily basis. You see, prayer is like
> talking to a friend.

These comments highlight several points. God is a best friend who is ever-present, always available, and welcoming. He is a friend with whom one can share and reveal anything. He provides all of the benefits of an intimate source of social support without the limitations that come with human supports. The act of praying draws God and the believer into a relationship that, in addition to being intimate and trusting, is also private and comfortingly exclusive.

Meditation and Prayer

In addition to the communication and relationship-building aspects of prayer, focus group participants also noted the importance of meditation as a part of prayer. In particular, they said that communication through prayer is an explicitly dyadic and interactive process. In addition to praying to God, one must also listen to God.

> And like I said, meditation to me is, the differences is in prayer, you're
> audibly or you're silently praying and you're making some type of
> statement to Him and meditation is Him talking back to you and being
> a still spirit when you can receive it.

> Also, I don't think that prayer is the only way of communication. Like I
> said sometimes you just gotta shut up and listen, you know, and I
> think that that in itself is hand in hand. It's not just the prayer itself.

Poloma and Gallup (1991) found 70% of Americans said that when they prayed they also spent time listening to God. The notion of listening to God is an established aspect of prayer and worship in many religions and faith traditions. In Christianity, the idea that one must listen to the "still, small voice" of God reflects this idea. The focus group discussion in Chapter 2 also notes the importance of meditation as part of a daily religious activity. Our use of the term *meditation* is distinct from current popular notions of meditation as a spiritual practice replete with specific breathing and postural practices. Instead, meditation is seen as a part of the process of building relationship and is an important element of the prayer experience. This use of the term in this context may be more aligned with the long tradition of contemplative prayer within Christianity. The emergence of this distinctive interpretation of meditation suggests that survey researchers need to be attentive to the various meanings that people may attach to meditative practice and its particular and distinctive manifestations within specific faith traditions.

Prayers of Thanksgiving

Another major theme that was discussed by focus group participants was prayer as a means of giving thanks. Prayers of thankfulness and gratitude are extremely common, are expressed by both individual churchgoers and ministers, and are a customary feature of a black church service. In some cases these are short, spontaneous prayers that reflect an ongoing, thankful attitude toward life (e.g., "an attitude of gratitude"). Prayers of gratitude can indicate being thankful for waking this morning, feeling the blood flow through your veins, and being thankful for the sun rising. Poloma and Gallup (1991) found that 78% of Americans prayed prayers of thanksgiving. The following comments from focus group members discuss the importance of using prayer to express one's thankfulness.

But like I said, there is so much to be grateful for. For one, that's the reason to pray, to be thankful.

First of all because the Bible commands us to pray. We are to bring our request to Him, to thank Him and to just praise Him sometimes, just a prayer of thanksgiving. Lord, thank you, for many things that He has blessed me with and sometimes I don't even ask, I just thank Him.

Typically, during the morning, I typically tend to pray about, you know, a bunch of different things. Somebody earlier said thanksgiving, giving thanks to God. Well, Lord, you woke me up this morning. Thanking Him for that.

The important part of prayer for me is, like you said just keeping that relationship and showing my thankfulness to Him. So, a lot of what I do in prayer is thank Him for all the blessings that I receive on a daily basis, which is so incredible, I'm so thankful.

Yeah, I think even almost every single day when I pray I always thank God for having another day because I always look back. S [another focus group participant] and I grew up around the same time and same area, and a lot of our friends have been shot, killed, stabbed, whatever, and I think those same people that just died, you know, if I wouldn't have started following God and confessing my sins and trying to be more Christ-like, I would be in those same places that they were. So I always sit back and thank God for it.

Prayers of Petition

Poloma and Gallup (1991) describe petitionary prayer as praying for material things that an individual may need. Though focus group participants used the terminology of petition, none of them used petitionary prayer to request material things or possessions. Focus group participants, however, did use petitionary prayer to ask for nonmaterial things or personal traits and characteristics such as strength, wisdom, and guidance. In other instances, petitionary prayer was used to address a problematic life situation or interpersonal relationship or to make a specific request for God's blessing and assurance of positive outcome (e.g., good health, safe travels). In contrast to the definition of petitionary prayer developed by Poloma and Gallup, it appears that focus group members employed a more elaborate definition and understanding of petitionary prayer. Here are three examples of what people said they prayed for:

I see prayer as a petition, you know, like you're not necessarily asking, but you're stating, just bringing it to His attention that you're in agreement with some things that maybe are happening in your life or some things that you want, to let him know that, Yeah, I'm aware of it Lord.

I can agree with X [another focus group member], because the scripture commands us to pray. And I pray to thank the Lord for different things. I pray to let Him know my requests. I pray for direction, you know, I just pray for the family. I pray for people, for health. I pray for instructions and I pray for relationships. I pray for him to work in me in order to improve the relationship because it's not always the other person, but it's probably me that needs something done on the inside of me. So there are various reasons why I pray.

I pray for wisdom, because to ease a lot of pride that comes to me. I know that in all my travels and all the things that I've seen as a man,

I'm not the end-all, the know-all, I am not all that I put in my mind
that I should be, I'm just what God wants me to be. And some people
don't like what I say, don't like what I do. I'm tempering my tongue,
and I'm tempering my tongue through prayer.

Prayer as Intercession

Focus group members also said that they prayed for others, such as
family, friends, and church members. These intercessory prayers allow individuals to extend the reach of support by enlisting God to provide support,
guidance, protection, and grace to significant others and acquaintances, as
well as to strangers. For example:

> Praying for my wife, you know, watch out for her today. Safety over the
> roads. Pray for general things, different things, pray for my church,
> brothers in my church, etc.

> I think you pray for, well I pray for others. I pray for myself. I think
> there has to be a constant prayer every day, in any situation, good,
> bad, or whatever.

Through such prayers, individuals actively cultivate intrapersonal orientations of caring and compassion for one another. Importantly, prayers of
intercession that are shared in public settings with others (e.g., benediction
and prayers said in parting for safe travel) also promote communities of
concern and care that extend beyond the individual to others.

Writing Down One's Prayers

In general, we conceive of prayer as spoken. However, several of the
focus group participants mentioned that they recorded their prayers in writing in the form of a prayer journal.

> I was just going to say, I like the idea of a prayer journal. It's something
> that I have started, but I do not always do it every day, but it is
> something about writing things down that helps you to focus more,
> whether it be giving thanks or things that you want to accomplish
> or grow closer with the Lord. I thought that was kind of a neat thing
> to do.

> A lot of times I do write, I write, I write most of my prayers just
> because it helps me to focus.

The Importance of Prayer

Findings from several surveys indicate that prayer is regarded as one of the most important religious behaviors. As noted in Chapter 2, when we asked focus group participants to discuss their daily religious activities, prayer was the first and most frequently mentioned activity. As evident in the focus group participants' comments about prayer helping to facilitate communication and build a relationship with God, prayer provides instruction, protection, support, and guidance. Prayer is an important aspect of daily life. Below is the comment from one of the participants who also notes the central and critical role of prayer in daily life. She notes, in particular, that without prayer, she would be more agitated and distressed (also see Chapter 4, "Prayer as a Source of Coping").

> So its kinda like, how could you not pray? I just, I can't, you know, if someone told me, "You can't do this anymore." This would be a real, real, real, grouchy black woman.

In short, prayer also helps people to regulate their emotional lives.

The Power of Prayer

Another theme that was evident in the focus group discussion was feelings about the power of prayer. Several of the focus group participants provided detailed accounts of how prayer helped them survive adverse circumstances. These participants discussed how religion in general and prayer, in particular, helped them cope in difficult situations:

> Basically my mother and my father was always out working. I was raised by my grandmother. She had like a third- or fourth-grade education. And she was, I mean almost every breath was something about, "I'm praying to the Lord, I'm praying for so and so." And I came up in a despicable kind of environment, too, in a ghetto, and I think that the only reason that I got into manhood is because of some of the prayers that she prayed for me and other family members. And all of us didn't make it out. I know guys that died at 13, 14 years old, and it was before all the hoopla that you get from the negative and the bad news. It was just happening, it was happening around us. And we had a covering. And the covering came from the people that were praying for us. The pastors would pray for us, they would come to our house to pray for us.

> I really didn't pray a lot, I didn't pray a lot until I got in trouble. I mean maybe that was wrong. I was younger, saying, I believed in God, but I

wasn't respecting God. You know what I'm saying? And how am I
going to say this, I'm not ashamed of this, I've been in prison before,
and to me, God saved me because the way I was going, I'd probably
end up dead or something. When I got in prison, I went back to school
and I graduated. And to me, He came, He told me even though I
believe in Him that wasn't good enough, I still don't know Him. So I
had to pray and come closer with God to come out of that place. I've
been home since, I've been out like two years now, out of prison. And I
think it's because God done slow myself down and respect the faith, I
fully respect as a grown man in religious preferences. Like I say, I tends
to pray about things I shouldn't pray about, I should of just praised
Him for letting me wake up in the morning....Like I said, I've been
through a lot in my life, you know what I'm saying, and I think it's only
because of God is why I'm sitting here today. Because other than that,
it can't be because of man, it can't because of my being cunning or
slick or anything like that. I found out a long time ago that's not it. I'm
here because God has a reason for me to be here.

These statements highlight the transcendent and transformative power of
prayer. Both personal and intercessory prayers are described as having the
capacity to protect and shield individuals from potentially overwhelming
events and forces in the environment. Beyond their ability to protect,
prayers also have the power to change people—to change their characters,
their behaviors, and their outcomes. Prayer, and its presumed role in ensuring the survival of the individual (whether actual physical survival, emotional resiliency, or spiritual renewal), is important in that it demonstrates
the power of prayer and figures in personal narratives as both a catalyst for
change and evidence of a divine purpose and destiny.

Focus Group Summary

The findings of our survey-based studies have consistently pointed to the fact
that prayer is a central component of the religious lives of African
Americans. However, these focus group findings help us to develop a more
nuanced picture of the meaning and significance of prayer in the lives of
African American adults. The responses offered by men and women who
participated in these focus groups highlight important points related to the
experience of prayer (e.g., prayer's private, intimate, supportive, and relational nature), prayer's role in building a relationship (e.g., the image of God
as a best friend), the many functions of prayer (e.g., communication, protection, guidance), the many forms of prayer (e.g., intercessory, petitionary),

the modes by which prayer is expressed (e.g., verbal expression, meditation, and writing), and people's reflections on the power of prayer (e.g., its power to protect and transform).

The focus group narratives remind us that prayer cannot be separated from relationship. Praying to or communicating with God is an act of intimacy. In addition, people use prayer, particularly intercessory prayer, as a means of creating—and including others in—a web of social, emotional, and spiritual support. The participants highlight the point that the relationship between God and believers mirrors, in important ways, the loving and nurturing relationships that exist between humans. In sum, bidirectional communication is seen as an important component of the God-believer relationship. Through prayer people make themselves vulnerable to God. They share their emotions, their needs, and their wants. They ask questions and seek advice, guidance, protection, support, and solace. They express their gratitude for graces received.

It is noteworthy that the narratives offered by these focus group participants challenge two important conclusions made by Poloma and Gallup (1991) in their study of prayer. First, contrary to Poloma and Gallup's assertion that petitionary prayers are used to seek material things, these participants use petitionary prayer to ask for guidance, support, and personal transformation rather than material goods. Second, although Poloma and Gallup suggest that conversational prayers may take the form of monologues, the focus group participants reported that they experienced prayer as a means of establishing a genuine bidirectional dialogue with God. These findings strongly suggest a need for future studies that specifically explore the complexities and nuances of the prayer lives of African Americans.

Chapter Summary and Conclusion

This chapter examined the importance and role of prayer in the lives of black Americans. Prayer is the most fundamental and frequently practiced form of religious expression. Survey research generally finds that 9 out of 10 Americans report that they pray, and about 1 in 4 Americans pray several times a day. There are significant differences in the frequency of prayer across various subgroups of the population, with older adults, women, and black Americans reporting that they pray more frequently than their counterparts. Research among blacks also shows the presence of significant age and gender differences in the frequency of prayer. The importance of prayer to black Americans is further seen in research that examines religious noninvolvement. This research shows that a significant percentage of those blacks who do not have a current denomination and who do not attend religious services nonetheless pray on a frequent basis. Research among blacks has also investigated the frequency with which individuals request that others pray for them. Requesting prayers from others is not as frequent as personal prayer, possibly due to the social nature of requesting prayer from others and the likelihood that requests for prayer are made only when an individual encounters a situation in which there is an expressed need for prayer. Personal prayer is therefore more spontaneous and immediate.

Analysis of the focus group narratives from the study, "Appraisals of Religiosity, Coping and Church Support," revealed several important themes regarding the nature of prayer. Most notable among them were the interrelated themes that: (a) prayer is means of communication with God; (b) through prayer, one can develop and maintain a relationship with God; and (c) the nature of that relationship is that of a friend or best friend. Other themes discussed in the focus groups involved prayer and meditation, prayers of thanksgiving, the use of petitionary prayer to ask for personal qualities and traits and to seek blessings, writing down one's prayers in the form of a prayer journal, the importance of prayer in daily life, and the power of prayer. Collectively, findings on the nature and meaning of prayer presented here, along with the work in Chapter 2 on the importance of daily prayer and Chapter 4 on the role of prayer as a source of coping, provide an elaborated portrait of the significance of prayer in the spiritual and religious lives of African Americans.

Part II

Functions of Religion

A s do all people, African Americans express themselves religiously both for the innate satisfaction of connecting with God and with a community of worshippers and for the positive functions that religion serves in their lives. Sociologists refer to these, respectively, as expressive and instrumental motivations. As among all people, moreover, religion serves a multiplicity of functions among African Americans. In Part II: Functions of Religion, we turn our attention to a discussion of several of the instrumental functions that religion fulfills for African Americans. Among them, we consider coping with life adversities and problems and participation in socially supportive interactions as two principal signs that religion is serving positive functions in people's lives. In the chapters in this portion of the book, we consider the broad topics of religious coping and social interaction within the church. The nature of and circumstances surrounding the use of prayer are explored in Chapter 4. Chapter 5 focuses on why and how individuals use ministers in relation to a range of problem situations and includes a discussion of why such assistance may be declined. We consider the issue of church-based support from fellow church members in Chapter 6, with a particular emphasis on instrumental, spiritual, and emotional assistance. Finally, we consider the types and consequences of negative interaction, such as gossip that occurs among church members, in Chapter 7. Findings from empirical studies and focus group transcripts are again drawn on to describe the various ways that religion is used to address life challenges and the nature and form of social interactions within religious settings.

Chapter 4

Prayer as a Source of Coping

Mounting empirical evidence indicates that religious cognitions and practices are important for coping with undesirable or threatening events and conditions (see Pargament, 1997, for the most exhaustive examination of religious coping). Individuals report using religious coping to confront a number of adverse life circumstances, including illnesses and physical disabilities (Pargament & Hahn, 1986), chronic pain (Kotarba, 1983), serious accidents (Bulman & Wortman, 1977), and bereavement (Mattlin, Wethington, & Kessler, 1990; Wuthnow, Christiano, & Kuzlowski, 1980). Although the majority of research on religious coping has focused on white samples, several studies show that, on average, African Americans are more inclined to employ religious coping strategies than their white counterparts (e.g., Conway, 1985–1986; Veroff, Douvan, & Kulka, 1981; Wood & Parham, 1990). Despite the fact that systematic empirical evidence in this area is scant, anecdotal accounts suggest that many African Americans draw on religious cognitions and practices to confront a wide range of stressful events and conditions, including chronic poverty and structural exclusion, as well as bereavement and health conditions (Griffith, Young, & Smith, 1984; Neighbors, Jackson, Bowman, & Gurin, 1983). Several researchers have called attention to the role of religious institutions and values in shielding black Americans from the harsh psychological effects of structural and interpersonal racism (e.g., Gilkes, 1980; Smith, 1981). Further, several scholars note that services in black churches may operate as a therapeutic community that functions as a mental health resource (Gilkes, 1980; Griffith et al., 1984; McRae, Carey, & Anderson-Scott, 1998).

The previous two chapters (Chapter 2, "African American Religious Participation," and Chapter 3, "The Frequency and Importance of Prayer") provided some basic information about prayer. Chapter 2 focused on the importance of prayer in the religious and spiritual life of black Americans. Chapter 3 provided a basic introduction to the topic of prayer, a general profile of the correlates of prayer, and a discussion of the forms and functions of prayer. This chapter addresses the role of prayer as a means of coping with serious personal problems and examines how prayer is used to handle these circumstances; in essence, how individuals actively use prayer to cope with life problems.

As part of an overall process of coping with problems, individuals may engage in a number of activities (e.g., religious print and broadcast media), use a variety of religious coping resources (e.g., fellow church members, ministers), or adopt specific religious coping orientations (i.e., positive religious coping and negative religious coping; see work by Pargament, 1997, for a review of religious coping) to address the problem. A profile of religious activities was presented in Chapter 2, "African American Religious Participation," and the general topic of prayer was covered in Chapter 3. Subsequent chapters in the book focus on various types of religious resources that individuals might use for dealing with personal problems (see Chapter 5, "Use of Ministers for Personal Problems," and Chapter 6, "Church Members as a Source of Social Support"). In this chapter, however, we specifically examine prayer, distinct from these other religious activities, as a means of coping with problems. We took this approach for several reasons.

Across all religious traditions, prayer is a fundamental activity of faith that is associated with, among other things, efforts to cope with life problems. Despite the prominence of prayer in both lay and scientific discussions, there are relatively few intensive and systematic investigations of prayer in relation to coping efforts. Investigations of prayer in coping are often limited to minimal assessments as to whether individuals report engaging in prayer for this purpose. We lack crucial information about the inherent meaning and nature of prayer for individuals, factors associated with the use of prayer in coping (e.g., social, personal, and problem type), and specific information about what the relevant outcomes and functional mechanisms are (i.e., emotional, psychological, behavioral, physiological) through which prayer operates in the coping process. In the absence of detailed information of this sort, we are left with largely utilitarian models concerning why people use prayer in coping with life problems. This extremely restricted and limiting view suggests that prayer is employed in highly specific situations defined by personal need or crisis for the express purpose of obtaining a particular valued outcome. Other popular characterizations of prayer is that it is a passive, emotion-focused coping strategy that serves to distract individuals from focusing on the problem, or that prayer is essentially palliative. The research evidence and focus group information reviewed in this chapter amply demonstrate that this view of prayer is inconsistent with the reports of individuals who engage in prayer and view it as a fundamental and vibrant form of religious expression.

The research examined in this chapter focuses specifically on situations in which individuals indicate that they have employed prayer (either exclusively or with other strategies and resources) in response to a problematic situation (e.g., a serious personal problem, an ongoing stressor) that they have confronted. We begin this chapter on prayer and coping with a brief review of the model of stress and coping processes that has guided our research—the life stress paradigm (Ellison, 1994). From there, we review relevant research from a number of sources on the general topic of religious coping and the use of prayer in coping with life problems. Two areas of research are given particular attention—coping with caregiving experiences and responsibilities and coping with health difficulties. Following this, we discuss situations in which religious coping, rather than being beneficial, may be associated with harmful physical and mental health outcomes for the individual. Next, we consider research findings from the National Survey of Black Americans Panel data on the use of prayer for coping with stressful episodes. Finally, information from the focus group study, "Appraisals of Religiosity, Coping and Church Support," provides specific insights from focus group participants on how they use prayer to cope with a variety of life situations and problems. We conclude the chapter with a summary and final remarks regarding the importance of prayer for individual coping efforts.

Coping With Personal Problems

Research and writing on the topic of coping encompasses a number of different ways of conceptualizing this construct and a diverse collection of findings related to stress and coping processes and outcomes. Our research, focusing on how religious involvement is associated with stress and coping, is based on the life stress paradigm (LSP). Briefly, the LSP posits that, in response to events that are perceived as stressful, individuals engage in a variety of behaviors to actively address the problem and/or enlist a number of personal and social resources in order to eliminate, ameliorate, or alter one's perception of the stressor (see Ellison, 1994, for a comprehensive treatment of religion and the life stress paradigm). Coping resources include both personal (i.e., personality characteristics and attitudes) and social (i.e., social support) assets that can be used in the coping effort. Recent writings suggest that examining these factors within the context of race and cultural factors would enhance our theoretical understanding of these processes and sharpen our appreciation of specific factors (e.g., group norms and expectations, cultural values and beliefs) that shape the nature of stress and coping experiences (Dilworth-Anderson, Williams, & Gibson, 2002; Janevic & Connell, 2001).

Given the importance of religious institutions for African Americans, it may be instructive to examine stress and coping processes within a religious context. First, social resources that are used to assist with coping may take the form of informal assistance from church members (i.e., coreligionists) and clergy, which provides individuals with various types of support in response to life difficulties and problems. Most notably, these include instrumental aid, emotional support, affirmation of self, and spiritual assistance (see Chapters 5 and 6). Social resources of this sort are helpful in dealing directly with a problem (i.e., tangible aid such as money or services), encouraging existing efforts to cope, modeling novel coping strategies, and helping individuals manage the emotional and psychological turmoil that often accompanies problematic situations (i.e., emotional regulation, maintenance of a positive sense of self). In the realm of personal resources, religious involvement may bolster the individual's sense of coping efficacy and beliefs about personal control. Specific religious beliefs, attitudes, and orientations, aspects of individual and group worship, and processes and rituals occurring within religious congregations may also positively impact various aspects of individual coping efforts (Koenig, 1994). With respect to social resources, individuals may use prayer to appeal to and communicate with God and religious figures in order to enlist the support of "Divine Others" in attempts to deal with life problems (Pollner, 1989). These efforts may result in higher perceptions of personal control in relation to problematic situations and an enhanced sense of self-worth. Further, recent research (Krause et al., 2000b) suggest that specific aspects of prayer that involve turning the problem over to God may be especially helpful for reducing the worry and resultant psychological distress associated with life problems and refocusing one's energies on those aspects of problems that can be addressed by active coping strategies. Clearly, the body of emergent research indicates that religious coping (of which prayer is one strategy) is a multidimensional phenomenon that can impact various facets of the stress and coping process.

Prayer and Coping With Life Problems

Prayer is a quintessential religious behavior that has a variety of purposes and recognized functions (e.g., praise, thanksgiving, petitioning, intercession). People often employ various aspects of prayer in response to adverse personal circumstances; for example, praying for someone who is experiencing ill health or personal tragedy. Our exploration of this topic will focus on reports of the use of prayer to deal with a situation or circumstance that is personally distressing to the individual. We will review a number of studies that have examined the use of prayer among African Americans to cope with particular life problems (including specialized subgroups such as the elderly and rural residents), as well as studies focusing on race comparisons in the use of prayer. Our goal is to understand how and why people use prayer to cope with personal problems, the circumstances associated with its use, individual beliefs about prayer, and perceptions of its effectiveness.

Research reviewed in Chapter 2, "African American Religious Participation," clearly shows that prayer is an integral part of the religious experience of black Americans and that they engage in prayer at higher rates than their white counterparts. As noted by Ellison and Taylor (1996), however, only a few studies directly focus on the use of prayer to cope with problems. Instead, much of the literature examines a number of religious behaviors and coping strategies that are used by individuals when they are experiencing life problems. Consequently, religious coping research includes a variety of approaches, from work that examines associations between global religious expression and commitment (e.g., religious belief, church attendance) and health outcomes, to research that focuses on the more proximal, specific, and functionally oriented approaches to religion (i.e., use of prayer) in response to specific personal problems. In addition, programmatic work by Pargament (1997) describes a typology of religious coping strategies, which gives more explicit attention to issues of both the beneficial and harmful consequences of religious coping.

The next two sections of the chapter review research on the topics on religious coping in relation to the caregiving experience and personal illness. Given the diversity of research focusing on religious coping efforts, these literatures do not specifically examine the use of prayer to cope with the caregiving experience or personal situations involving ill health. They do, however, provide a number of useful and interesting insights regarding how religious coping varies across racial and ethnic groups and the specific ways in which such strategies relate to stress and coping processes under these circumstances.

Religious Coping and Caregiving

Dilworth-Anderson and colleagues' (2002) review of race, ethnicity, and cultural factors in caregiving research provides an overview of the informal and formal resources, coping strategies, perceptions, and experiences of those caring for dependent elderly. Despite the fact that cultural factors in caregiving are indeed important considerations that influence caregiving experiences and outcomes, a clear picture of caregiving experiences in diverse groups has yet to emerge due to persistent theoretical questions and methodological difficulties. However, one area of research on race and cultural differences in caregiving has been of particular interest to researchers. A number of studies have shown that African American caregivers are less likely than whites to indicate that caregiving is stressful and more likely to indicate that they derive particular benefits and rewards from their experiences (Janevic & Connell, 2001; Lawton, Rajagopal, Brody, & Kleban, 1992; Picot, Debanne, Namazi, & Wykle, 1997; White, Townsend, & Stephens, 2000). Several researchers have suggested that African Americans' use of religious coping strategies may account for differences in overall appraisals of their experiences (Connell & Gibson, 1997) and other aspects of caregiving, such as satisfaction, burden, and role strain (Aranda & Knight, 1997; Miltiades & Pruchno, 2002; Navaie-Waliser et al., 2001; Picot et al., 1997).

Research on caregivers for family members with dementia (e.g., Alzheimer's disease) generally reveals that religious involvement helps them cope with stress (Koenig, McCullough, & Larson, 2001). One study of black caregivers for family members with dementia found that the most prevalent method of coping with the stresses of caregiving was prayer or faith in God (Segall & Wykle, 1988–1989). Wood and Parham's (1990) study of rural caregivers for family members with Alzheimer's found that religious coping was common among both black and white caregivers. Black caregivers, however, were considerably more likely than whites to pray, think about religion, receive support from their ministers, and consider God a member of the social support network. Similarly, a qualitative study of African American caregivers (Sterritt & Pokorny, 1998) found that God and religion was the first source of informal aid mentioned.

Although a comprehensive review of the literature on religious coping and caregiving is beyond the scope of the present chapter (see, in particular, critical reviews by Dilworth-Anderson et al., 2002, and Janevic & Connell, 2001, and articles by White et al., 2000, and Picot et al., 1997), several general conclusions can be made about this body of research. After several decades of research on caregiving, researchers are beginning to develop a more complete understanding of the complex factors and processes involved in the caregiving experience. While still in its infancy, the more systematic focus on racial and cultural factors in caregiving promises to clarify how various population groups differ with respect to caregiving norms and expectations, cultural values and beliefs, and coping resources and their consequences in terms of relevant processes and outcomes. Information of this sort will enrich the theoretical understanding of stress and coping processes and enhance our efforts to develop practical approaches to assist caregiving individuals and families.

As an overall assessment of the literature, current evidence suggests that religious orientations and coping strategies are relevant for understanding several aspects of the caregiving experience, including primary appraisal processes (e.g., assessments of stressfulness), evaluations and enhancements of personal resources such as mastery and control perceptions, use of social resources such as support from others (e.g., church members, God), and individual perceptions of the rewards and benefits of caregiving. However, much work remains to be conducted in order to understand more fully the various types of religious coping strategies employed (e.g., prayer, beliefs) and their mechanisms of operation, the relevant personal and social circumstances (e.g., gender, education, region, denomination) and caregiving contexts (e.g., mix of formal and informal resources, unmet needs, intensity of caregiving) that may influence their use and effectiveness, and the specific outcomes (e.g., stress, burden, depressive symptoms) for which religious coping strategies appear to be most useful.

Religious Coping and Health and Illness

A prodigious amount of research examines the relationships between religious involvement and mental and physical health outcomes (see Chapter 8, "Impact of Religion on Physical Health," and Chapter 9, "Impact of Religion on Mental Health and Well-Being," in this volume, and also Koenig et al., 2001). In this section, we provide a selective review of research that examines how individuals perceive the role of religion and faith in matters of health and illness and, specifically, their perceptions of religion and use of religious strategies in their efforts to cope with health problems. Interest in understanding the role of religious strategies and prayer in coping with illness comes, in part, from concerns that religious coping efforts may interfere with or cause delays in seeking medical help. For example, particular religious teachings and coping strategies may proscribe certain medical procedures and treatments, negatively influence patterns of informal and self-care, hinder professional help seeking for health care, or encourage exclusive treatment by clergy (e.g., for mental and emotional problems). On the other hand, research on religious coping strategies has also focused on the potential benefits and salutary effects of these efforts on the health and well-being of patients (Koenig, 1994). Accumulating evidence suggests that religion (e.g., beliefs and attitudes) and religious coping (e.g., prayer) are important for the health of patients (see Koenig et al., 2001) and are associated with a variety of health behaviors (e.g., general self-care and informal care, the use of professional health services) and health outcomes.

Several studies suggest that religious beliefs and practices become more salient to people when they are in poor health (Mansfield, Mitchell, & King, 2002; Oyama & Koenig, 1998) and are related to overall better coping and mental health outcomes (Koenig, 1994). Ai and associates (Ai, Dunkle, Peterson, & Bolling, 1998; Ai, Peterson, Bolling, & Koenig, 2002) explored the use of private prayer by middle aged and older cardiac patients. Ai et al. (2002) found that beliefs about prayer (i.e., importance, efficacy, and intention to use prayer to cope with surgery) were associated with optimism among presurgery cardiac patients. Prayer was also important in postoperative recovery from cardiac surgery; prayer about postoperative difficulties was associated with decreases in depression and general distress one year following surgery (Ai et al., 1998).

A collection of research studies shows that medical patients are, on the whole, more religiously oriented than their physicians and further desire to know their physicians' religious orientations and to have their physicians inquire about their beliefs and engage in mutual prayer (Maugans & Wadland, 1991; Oyama & Koenig, 1998). Bearon and Koenig's (1990) study of religious cognitions and prayer among older adults found that prayer was used in response to recent physical symptoms and was associated with being Baptist and having lower levels of education. In addition to praying about these symptoms, respondents were also likely to both use medicine to treat the symptoms and to discuss them with their physician. Finally, respondents endorsed a view of God as benevolent but were unclear about God's role in health and illness.

In contrast, Mansfield et al.'s (2002) study of spiritual practices and beliefs in relation to healing among black and white residents in eastern North Carolina found ample evidence that people use prayer for personal healing and the healing of others. In addition, respondents endorsed the belief in divine intervention in healing, as well as the belief that God acts through doctors to cure illnesses. Although these practices and beliefs were evident among both black and white respondents, blacks held these views more strongly than their white counterparts. A qualitative study of religion and health among rural samples (McAuley, Pecchioni, & Grant, 2000) found that black and white elderly differ in important ways as to the centrality of religion and God in their lives and the role of religion and God with respect to health. On the whole, older blacks were more likely than older whites to describe their relationships with God in personal terms and to say that religion permeated their lives. For African American elderly only, God assumed a number of roles in relation to illness, including that of comforter (ameliorates the effects of illness, makes illness easier to manage), guardian/protector (protects against illnesses), health communicator (provides health-relevant information), and miracle maker/healer/answerer of prayers (heals illness). Prayer was mentioned as the medium through which God's role as a miracle maker/healer/answerer of prayers, in particular, was manifested. Similarly, a qualitative study of older adults in rural North Carolina (Arcury, Quandt, McDonald, & Bell, 2000) provided support for the role of prayer in the maintenance of good health and in healing illnesses. Finally, a survey of black and white community-dwelling older adults in eastern North Carolina found that black respondents were significantly more likely to believe that religious faith was important in treatment (e.g., use of prayer, God works through doctors) and religious interventions in illness were effective (e.g., prayer heals, God's will in healing).

This brief review of research findings on the relationship between religious coping strategies (e.g., prayer) and health suggests that there are a number of ways that individuals think about and employ religious resources in response to illness. Prayer, as one form of religious coping, is a primary method through which individuals attempt to manage or ameliorate the effects of ill health. In addition, use of prayer is implicated in attempts to bring about instances of divine intervention. Across a number of different study samples (e.g., older and younger, black and white, community-dwelling and hospital patients) it appears that the use of prayer in circumstances of poor health is a robust and pervasive phenomenon. However, these studies also demonstrate demographic variability (e.g., race, age) in both the use of prayer in illness and beliefs about its efficacy. Of particular note with respect to African Americans was the observation that prayer, and religious activities more generally, were not regarded as something that was separate from one's normal, everyday life. As described in one of the qualitative studies (Arcury et al., 2000), prayer and religious faith were not things that you "used" to effect specific health outcomes. Prayer and religious faith were, instead, regarded as givens in one's life and were simply a fundamental aspect of one's being. These and other themes will be revisited in the analysis of the focus group information exploring the use of prayer in coping.

Harmful Effects of Religious Coping

Like any phenomenon, religious coping can have both beneficial and harmful effects. The majority of this chapter, and research in general, investigates the beneficial impact of religious coping. We would be remiss, however, if we did not discuss the negative impacts of religious coping. To date, very little research has examined the harmful effects of religious coping among blacks. Available research has investigated how religious coping may prevent individuals from acknowledging and confronting domestic abuse (Pargament, 1997) or cause delays in seeking treatment for medical conditions (Koenig, McCullough, & Larson, 2001). With regard to domestic abuse, battered women may be less likely to confront their situation because they believe that they are being punished by God, they are not religious enough, or that they must honor their husband (Pargament, 1997). A study by Lannin and colleagues (1998) found that religious coping could lead to higher rates of breast cancer mortality among African American women. Black women were more likely than white women to endorse the statements "The devil can cause a person to get cancer" and "If a person prays about cancer, God will heal it without medical treatments." Religious beliefs of this sort may seriously delay diagnosis and treatment of serious illnesses, which contributes to untimely deaths. Pargament (1997) notes that although religious coping that involves prayer and Bible reading are helpful when confronting a serious problem, it can become problematic if it is the only type of coping strategy that is employed. Further, religious coping that leaves no room for other coping strategies (e.g., not seeking medical assistance) may lead to serious problems, especially for health situations that are, in some sense, controllable (Pargament, 1997, p. 328).

Prayer and Coping Among Black Americans

A series of studies from the National Survey of Black Americans focus on individual efforts to cope with serious personal problems. After reporting that they have had a serious personal problem, respondents were told, "I am going to read some things a person might do to deal with a personal problem. As I read each one, please tell me if you did any of these things to try to make the problem easier to bear." Respondents were then asked about a number of things they could have done to make the problem easier to bear, such as: (a) relaxed, (b) tried to put it out of their mind, (c) prayed or got someone to pray for them, (d) drank liquor, took pills or tried to get high, (e) kept busy by doing other things like watching television, reading books, and (f) tried to face the problem squarely and do something about it.

In a preliminary analysis of these data, Neighbors et al. (1983) found that prayer was used by 44% of adults to cope with a serious personal problem and was considered the most beneficial coping strategy. Prayer was mentioned more often than other strategies, such as facing the problem squarely, doing something about the problem, keeping busy, or staying relaxed. Further, as the seriousness of the problem increased, individuals were more likely to use prayer as a coping response. In a study of personal problems among older adults, Chatters and Taylor (1989b) found that the majority of respondents reported that they had recently experienced a problem and that difficulties in the areas of health and finances were the most significant. One in six older persons used prayer to cope with money problems, and 2.6% of respondents reported using prayer to cope with a health problem. These initial findings on coping with personal problems suggested that prayer, and more generally religion, were important coping resources for black adults.

Ellison and Taylor (1996) conducted one of the most in-depth studies of prayer as a source of coping among black Americans. In contrast to other efforts that examine a variety of religious coping efforts, their work focused exclusively on prayer as a source of coping and utilized a multivariate analysis strategy to identify the factors associated with the use of prayer. Five major findings emerged from this study. First, when confronting a serious personal problem, African Americans frequently use religious coping in the form of prayer and asking others to pray on one's behalf. Second, women are significantly more likely than men to utilize prayer when coping with problems, even when controlling for other important predictors of religious coping. However, age and educational differences were not important in distinguishing who uses prayer as coping when controlling for other relevant variables. Third, the type of life problem involved is important in predicting the use of prayer. Black Americans who are coping with the death of a loved one, their own health problems, or the health problems of loved ones are more likely to use prayer or have others pray for them, than for other types of life problems. Fourth, those who had lower levels of mastery or feelings of control over personal affairs were more likely to turn to prayer in coping with problems. Lastly, blacks who are more religious overall (i.e., higher levels of organizational, non-organizational, and subjective religiosity) were more likely to use prayer. However, this was not a perfect relationship, which suggests that religious coping is not merely an indicator of overall religiosity.

Finally, findings from the National Survey of Black Americans Panel data provide a sense of whether the use of prayer to cope with personal problems has changed over a number of years. Subsequent waves of data collection for the NSBA Panel Survey contain the set of questions about coping in response to serious personal problems that were included in the original study. Recall that respondents were asked about what they could do to make the problem easier to bear (e.g., relax, put out of mind, pray/get someone to pray for them). Table 4.1 shows that in each wave of data, prayer was the most utilized form of coping, with 9 out of 10 respondents indicating that they prayed or asked someone to pray for them to cope with personal problems.

Lastly, the National Survey of American Life contains a question about the use of prayer when coping with stress. Respondents were asked "How important is prayer when you deal with stressful situations?" Nine out of 10 blacks said that prayer was very important in dealing with stress. This was considerably higher than the levels reported by whites, in which 7 out of 10 said that prayer was very important when dealing with stressful situations.

Focus Group Findings

As we saw in the previous section, a collection of primarily quantitative studies has provided a general profile of the use of prayer in efforts to cope with problematic life situations (e.g., personal illness, caregiving experiences, ill health of a loved one). This research also provides us with information about how sociodemographic statuses (e.g., age, gender, education), religious factors, and problem type (e.g., illness, bereavement) are associated with the use of prayer. However, except for a few qualitative investigations (see, for example, Arcury et al., 2000; Krause, Chatters, Meltzer, & Morgan, 2000b), we know very little about how people think about using prayer to deal with problems and what they identify as being important about these activities and resources. Simply put, we don't know when people use prayer, how they make decisions to use prayer, what the content of their prayers is, and how effective they view these efforts. The focus group participants in the study "Appraisals of Religiosity, Coping and Church Support" were asked to discuss how they used prayer to cope with life problems. As demonstrated in the following comments, this was a rich source of information about why and how people pray.

Prayer Is an Ongoing Coping Activity

Several important and consistent themes emerged that illuminated the role of prayer in participants' lives. As described in the previous chapter,

Table 4.1   Coping Strategies Used Across National Survey of Black Americans Waves II-IV

Coping Strategy	Wave II 1987–1988	Wave III 1988–1989	Wave IV 1992
. . . relax, not let it bother you ?			
Yes	75.3	76.2	72.9
No	24.7	23.8	27.1
TOTAL	100.0	100.0	100.0
N	506	260	269
. . . try to put it out of your mind?			
Yes	70.4	71.5	76.3
No	29.6	28.5	23.7
TOTAL	100.0	100.0	100.0
N	507	260	270
. . . pray or get someone to pray for you?			
Yes	90.5	89.2	90.7
No	9.5	10.8	9.3
TOTAL	100.0	100.0	100.0
N	507	260	270
. . . drink liquor, take pills or medicine or try to get high?			
Yes	15.4	7.7	11.8
No	84.6	92.3	88.2
TOTAL	100.0	100.0	100.0
N	506	260	271
. . . keep busy by doing other things like watching T.V., reading books, and going places?			
Yes	88.4	84.2	88.1
No	11.6	15.8	11.9
TOTAL	100.0	100.0	100.0
N	507	260	271
. . . try to face the problem squarely and do something about it?			
Yes	89.5	85.8	87.5
No	10.5	14.2	12.5
TOTAL	100.0	100.0	100.0
N	504	260	271

both men and women indicated that prayer was an important and customary part of their daily life. In a similar vein, in discussions of coping with problems, participants said that prayer was important for dealing with a range of personal issues that they confronted on a daily basis. Accordingly, several participants spoke of prayer as an ongoing coping activity that could be engaged in at any point during the day as dictated by circumstances. A second theme emphasized the view that prayer was a means through which participants communicated with God in much the same way that one might converse with a friend or family member (i.e., relations with Divine Others; see Chapter 3). Through prayer, participants were able to draw upon God as an important resource for support and motivation and as a means of relieving stress. Two black men discussed both the importance of prayer in coping with the hassles of daily life and in maintaining ongoing communication with God.

> And I've learned that we, as black men, probably are the last ones that will run to a psychologist, a social worker, so in those instances, and I am counted in the number as well, I tend to rely on God to take care of a whole lot of those issues that I have, and to relieve a lot of the stress that I have to deal with on a daily basis and just to get me started and keep me going, keep me motivated.

> I consult with God about decisions about my family and just from getting up in the morning day-to-day things, struggles. Sometimes you can't tell your best friend everything. Sometimes friends have a habit of letting you down, but God does not fail. And to put your faith in a God that does not fail helps you to overcome a lot of different things and it makes you stronger because you know you have a relationship with a God that is tangible, that's existing, that you can talk to. You don't have to be threatened by him and he's going to tell you what is beneficial for you to overcome and to also, to be, to help other people. He's never going to tell you something that is going to hurt you or hurt other people. He's going to advise you or give you the wisdom or knowledge to make the right decisions, and its up to you to make those decisions. He's not going to twist your arm to do it. Ultimately, it's still up to you, and I find that prayer is a great means of communication with God.

Information from the focus groups revealed two different perspectives concerning the use of prayer as a coping strategy. The first perspective describes individuals who pray in response to specific problems, while the second perspective reflects the view that prayer should be an ongoing activity and an integral part of one's daily life. Among this latter group, participants may not necessarily indicate an increase in frequency of prayer during a personal crisis, as they already have an established and intense prayer life. This does not mean that they don't pray for help when dealing with specific problems, but that these special prayer circumstances are integrated into a committed practice of private devotion. This second pattern was discussed in several of the focus groups. The following statements from men in the focus groups fairly succinctly express this point of view.

> Most people, well a lot of people, will just pray when they are in trouble. Something they had go on in their life that they can't handle on their own and they might seek out the help of a pastor or another church member and say will you pray for me about such and such a thing. But I found myself that I do that too and I pray for other things, not just when I am faced with a difficult situation.… But anyway, I think for most people they pray when they are faced with a crisis more so than just praying all the time, even though that is what you are supposed to do, pray all the time. A lot of people just pray when they are faced with a crisis.

> That's what happens a lot of times, we wait till we get in dire straits, our back's up against the wall. But if we get in the habit of presenting little things. You see, he who is faithful in least will be faithful also in much. I mean little things, I have had situations where I dropped my keys outside in the winter, thought I had my keys in my pocket. Came outside, everything is covered and I'm like, "Lord you know I need to get to work," walked and kicked the keys in the snow, you know, I mean little things, I mean the Lord is interested in every little aspect.

> I pray out of my heart, "Lord, help me!" Sometimes, "Have mercy, Lord!" You know what I'm saying? So what I was saying, that we pray continually, not just when we have a problem, but just talking to God. "God, I love you," that's praying.

> Every walk of my day, every second of my day, I remember being told as a child that Paul prayed all the day long. When he wasn't praying and realized he wasn't praying he prayed some more. So this is the philosophy I've pretty much had. That when I found myself not praying, Oh, I'm not praying, I gotta figure something to pray about and there are so many things to pray about and that's what I try to do, problem or not.

In one of the focus groups, two men also discussed the fact that prayer should be a part of daily life and that prayer should not be an activity that is reserved for crisis situations.

> That's a good point. I think oftentimes we think God is a Santa Claus, too.

> That's what I used him for. Like I said, I'd pray for Him when I got in trouble, I talked to God when I needed God, and see, that's what I was wrong about.

The same sentiment was expressed by a man in another focus group:

> And yeah I used God too, because I didn't pray until I got in trouble, you know, but then, you know, as I matured in Christ, I learned that it's a lifestyle and it's no longer a Sunday ritual, it's no longer when I go to choir rehearsal or I'm involved in something that has to do with the church, then I need to change and put on this other face and clothes.

Although many people pray more often during stressful periods, one woman said that she actually prayed *less* frequently during difficult times. Her response speaks to the notion that because God is omniscient, there is no need to prepare a formal prayer.

> Just one little thing I can add is during my toughest times, I find that I don't pray as much because knowing, I feel like God knows my heart, so I usually only speak two words. It could be one or two words. It's either "Lord" or "Lord, Lord." And, I don't feel like I need to say anymore because he knows what's going on.

As demonstrated by the previous comments, prayer was not a compartmentalized behavior that was used only under special circumstances, nor was it considered a rote activity or an empty ritual. We had anticipated that individuals would discuss specific instances of praying in response to health, money, or other problems. Although participants clearly prayed about these larger issues, they also prayed about numerous events that occurred in their daily lives. Further, rather than thinking about prayer as a formal, separate activity, they talked about prayer as being a critical component in communicating with God and as an important part of having a "prayerful" attitude throughout one's daily life.

Interpersonal Conflicts on the Job

Although focus group respondents on the whole tended not to mention specific problems that they prayed about, one of the most frequently discussed issues concerned interpersonal conflicts occurring on their jobs. The first two statements are by women, and the third comes from a man.

> On the job, I need prayer every day before I go in sometimes. My boss sometimes is grumpy a lot and he'll come in my office complaining about things and I am like, "Lord, I am not going to let him steal my joy...you know ruin my day for the rest of the day." So, I have to kind of step back like that cause he'll ask me sometimes, "Are you this happy all the time?" and I am like, "No, I get frustrated too, I just close my door and say a prayer so I calm down a little bit before I have to go on to the next thing."

> I certainly pray for when there's problems and the one thing that comes to mind is that I've been having problems with a lady on the job and she is a Christian, too. And sometimes we just seem like we buck heads. Now just this week, I said, Lord you got to help me deal with this lady, and so I prayed because I know that sometimes my flesh want to rise up and I ask the Lord, please, bring that flesh into subjection because I know she is a Christian, and I'm a Christian. And sometimes I just have to just hold myself or just let her speak and agree. So I will just let her talk and I'll agree and I'll say okay, just chill. Let her have her way, you know, if it's gonna create peace.

> Specifically at work, well, I won't go into specifics, but basically a couple of things happening at work, a couple people, and I had to pray to God to focus on my attitude, because I was getting so bent out of shape worrying about this person trying to do stuff to me, I just started praying for that person and started praying that the situation would change and then I would change my attitude in the whole process. And once I started changing my attitude, then everything started changing—the person started changing, things stopped bothering me so much—and so I think the prayer was important because like you say, it releases stress and you know you're giving it to God and you ain't gotta worry about it anymore because it's taken care of.

Another issue that was mentioned was praying because of health concerns.

> I had been sick and just prayed, you know, and then been healed from prayer, through praying not specifically nobody laying their hands on me or going to no preacher or nothing, just praying for myself.

Overall there was not a lot of discussion of prayer concerning health problems. This could be because the participants were relatively healthy or they were not willing to discuss specific health problems with other participants.

Prayer Gives Strength, Wisdom, and Guidance

In discussing the various ways that prayer helps them cope with problems and deal with daily life, focus group participants mentioned that prayer gives them strength, guidance, and wisdom. In the following responses (the first by a man and the second by a woman), participants also said that praying provides a sense of assurance and equanimity regarding the decisions they make and the actions they pursue.

> For me, it's just getting through everyday life, because everything that goes on, I mean for you to try to handle it yourself, you couldn't do it. I pray for the strength to make the right decision along with the wisdom to know whatever it is that God wants me to do. And I pray that he'll just give me the direction to do, to do his work, for me to work for him just to get through my everyday problems, and make sure every decision that I make is a Godly decision.

> I think people pray sometimes, they pray more when they're in distress. But I pray and I have problems and things and I just ask the Lord, "If it's got to be this way just give me the strength so that I can get through it." And that makes me feel better. And things are not always going to be perfect and it's not always going to be the way that you want it, so you know, I just let him know, "Let your will be done and just give me the strength to get through this. Maybe it has to be this way. I don't know why, but maybe I don't need to know why. Just give me the strength to get through it." And that makes me feel better right there.

Prayer Reduces Stress

The next group of comments from focus group participants centers on a number of related themes. Participants particularly underscored the ways that prayer helps to reduce the stresses that are associated with the problems and issues of daily life. Also evident in these comments is the notion that prayer provides individuals with a different perspective on the problems they face, which then enables them to begin to deal more effectively with the issue at hand. Prayer also works to strengthen and sustain one's endurance in order to deal with life issues. Finally, the importance of prayer as a means of communicating with God was again mentioned as an especially calming aspect of prayer. Communing with God in this manner reinforced a deep belief and understanding that God is all-knowing and always available to help with problems.

As a man and, you know, having to support your family and all these different things typically, men, I find we don't typically particularly share things with each other too well, and for me being able to share things with God has been just awesome. I think, again like you said, the ability to relieve stress through that, there is a piece of God that you get from communicating with the Father and to me that, I used to hoop all the time, and I thought that was the way I relieve stress. But, I used to get so hyped in the court and get done and I'd still be you know, stressed. So, to me prayer is really, that ability to communicate with God is a stress reliever for me.

Also prayer releases stress, you know, it releases frustration. Old folks have a saying, they say, "No prayer, no power; little prayer, little power; much prayer, much power." You know, I believe you get the power to be able to deal with the everyday problems in life. You know, it strengthens you, it gives you strength. It gives you a new outlook on life. It gives you moral fortitude to be able to deal with life. You know, prayer.

One dimension of it for me is when I'm praying about a problem, I think it makes it a lot easier to deal with, cause if I have a problem I'm thinking it's like the end of the world or whatever, you know, like I'm just ready to lose my mind. I can't really function until I start to pray and understand it's really not that big. The Lord always has my back, he is always going to make a way. He is going to find a way out of this for me. So it's, it's like a calming type of, coming back to reality type thing, a soothing type.

I'll tell you this much, it's better than punching your fist through a wall, beating on your family member or wife. It's better than taking out that stress and aggression on things and people around you. I call God the ultimate stress-reliever because God knows what you are going through. He knows, and if you come to him, he will try and give you a way out. He will say, this is what you need to do. Maybe you need to change some things in your lifestyle that creates stress. God will give you the wisdom to do those things. 'Cause you hear so much about domestic violence, but, I wonder about do those men that engage in domestic violence really pray? I wonder about that. Maybe we will see our domestic violence rates drop in our households if some men pray, because you do not have to beat on your wife or your mother or your children when you are stressed out. You can go to God.

Elaborating further on the notion that prayer can alter one's perspective on a problem, one woman said that silent prayer gave her the opportunity to reflect and reassess the problem. This process is particularly important in handling the emotional turmoil that can accompany distressing situations that can, themselves, cause stress. It is apparent from her comments that she undertakes a fairly thorough reappraisal of the problem situation, including her potential contribution to the issue, as well as others' opinions and experiences with the problem.

> And I found that when I pray silently and meditate that it gives me the opportunity to calm down, sit back and, you know, evaluate and actually listen to not just God, I listen to other people, because sometimes things are not, I mean, the same problem that you think you're having, someone else is having already. They've been through it and if you sit back and listen long enough, it doesn't seem to be a problem if everybody is having it, you know. But I think through prayer it gives me that strength to be able to identify and discern different things that are actually, I feel are caused by myself or my reaction or response as opposed to just being a life experience.

Focus group members also indicated that one of the mechanisms that made prayer an effective coping method is that, through prayer, they could give their problems up to God. In prayer, they would acknowledge that this is a problem that they could not handle. So they would give the problem up to God, put the problem in God's hands, or "put the problem on the altar." In doing this, they would attempt to stop worrying about this issue and thereby regain some degree of control over the problem. In this way, engaging in prayer can relieve the stress that is associated with excessive worry about a problem (see Krause, Chatters, Meltzer, & Morgan, 2000b). For example, one woman said:

> I pray for different things. I pray when I have problems. I pray when other people have problems. I pray and thank him for things that went good and for the potential. I say, "Let Your will be done," and then I just feel relieved because I'm done with it. After I do that, I'm done with it.

In the following exchange with the group facilitator, a man discusses how prayer can relieve stress even though the problem may still exist after prayer. Further, he says that using prayer in response to a problem provides one with cognitive and emotional resources to deal with the problem.

> Honestly, I just feel like when you pray, if you really believe in God, I do not really feel you know it's possible that you can feel worse than you did before you started praying. I mean to me honestly, I just feel like if you really believe in God, when you get through praying if your

problem is still there if you open your eyes or however you go to him, you at least feel a little bit better about it you know.

Facilitator: How so? I mean when you say you feel better. Let's say the problem is still there.

Because I feel like you, you know that you have help. Even though it's here, and in a matter of time, you will receive a thought or a direction or guide on how to resolve that problem. I mean some people have problems and other people have the same problem, but they sometimes feel different about it. Some people are more stressed than others about it you know because they do have God in their life to make them feel better and know that they do have someone to lean on or call to. I just feel like whatever it is that you pray about, you will feel different, if you really believe in God, after you get through praying.

Spiritual Component of Prayer

It is also critical to remember the religious and spiritual component of prayer. Although there is a psychological component to prayer that helps relieve stress, our focus group respondents indicate that the spiritual component of prayer is the most important in helping cope with personal problems. This was stated succinctly by one man.

Prayer is more of a divine, it brings a divine intervention from God, you know, in revelation to you regarding what the answers is to your problem. There's more to it than just meditation or to make you feel good. There is actually a relationship with an Almighty God.

Loving Your Enemies/Forgiveness

Several individuals mentioned that one of the other ways that prayer reduces stress is in helping them to handle interpersonal conflicts. Here is one example in which an individual mentions praying for one's enemies and turning the problem over to God as being a way to reduce stress.

I was going to say, yeah, especially that one about praying for your enemies. I find that works, too, and I don't know if it's because it's relieving stress from me and I just give it to God and forget about it.

The comments of focus group participants on loving your enemies is an acknowledgement of the importance of forgiveness. Forgiveness has been generally defined as abandoning negative assessments toward an individual who has unjustly hurt us and showing compassion toward the person (Enright, Freedman, & Rique, 1998; see also McCullough, Pargament, & Thoresen, 2000). Forgiveness is an important aspect of mental health; researchers have fairly consistently found that individuals who can forgive others have a lower likelihood of experiencing psychological distress than individuals who are unwilling to forgive (Krause & Ellison, 2003). Krause and Ellison (2003), using the research of Scobie and Scobie (1998), note that the "Christian Model" of forgiveness is based on the belief that people should forgive unconditionally. This unconditional forgiveness may enhance psychological well-being, because it allows individuals to let go of the hurt and resentment associated with a transgression and consequently avoid ruminating over these events (reliving the hurt over and over; Krause & Ellison, 2003).

In the following example, one man discusses how prayer helped him deal with an unexpected marital breakup. This passage reflects many of the themes that have been previously discussed, including using prayer to cope with a serious problem, prayer as an activity that relieves stress, and turning the problem over to God.

A Let me tell you, I was going through a divorce years ago. My wife left me for another man. I come home, she was gone. The furniture was gone, I had no concept she was leaving at all. You know, the cat said meow, she's gone. Everything was gone, you know what I'm saying? And I was hurt, and I went to a psychiatrist, and we sat there and he was talking over the same thing week after week, "How do you feel about this? How do you feel about that?" And my father come, he said, "When's the last time you been to church?" I said, "Daddy, it's been a while." You know, because we all get grown and leave church for a while. I went back to church and started praying, and I learned you turn it over to God and leave it there. See, I was going to a doctor, going over the same thing, rehashing the same thing week after week, "Well, how to you feel about that? How do you feel about this? How do you feel about that?" I was like, "I'm getting tired of going to the same thing over and over again." But I went to church and I turned it over to God, and I began to grow. I left the psychiatrist, you know, and I'm here today because of prayer. Because of prayer.

Facilitator: Can you say a little bit more about how the prayer helped in that situation?

A Yeah, it strengthened me, you know, because day by day I realized that the pain went away. I told the Lord, "Take the pain away." I was really hurting,

I contemplated suicide, and day by day and I trusted the Lord, the days became brighter and I had more hope through prayer, prayer with God.

Later during the focus group the same man continues his discussion about his divorce and the way that prayer affected his life.

My wife, when she left me, she went to another man in [a city in Michigan], and we stayed in contact. And over the years the man developed [a fatal disease]. And he was in the hospital. He called me, he knew that I was saved, you know, he said, "Will you come to visit me and lead me to the Lord?" Now my old self was saying, "Man, you must be crazy!" You know what I'm saying? But through prayer the Lord had changed me over the years. And I went to him, and witnessed to him, he accepted the Lord. He died two days later. So I'm saying, the Lord will, through prayer, allow you to love your enemies you know, prayer will change you.

Power of Prayer

Finally, focus group members provided several examples of the power of prayer to effect change in potentially catastrophic circumstances. Both of these examples are from men.

When he was saying God knows but he wants you to know. It was about two years ago, I didn't know why, but you know, when I went to Bible study in the church I prayed for three weeks straight for my family. After that three weeks, my stepmom and my little sister was in an accident, a car accident. And, if you could have seen the car, it was no way possible anyone could have survived. But, they did, no broken bones or anything you know. It was like, I knew I was praying for a reason, and I guess that's what that was for. Like you said, God knows already what he wants you to know.

This is a situation that I was in. Even though I prayed before it happened, but I was on my way home from the West Coast. I was driving by myself. I had a little car, it was little, the tires blew out and there was a semi coming. And I prayed right then because I almost went over the turnpike exit, and I bounced back and I almost hit the semi, and I just prayed, I said, "If it's my time, then let it be, but I want you to know that I am confessing my sins." I was just praying in my mind. And my tires blew out, I mean, just like that, and when they blew out it saved me because if my tires would have been able to roll, keep going, I would have been hit by the semi because it was a bad storm.

But then I was traveling along, following some friends. So I packed my stuff up, put it in their car, and there was a van that had just went past me and looked over, there were like four or five bodies, three little kids and like the dog, and I was like, I had just missed the point of . . . And right then I was like, why did it happen? I mean at that point no one can say why did that happen, because it was like I was witnessing it, it was like you can see your life getting ready to come and go, and it was just like boom, my tires just blew out. So I guess it was the light. He was saying, "It ain't your time, it's not your time."

Focus Group Summary

The focus group information on prayer and coping was particularly informative and instructive about the nature, content, and process of this religious activity. The information was especially helpful in revealing a much more differentiated picture of the use of prayer in coping, because it is often portrayed fairly simplistically in the research literature. This may be the case for several reasons. First, as noted by Pargament (1997), some studies that have been cited as examples of religious coping merely reflect correlations between the presence of one or more stressful circumstances and reports of prayer behavior. Studies are needed in which the problem and the use of prayer to cope with the problem are more proximally related to one another. Second, other studies of prayer and coping that involve samples of individuals who are medically ill or otherwise experiencing dire personal circumstances are examples in which the problem and prayer are more closely linked. However, when individuals are asked to report on their use of prayer to cope with the illness or other trauma, they may report only on whether or not they have prayed and the frequency of prayer. Crucial data about the content of prayer, which is often not assessed, may provide important information about issues of personal control in illness and coping beliefs and behaviors.

Moreover, the emphasis on prayer as coping in the context of illness, hardship, and serious personal difficulties has biased research toward examining events of this type and neglected possible other uses of prayer in relation to more mundane events and circumstances. The focus group data clearly showed that individuals pray for a variety of concerns, some of which are related to the everyday stresses and hassles of living and that involve important social roles (e.g., spouse, parent, worker). Other uses of prayer involved the resolution of interpersonal difficulties and appealing to God to transform one's attitude regarding another or about a relationship (e.g., prayers to help one to forgive another). Perhaps the most remarkable responses concern the use of prayer to maintain ongoing communication with God and the psychological and emotional benefits derived from these relations, such as a sense of calm assurance and confidence of God's presence and support. Related to this, several members told us that they engaged in prayer on a constant basis (i.e., pray unceasingly) and conveyed the idea that being "prayerful" in all aspects of their lives provided them with constant moral direction and behavioral guidance and instilled an ongoing awareness of God's presence. In a situation of close communication with God, several group members said that their prayers might be particularly succinct because God was already aware of their needs (i.e., "He knows your heart"). These prayers might reflect a simple appeal for help or an outpouring or expression of absolute faith.

Focus group participants also talked about prayer in a manner similar to that used in research on stress and coping processes. God was mentioned in several instances as being an important source of social support and as providing unfailing and constant support. Prayer was used in a number of different ways as part of the coping process. Some individuals spoke of prayer as helping them manage the emotional distress that is associated with personal problems. In this regard, they spoke of the sense of calm that prayer provided them and that by communicating with God through prayer, they developed a sense of hope that the problem would be resolved. A prominent response from the group members was the reference to prayer in relation to stress relief and the sense that prayer was a viable and preferable means of responding to stressors. Obviously, the focus group data did not include appropriate measures to assess the action of prayer with respect to known physiological mechanisms (i.e., the relaxation response) and pathways (e.g., neuroendocrine function, cardiovascular system). However, the repeated and consistent references to feelings of calm and peace and reductions in feelings of stress strongly suggest that focus group members were reporting on meaningful and authentic phenomena. Finally, comparable to the processes of cognitive reframing and threat appraisal, other group members talked about how prayer helped them to see the problem in a new and different light. Prayer was effective in helping them see that the problem was, indeed, manageable and within their ability to handle.

Group members spoke frequently about issues of personal control in their efforts to handle life problems. Many of the comments indicated that prayer was empowering and gave them the means of approaching and coping with these problems. These comments were similar to the notion of having a collaborative relationship or a partnership with God in terms of facing life difficulties (Pargament, 1997). Group members also mentioned that, for particular problems, they relinquished their attempts to directly change the situation and turned the problem over to God (i.e., "let go and let God"). This approach seemed to be particularly beneficial in terms of reducing the negative emotions (e.g., worry, sorrow) that often accompany life problems. In other instances, turning over a problem was an appeal to God to change the individual's attitude or perspective about a relationship or situation (e.g., forgiveness of others). These interpretations of turning a problem over to God are distinct from largely negative characterizations in which individuals are thought to surrender control and abandon personal attempts to change a situation. Finally, group members said that they might say a prayer of deference to God's will in certain circumstances (i.e., "Your will be done"). Rather than indicating a sense of fatalism or resignation, this prayer reflected a mature and informed acceptance of the problem situation and a belief that the outcome, because it was conceived by God, would ultimately be the correct and appropriate one.

In summary, focus group participants provided important information concerning the diverse and highly developed uses of prayer in coping with a number of life situations and circumstances. The picture of prayer that emerges is more nuanced than is currently available in the literature and indicates that prayer is used to cope with everyday life occurrences (i.e., daily hassles), ongoing and chronic stressors, as well as serious life problems (e.g., health and financial hardship). Further, for some individuals, being prayerful is a way of living in the world that both personifies their approach to dealing with life issues and gives witness to their religious beliefs and commitment. These data documented that using prayer to cope with problems is a varied and complex phenomenon. Prayer is intimately involved in a number of aspects of the coping process, including the formulation and use of cognitive strategies and approaches to problem solving, marshaling social support from God, appraising the threat potential of particular events, and regulating one's emotional response. The focus group information clearly illustrated that prayer, when used in the service of coping with life problems, provides many opportunities for self-reflection and examination and spiritual growth.

Chapter Summary and Conclusion

An impressive amount of research has demonstrated that religious coping of various types is important in helping deal with the stresses associated with undesirable or threatening conditions such as physical illness, accidents, disability, and the death or illness of a loved one. Religious coping is particularly common among black adults who are caregivers for family members who are suffering from dementia, as well as among persons who are themselves experiencing poor health. Research using the National Survey of Black Americans and the National Panel Survey of Black Americans shows that prayer was one of the most frequently mentioned coping responses. Ellison and Taylor (1996) found that women, respondents who had personal health problems or loved ones with health problems, and persons who were dealing with the death of a loved one were more likely to use prayer as a source of coping. Further, they found that lower levels of personal mastery or feelings of control over personal affairs significantly increased the likelihood that an individual would turn to prayer when coping with problems.

Analysis of focus group information provided important insights into the nature and meaning of prayer for participants. First, these data indicated the presence of two distinct patterns for using prayer to cope with life problems. The first pattern of prayer was represented by individuals who prayed in response to specific problems that they encountered. In contrast, the second pattern of prayer was represented by individuals who prayed very frequently and intensely and for whom prayer was an integral part of their daily life. This latter group prayed all of the time and felt that prayer should not be reserved for crisis situations. Second, participants said that they used prayer for a number of life problems (e.g., job problems, health difficulties, relationship issues) and provided a number of reasons why they used prayer to cope with a range of problems from job to health difficulties. Prayer was regarded as being very effective in imparting strength, reducing stress, and helping to ease their worries about a problem. In addition, prayer was effective in helping participants pray for and ultimately forgive their enemies.

Finally, the survey data and the focus group information provide an overall picture of the use of prayer in coping with life problems that is both complex and multifaceted. Prayer is clearly regarded as an important and primary response for coping with life problems. However, although prayer is used in efforts to deal with life problems, individuals may not use prayer specifically to request a particular outcome. In fact, a number of focus group participants said that their prayers focused instead on individual qualities and traits that might help them cope with a problem or to accept whatever outcome might transpire. Of particular significance, when confronted with a problematic life situation, many focus group members described an attitude of "turning the problem over to God" and accepting God's will. Rather than a fatalistic orientation or a sign of resignation, these perspectives may allow participants to manage more effectively the psychological distress (i.e., worry) associated with problems and redirect their coping efforts to aspects of the problem that are amenable to change (Krause et al., 2000b). Given these perspectives, previous findings (Ellison & Taylor, 1996) indicating that the use of prayer in coping was associated with lower levels of personal mastery and control over personal affairs are cast in a new light and suggest a more complex interpretation of this relationship.

Chapter 5

Use of Ministers for Personal Problems

African American ministers are an important and vital resource for individuals and the African American community. A long tradition of work documents the diverse roles that clergy have played with respect to community leadership, development, and empowerment, and in brokering relations between black communities and social institutions and organizations within the broader society. Clergy have also played an important role in spearheading the provision of services to their congregations and surrounding communities through programmatic efforts organized by churches (Gilkes, 1980; Levin, 1984; Olson, Reis, Murphy, & Gem, 1988). Of particular note are antipoverty and material aid programs (Chaves & Higgins, 1992) and a range of church-sponsored programs and initiatives including youth programs (McAdoo & Crawford, 1990), programs for the elderly and their caregivers (Caldwell, Chatters, Billingsley, & Taylor, 1995; Haber, 1984), and community economic development initiatives (Billingsley, 1999). In the area of health programming, there have been a number of health care screening and programs to poor blacks (Levin, 1984, 1986) and other efforts that focus on ameliorating hypertension (Perry, 1981), controlling weight (Kumanyika & Charleston, 1992), and general health promotion activities (e.g., Eng & Hatch, 1991; Eng, Hatch, & Callan, 1985). A recent survey identified more than 1,700 outreach programs offered by churches; roughly two thirds of the churches sponsor at least one community outreach program (Billingsley & Caldwell, 1991;

Caldwell et al., 1995; Thomas, Quinn, Billingsley, & Caldwell, 1994). These church-based programs provide basic needs (e.g., food and clothing distribution, home care) assistance, income maintenance programs such as financial services, and low-income housing and counseling and intervention for community members, such as family counseling, parenting/sexuality seminars, youth-at-risk programs, and aid to the incarcerated and their families. Other initiatives include various types of education and awareness programs (e.g., child care, life skill and academic tutoring), health-related activities (e.g., HIV/AIDS care, substance abuse counseling), and recreation and fellowship for families and/or individuals. In addition to sponsoring a diverse array of programs, many congregations also report cooperating with a range of community institutions and government agencies via referrals and other means (Billingsley, 1999).

These and other types of church and community partnerships recognize that, within black communities, religious institutions and clergy are both trusted and respected. Working in collaboration with black churches and their clergy and other resources, these initiatives have tapped into the traditions of mutual assistance and self-reliance to improve the health of community members. However, it is important to recognize that, in addition to these programmatic efforts, clergy also provide assistance to individual members of their congregations in the form of counseling and assistance on a range of personal issues from marital and family concerns to drug abuse and mental health problems. In fact, a number of studies indicate that clergy are not only a preferred source of assistance among African Americans, but in many cases are the only forms of professional help-seeking that is enlisted.

Despite the prominence of clergy assistance, we know little about the process whereby individuals actively choose and seek out support from clergy (Taylor, Ellison, Chatters, Levin, & Lincoln, 2000). Specifically, we have little reliable information about why certain individuals choose to use ministers to assist them in dealing with personal problems, the types of concerns people take to ministers, the ways in which clergy help, and perceptions regarding the general efficacy of ministerial assistance (Williams, 1994). This chapter is an initial exploration of the circumstances involved in using ministers for personal problems. Stated another way, we are interested in who goes to ministers for help, what sorts of problems concern them, their reports of what ministers advise or actively do in these circumstances, and whether those seeking help view these efforts as effective.

The chapter begins with a brief overview of the research literature on the role and importance of clergy with respect to formal systems of care and treatment. This work provides a background for understanding not only the types of issues that clergy encounter, but also ways in which these are managed. Following this, we discuss the literature that examines individual efforts by clergy to assist individuals who are coping with life problems and difficulties (i.e., clergy as a coping resource). Next, we explore two data sets that are pertinent to the question of clergy assistance. First, we examine multi-wave data from the National Survey of Black Americans on the different sources of assistance that respondents report using to handle a personal problem. These data provide some indication as to changes over time in the prominence of clergy assistance as one of several strategies used to cope with personal problems. Following this, we examine, in depth, focus group data on the use of ministers for personal problems. The focus group data provide an extremely rich source of information about how individuals think about both the benefits and drawbacks associated with enlisting clergy in the help-seeking process. We use the focus group data to explore relevant themes and issues in the use of clergy assistance that have been identified in the literature. Finally, we conclude the chapter with a discussion of both the theoretical and practical significance of the findings and their implications for future research and for developing a comprehensive understanding of clergy's role in helping individuals contend with life difficulties.

Clergy and Formal Support Systems

Clergy counsel on a wide range of problems, including alcoholism and other forms of substance abuse, depression, marital and family conflict, teenage pregnancy, unemployment, and legal problems. In fact, the type and severity of psychiatric problems that clergy encounter in counseling do not differ significantly from those seen by mental health practitioners (Larson et al., 1988). However, given the heterogeneity of this group, the counseling and referral practices of individual clergy diverge considerably (Gottlieb & Olfson, 1987). Even ministers who have received post-graduate education receive minimal training in counseling individuals experiencing basic problems of daily life (e.g., marital relationship problems) and are totally unfamiliar with psychopathology and the symptoms of severe mental illness (Bentz, 1970; Gottlieb & Olfson, 1987; Virkler, 1979). Moreover, clergy tend to underestimate the severity of psychotic symptoms (Larson, 1968) and, compared to other mental health practitioners (e.g., physicians, psychologists, social workers, psychiatric nurses), are least likely to recognize suicide lethality (Domino & Sevain, 1985–1986). In many instances, their religious and ministerial training may lead them to interpret mental or emotional problems in purely religious terms (Hong & Wiehe, 1974) or to interpret clinical symptoms (e.g., hallucinatory behaviors) as evidence of religious conflict (Larson, 1968).

However, a number of studies suggest that characteristics of ministers may impact their counseling and referral activities with individual church members. Ministers' level of education is an important predictor of their level of knowledge regarding mental health issues and services available from professionals and public agencies. Further, ministers with more education are more confident in their understanding of these issues and interact more frequently with the mental health community than do their less-educated peers (Gottlieb & Olfson, 1987).

Nevertheless, few clergy refer their clients to mental health professionals overall; only 1 in 10 cases are referred to mental health professions for more specialized services (Mollica, Streets, Boscarino, & Redlich, 1986; Veroff, Douvan, & Kulka, 1981; Virkler, 1979). Further, clergy are also generally unaware of the availability of services offered at community health centers and university clinics (Mobley, Katz, & Elkins, 1985) and unfamiliar with required referral procedures (Winett, Major, & Stewart, 1979). Clergy with advanced education and liberal theologies have a higher probability of making referrals, whereas those who are less educated and who have more theologically conservative perspectives are more likely to attempt treatment of individuals exhibiting symptoms of psychiatric disorder (Gottlieb & Olfson, 1987).

Despite these factors, the research literature also shows that clergy are very successful in responding to the general needs of their congregants and securing appropriate services. They provide a wealth of supports to congregants, including financial assistance, emergency shelter, and food, as well as assistance in dealing with problems of living. Moreover, there is a growing recognition among clergy of the importance of addressing the mental health needs of their congregants, as reflected in the growth of the field of pastoral counseling and the provision of graduate training in clinical counseling.

Clergy as a Coping Resource

When confronted with a serious personal problem, an individual can choose from among a broad array of professional helpers, including psychiatrists, clinical psychologists, social workers, physicians, lawyers, marriage counselors, and vocational guidance counselors. For many Americans, however, clergy play a critical role in addressing a diverse array of personal problems and concerns (Taylor et al., 2000). In one of the earliest systematic examinations of this question, Veroff and associates (1981) found that

39% of Americans who had a serious personal problem sought help from a member of the clergy and clergy were consulted more often than other categories of professional helpers (e.g., psychiatrists, psychologists, doctors, marriage counselors, or social workers). As might be expected, clergy are consulted for life problems and concerns that are consistent with their traditional ministerial roles and training, such as comforting the bereaved and advising those who are physically ill. However, clergy also counsel individuals concerning interpersonal crises such as martial and family issues and serious mental health problems (Chalfant et al., 1990; Veroff et al., 1981). Information for African Americans, in particular, indicates a reliance on clergy to address mental health issues (Neighbors, Musick, & Williams, 1998). Finally, clergy are instrumental in marshaling material goods, resources, and services to meet daily needs for food, shelter, and clothing and in providing educational and job training opportunities. African American clergy, in particular, are involved in a multitude of ways in assisting their congregation members and ensuring their spiritual, emotional, and physical well-being.

The preference for asking clergy for assistance with life problems may, in part, be related to several factors, including treatment expense, access, and experience and familiarity with help of this type. For those who are poor, the clergy hold a distinct advantage over other professional counselors as a preferred source of assistance because, unlike most other sources of professional help, they do not charge for their services. Veroff et al.'s (1981) analysis found that among individuals who had a serious problem but failed to seek help, treatment expense was mentioned as a reason for not consulting a psychiatrist or psychologist. Even for those who are not poor, difficulties with access to professional assistance may be an additional factor in choosing clergy over other sources of help. For example, clergy do not require insurance coverage, co-payments, or other bureaucratic procedures for a consultation. In contrast to psychiatrists, psychologists, marriage counselors, and other mental health specialists who are typically approached after prior consultation with a referral source, the pathway to clergy is generally a direct one that is rarely mediated by either formal or informal referrals (Veroff et al., 1981). Further, individuals who seek assistance from clergy generally do so within the context of a meaningful personal relationship with their minister in which there is rapport and trust. Finally, individuals may be more inclined to seek clergy for help in dealing with a personal problem because of a common ethos with regard to helping others, shared worldviews about the nature of problems (e.g., beliefs about the origins of and responsibility for problems), and customary and accepted ways of coping (e.g., prayer) with life difficulties that are expressly religious.

With regard to social status factors, the available evidence indicates few associations between sociodemographic status and the use of clergy for personal problems. Neighbors et al. (1998) reported that an initial bivariate association between gender and seeking help from clergy (women were more likely than men to say that they turned to clergy to deal with personal problems) was rendered insignificant in the presence of controls for other demographic factors and problem type and severity, while the relationship between education and clergy use bordered significance (persons with a college degree were more than 1½ times more likely than those with less than 12 years of education to say that they used ministers for personal problems). Veroff and associates' analysis indicated that religious denomination and church attendance were relatively strong and consistent predictors of the use of clergy and mental health specialists. Specifically, Jews had a high likelihood of seeking help from psychiatrists/psychologists and were the least likely to use clergy, whereas Fundamentalists were among the highest users of clergy but among the least likely to use psychologists or psychiatrists. With respect to religious involvement factors, frequent church attenders were more likely to seek assistance from clergy, whereas infrequent attenders were more likely to seek assistance from psychologists or psychiatrists (Veroff et al., 1981).

Systematic research on the use of ministers among African Americans is scant. This is despite the acknowledged role of religion and religious institutions in the lives of African Americans and information indicating that clergy can be a pivotal link to social resources both within the church and outside (i.e., community) of it. Further, given a high level of unmet need for mental health and other services among the black population (Neighbors, 1985), ministers may play an integral role in health and social welfare delivery systems for African Americans. Although several studies have examined the counseling and referral practices of clergy (see Meylink & Gorsuch, 1988, for a review), few address these issues among black ministers. One exception is Mollica et al.'s (1986) study of 214 ministers, one of the most comprehensive to date of mental health counseling activities among black and white clergy. The counseling and referral practices of black ministers were distinctive in several respects. Black ministers were more heavily involved in counseling, with nearly 70% spending more than 10% of their time in counseling activities. Black ministers were involved to a greater extent in crisis intervention and in counseling persons with diagnosed mental illness. Compared to their white peers, African American clergy placed greater emphasis on the use of religious practices such as church attendance as a strategy to treat emotional problems. Although the rate of referrals made and received were low among both black and white clergy, referral patterns varied by race: Black ministers were much more likely to make referrals to community mental health centers.

Neighbors and colleagues' investigations of the use of ministers using data from the National Survey of Black Americans (Neighbors, 1991; Neighbors et al., 1983; Neighbors et al., 1998) found, using bivariate analysis, that ministers were frequent sources of help to persons with a serious personal problem (Neighbors et al., 1983) and were significantly more likely to be used when the problem involved bereavement (multivariate analyses; Neighbors, 1991). More recently, Neighbors et al. (1998) examined the impact of demographic and problem type and severity on reports of using clergy for personal problems. They found that, in comparison to an economic problem, respondents with a problem involving death/bereavement were three times more likely to consult clergy, while those with an interpersonal problem were two times more likely. With respect to problem severity, respondents who felt that they were "at the point of a nervous breakdown" were twice as likely as those indicating that they "felt nervous" to report that they sought out clergy to help with their problem. For persons who went to only one source of assistance, roughly half used clergy to deal with a problem. Further, those who went to clergy first were more likely to forgo other sources of assistance, especially for death, health, and emotional problems and for difficulties in which respondents characterized themselves as being at the point of a nervous breakdown, feeling nervous, and feeling depressed. The type of assistance received from clergy included religious coping (i.e., prayer, reading the Bible), counseling advice (i.e., listening, giving advice, comfort), and taking specific action to help the individual. Finally, persons who used clergy exclusively were more likely to report satisfaction with that encounter and to say that they would refer others to this source of assistance. Collectively, these findings show that clergy provide direct and beneficial assistance to individuals with particular types of personal problems and circumstances. In addition, however, the literature indicates that it is important to encourage communication between clergy and other professionals, such as specialty mental health workers, to increase access to other forms of professional services (Neighbors et al., 1998).

In summary, the growing body of systematic attempts to examine the factors associated with the use of clergy for personal problems among African Americans has provided a number of interesting and provocative issues for further study. Central among them are questions as to the role of status factors (e.g., gender, education) and problem characteristics (i.e., type and severity) in the decision to seek help from clergy. In addition, we have little information about how religions' involvement factors (e.g., church attendance, degree of religiosity) and connections to specific religious institutions (e.g., denomination), may influence choosing clergy versus other types of helpers. Although the research literature provides a number of very interesting suggestions, an in-depth examination of factors associated with the use of ministers for personal problems has yet to be completed. The next section of the chapter explores a number of these issues using multiwave survey data on the use of ministers and in-depth focus group information.

Survey Data on the Use of Ministers

Data from Waves II (1987–1988), III (1988–1989), and IV (1992) of the National Survey of Black Americans were examined to answer the question concerning the prevalence of the use of ministers among African Americans and whether this percentage has changed over time. In response to a series of questions regarding the experience of a serious personal problem, NSBA respondents were asked to indicate whether they had ever gone to a number of places or organizations for help. The listing included (a) hospital emergency room, (b) medical clinic, (c) social services or welfare agency, (d) mental health center, (e) private therapist, (f) doctor's office, (g) minister or someone else at your place of worship, and (h) some other place.

First, examining the percentages within a particular wave of data reveals that the most frequently mentioned sources of assistance are the doctor's office and the minister (or someone else at your place of worship; Table 5.1). This is consistent across all three waves of data, with these two groups virtually identical with respect to the percentage mentioned as a source of assistance. Within each wave of data, other medical resources (i.e., medical clinic and hospital emergency room) are mentioned next, followed by private therapist. The two exceptions are noted in Wave III where "some other place" was mentioned more frequently than "private therapist," and in Wave IV where the percentage of respondents who report seeing a "private therapist" is greater than those going to a "hospital emergency room." Overall, however, the pattern of findings is largely consistent across waves of data collections in demonstrating that private doctors and ministers are the most frequently cited sources of aid, followed by other medial resources and mental health specialists.

Focus Group Findings

A portion of the focus group protocol for the study "Appraisals of Religiosity, Coping and Church Support" was devoted to exploring group

Table 5.1   Use of Formal Help-Seeking Resources Across the National Survey of Black Americans, Waves II-IV

	NSBA Data Waves		
Formal Help-Seeking Resource	Wave II 1987–1988	Wave III 1988–1989	Wave IV 1992
Hospital emergency room			
Yes	17.9	11.9	13.7
No	82.1	88.1	86.3
TOTAL	100.0	100.0	100.0
N	506	260	270
Medical clinic			
Yes	18.1	14.2	16.6
No	81.9	85.8	83.4
TOTAL	100.0	100.0	100.0
N	509	260	271
Social services or welfare agency			
Yes	9.0	7.3	8.5
No	91.0	92.7	91.5
TOTAL	100.0	100.0	100.0
N	509	260	270
Mental health center			
Yes	7.5	3.1	7.4
No	92.5	96.9	92.6
TOTAL	100.0	100.0	100.0
N	509	260	270
Private therapist			
Yes	13.6	8.5	15.5
No	86.4	91.5	84.5
TOTAL	100.0	100.0	100.0
N	509	260	271
Doctor's office			
Yes	33.5	25.4	33.3
No	66.5	74.6	66.7
TOTAL	100.0	100.0	100.0
N	507	260	270
Minister or someone else at place of worship			
Yes	32.2	26.9	32.2
No	67.8	73.1	67.8
TOTAL	100.0	100.0	100.0
N	509	260	270
Some other place			
Yes	7.9	8.7	9.4
No	92.1	91.3	90.6
TOTAL	100.0	100.0	100.0
N	504	260	267

members' perceptions and attitudes about the use of ministers for personal problems and their experiences in consulting with clergy for problems. For this section, the focus group facilitators were instructed to say the following: "Ministers often help people deal with different types of problems that they face in life. Have any of you ever gone to a minister (during times of trouble or tough times)? Why did you go? Can you tell me about that?" One of the enormous benefits of using the focus group methodology is the ability to learn from group members something about the context and process of clergy assistance. In particular, the content of the focus group information was evaluated in terms of the specific insights it provided concerning the group members' views regarding clergy assistance as a viable source of aid, their attitudes and beliefs about approaching clergy for help with personal problems, the particular problems for which they are likely to ask for assistance, factors that may facilitate or hinder their willingness to do so, and the perceived efficacy of clergy assistance. As described in the following sections, the analysis of the focus group information verifies the relevancy of these themes to participants' perceptions about consulting with clergy for personal problems. This material is organized into three main sections: (a) patterns and circumstances in using ministers, (b) deciding to forgo clergy help, and (c) choosing to disclose problems.

Patterns and Circumstances of Using Ministers

This section explores focus group responses to illustrate various patterns of minister use for personal problems, the types of problems mentioned, and the forms of help provided, as well as the factors that facilitate the use of ministers (e.g., accessibility, rapport, and trust). Many of the focus group participants said that they had sought assistance from their pastor or minister in the past. As indicated below, some did so on a fairly frequent basis, while others were more selective in their use of ministers:

> So, yeah, man, I have been to my pastor. I would say over the last four years, I think I may have had with either my fiancée or just me combined, maybe about five or six times.

> My reason is because I really, I really trust my minister and I really know that he can really relate to everything that I am going through because I feel that he is knows me. But, you know, in the same sense, I don't really look at him as like a high, like he's God or like a higher being you know. And, I really understand that he's just a person that was chosen to go through and relate to God. I go to my minister quite often when I do have problems.

Yeah, I, really I thank God for my pastor because he's a pastor that stresses teaching and knowledge. He is a knowledgeable man and he stresses that to each of his members. I've gone to him concerning different things.

I was just thinking, I've been saved now for 24 years and I maybe can tell you, maybe three, maybe four times out of my whole saved life that I've gone to talk to the pastor about something. Generally, like she say, you know some things I just don't think I need to bother him with. But if I am sick or in trouble or my children, you know, need help or something then I've gone, but not often.

One man stated that ministers were only one of several sources of help that he would use to discuss personal problems, suggesting that his help-seeking process may involve a sequence of multiple sources of assistance:

For me, it's just that, I don't want to say I would never go, but that's not necessarily the first place I would go or the only place. I might go to multiple people, my wife maybe. In fact my wife is usually the first person I go to. So I wouldn't say that I would never go or I'm not likely going or have never gone, but it's just, that's not the first place and it would rarely be the only place that I would go.

Participants in the focus group study offered a number of reasons why they utilized ministers and pastors. One reason was the perceived stigma that was associated with discussing problems with a psychiatrist or other mental health professional. In contrast, seeking help with personal problems from a pastor was viewed more positively and as a normative feature of church life.

I think, I don't know if it is media based or just the way I grew up in the hood, but there is a stigma of going to see a shrink, you know what I am saying. However, and I do not know if this is like this in other churches, but in our church there is no stigma associated with going to see the pastor, you know. But just the fact that you can go to somebody, you know when you going to see a psychiatrist, what's wrong with you? Where like, you know, in the church don't everybody go talk to the pastor once in a while?

Another reason for seeking help from pastors was their accessibility and availability during times of need. This might be in the form of regularly scheduled opportunities to discuss concerns or immediate response to emergency situations.

You know, in our church there is open counseling every Wednesday from 1 until 8 P.M. or probably at least until 7:00. He's counseling and talking to folks. So that could just be a thing where it's open to where you go to and that could be the difference.

One thing about our church that I really thank God for, is that my pastor he offers counseling on Wednesdays from 1–5 every week.

But, just to know that they will come as soon as you call and sometimes if the pastor is out of state for instance, then the elders will come. Whether it is sickness, illness, family problems.

You can call her anytime of the night, in the morning. She would pray, she would have consultation with you and there's other people in church too that are prayerful and are, centered so that you can go and reflect and talk to.

I have gone through many surgeries and one particular time, they had did surgery and they was threatening to take me back in surgery. And they had worked with me, and I ended up in the hospital three weeks. My blood pressure, I mean, my fever kept growing. They come that morning to tell me they said, We are getting ready to take you back to surgery. And, I had enough strength to muscle up to call my pastor. Must have been about three or four o'clock in the morning. And he prayed. And by early that morning, before they got ready to take me for surgery, two of the young ministers, two evangelist came, and they prayed for me. And, when they got me back to the x-ray to look at the thing, it was gone.

Apart for the benefits of seeking counseling and advice from one's minister, recognition of the religious dimension that is conveyed as part of counseling and assistance was an important concern in seeking help from clergy:

You know, we've done that, we've been in one church for approximately eight years, you know, and whenever there is an issue we [he and his wife] just can't seem to hammer out at home, we seem to be able to go to a counseling session with our pastor and all of a sudden, issues just come up there that would never come up at home. Part of that is just having a mediator, just having somebody there to listen. But then to have a Godly mediator who can not only hear you, but can hear what God is saying, I think that adds extra power to the fact that I am going to see somebody.

And again in counseling there has to be a spiritual dynamic to it since we are spiritual beings.

Several focus group members indicated that they were more likely to seek assistance from their pastors because they had developed a close personal relationship with them. As expressed here, the connection to one's pastor can take the form of a kinship relation (father figure) and involve ongoing encouragement and positive emotional support. Further, the presence of a caring personal relationship may instill a feeling of personal accountability to others that promotes a more effective helping relationship. These considerations were extremely important, as three men noted:

> I didn't grow up with a father, you know what I am saying. So, I had no earthly man in my life that I could go to and talk about, you know, about little stuff about hooping and nothing like that, you know. So, for me, I look at my pastor not as God, but as a father figure, and not so much a father figure as in, loan me some money, but as a father figure in terms of integrity, you know.

> You know, I think that at least I have a pretty decent relationship with our pastor, but I think a lot of it has to do with the fact that he opens himself up to us. So he's not one that just you know, "You go to all the rest of the people in church and if it's a real serious problem come to me." I think he mingles with us, he fellowships with us a lot, and I feel comfortable telling him a lot of stuff. And the stuff that I'm doing wrong or that was doing wrong. I mean, if you're accountable to somebody or if somebody's accountable to you, if you tell that person, then you'll be less likely to do it.

> But sometime, man, you get a phone call or your pastor stop by your job or preach inside and say, "You know brother, I was praying for you." And how uplifting that is for your pastor just to say, "Man I was praying for you." And that just like makes your week, makes your month, even though not taking nothing away from God. But I'm just saying for your pastor just to say, "You know brother, I was praying for you." You know, I mean that's just good to have a pastor to say things like that to you and always talk, you know, positive and encourage you along the way. But we know ourselves sometimes you got to encourage yourself. But you can't take nothing away from God and you can't take nothing away from your pastor.

Similarly, a woman's comments indicate that a personal relationship in which one is individually known by the pastor is important:

> So, he [the respondent's husband] hadn't gone to church in a few weeks and our minister called. That's why I like small churches because

> I, me personally I would never go to a church with ten thousand members and satellites because I believe that ministers should know that, "Hey, K. is not here in church this week. She hasn't been here in two weeks and I want to know why." And, they call your house. See, I like that and that's what he did.

Another woman expressed a similar sentiment in discussing the types of relationships that can develop with pastors in small, as opposed to large, churches:

> And being involved in a lot of big churches, some of them get involved in politics and money. I feel they do their job, but I just don't feel that they're the best person for me to speak to, so I usually find myself going to deacons or other people, whether they be people I work with who have strong faith. Some of these big churches get into politics and money, and like I said, I just feel like it'd just be a burden.

With respect to active counseling, focus group respondents said that they received a variety of advice from their pastors:

> But, yeah, I've used my pastor. Once before I went to him and that was when I was deciding whether or not I was going to go to school locally or go away. I felt obligated to myself personally to stay at home because my mom was raising, you know, like five of us, so I wanted to help out financially. So I felt kind of guilty about thinking about leaving. So anyway, I went to the pastor about that, you know. The answer was, Is the situation at home unbearable, you know, with all the distractions, with my friends coming by and all these other sort of things. So I decided, after talking with him, I decided to go away to school after our conversation.

> Within the last year, my parents went through a divorce and it broke me...And I didn't understand, I didn't understand it. And then going to him [her pastor] and receiving counsel and just sharing and what he gave in term of to help console me, you know, in dealing with my parents.

> I have been to ministers in the church specifically on marital issues because they've been there, they've done that and I wanted to get a certain, you know, perspective from them.

According to the following response, in addition to advice, encouragement, and counseling, black ministers provide instrumental assistance such as monetary help with bills, finding a place to live, and interfacing with the legal and welfare systems:

> So, he was very helpful in natural ways as well spiritual. He's always got good wisdom, but when I needed a car he gave me one... and like there was a time when I got in debt and I was a baby in Christ and I said they fixin' to call. So, you know, we made arrangements and... he gave me the money and I paid him back.

Similar to analyses reported from the National Survey of Black Americans, one of the major problems that individuals seek assistance for is coping with the death of a loved one. Several of the focus group respondents mentioned the importance of their pastors when they were dealing with death and bereavement issues:

> Well, I lost a child last year in a car accident, and our pastor was very instrumental in assisting us to get back up on our feet.

> My wife, she, in a short period of time lost both her parents to cancer. So, you know, in a situation like that, yeah, I mean, she went and she, she... and you know... Everyone before you get married you consult with your pastor, but I think um the death of a parent, especially in a short time period, I mean, you know. And I really couldn't, I felt inadequate because I really couldn't, you know, tell her, I mean what it's like, "Well you know, you just pray about this, that or whatever," you know, because I wasn't in that situation. And she is like, "Well how would you know," and she would tell me, "You don't know how I feel because you haven't been there." So she, when she talked to the pastor and basically told him the same things, but I, I guess it was a little bit more credible coming from him and I wasn't offended by it or anything. My main concern was her well being.

> I lost my husband a little more than 2 years ago. And, I got the call early on Saturday morning, and he [the deceased husband] was in another town so I had to go to where he was and had to deal with that. But, as soon as I got back home that evening, I called for the elder, for the minister, for my pastor, and in five minutes he was there. And in another hour, some of the other ministers that we know were there. Yeah, I needed them.

Addressing the spiritual dimension of life, another reason for seeking help from pastors was to help with crises of faith:

So now that I have become more mature in my faithfulness, I'm starting to do things like I'll seek people out, seek out ministers, to help me with my trials and to talk about God because, I mean, actually today because I'm going through a major problem right now. I went to go talk to my pastor to see if he could ah give me some words of wisdom to help me increase my faith in God…to have him pray for me.

My husband had issues that he was dealing with about religion in general because some key people in his life were being affected by illness. So, he was questioning God, he was questioning faith you know, here's my grandfathers, he's a minister, he's had both legs removed, why?…And so he was able to talk through his problems with our minister.

There are times that I have had such battle in my mind that I had to get some instruction, and when I called the men of God, by the time they give you that word, you see that word is what works.

Deciding to Forgo Clergy Help

Distinct from the previous set of responses, the next section describes the comments of several individuals who said that they did not use ministers and their stated reasons for not seeking help from them. Stated reasons for not asking ministers for help were varied and included issues of personal choice, a belief that problems should be addressed to God exclusively, a lack of trust in the minister around issues of confidentiality, and fear that disclosure would alter their relationship with their minister or pastor. Several participants also provided reasons why it is important to seek assistance from one's minister. With respect to personal choice, one man felt that the concept of machismo prevented a lot of men from seeking help from anyone, including pastors:

Sometimes men don't seem to relate to other men. We hold a lot of things inside ourselves. We say, "I can handle it, I can handle it." I was going through a divorce, I tried to hold everything in, and, "I'm macho, I'm tough, I can deal with it, men don't cry. Real men don't cry." Real men do cry, you know, and get that frustration out. I think a lot of men just won't talk to a pastor or talk to anybody, but they want to hold it in and they're ashamed of what people will think about them. "I can handle it." All the times you can't handle it. And sometimes just talking to somebody will help you release the frustration and the problem. And talking to your pastor because he'll tell you what the Bible says and how to deal with your life spiritually, how to be successful in the spiritual life. I watch the church at benediction, when we're getting ready to close our service, and oftentimes men hold hands. Some men will pull their hand back, like, "I ain't holding your hand." Man, we're just too macho. We think we're being a homosexual because we hug one another in church. You know, macho-ism, you know.

Another man noted that even though he had a close personal relationship with his pastor, he discussed his problems exclusively with family members.

See, I love my pastor. He's a good pastor. He allows you to talk to him. As a matter of fact, he asked me to come in and sit down and talk to him. But my thing is the love line, for me is family first, you deal with your family and talk with your family about your problem, and that's why I don't go see my pastor, because I do have a lot of uncles, a lot of them will sit down and talk to me, or else I'll just get a friend who will listen to me. He does let the doors be open, open line, give him a call anytime basically, but I just, to me he's not my family, so I just don't deal with him.

Several focus group members said that they would not seek help from pastors because pastors/ministers were simply "middle men" and they preferred to talk directly to God. According to several men:

I mean my idea has always sort of been, rightly or wrongly, knock out the middle man and talk directly to God myself.

And so I have this discomfort and I guess the only person I'm comfortable being naked with, as R. said earlier, is with God or my wife.

I look at spirituality as something between me and God. I don't think I need to bring somebody else into the picture. Maybe, maybe they might have insight that might be beneficial, but it always seems to me, if I have an issue, I just go to the source.

I mean, I don't want to have to go through, some mediator to get to this solution.

One woman said that she does not seek assistance from ministers because of a lack of trust:

> This might add a sour note, but I'm a little leery of ministers.
> Something happened, my grandmother raised me and something
> happened to her and I was raised up knowing all of this and so I really
> can't...I try to respect them and keep it on a spiritual level, but I'm a
> little leery of a lot of ministers. I just don't feel real comfortable with
> them. So, I just try to keep a personal relationship with God.

The issue of whether one should discuss problems solely with God or with God and ministers was debated in several of the focus groups. Some of the men in the focus groups felt that it was important to talk to both ministers and God:

> Well it's good to talk about some things. You going to have to talk to
> someone, even though you go to God, it's good to get a sin and just
> talk about. Some things you just want to just talk to a person about.
> You know what I mean?

> Sometimes he [God] wants you to go talk to someone. Because
> sometime man, a person do have your answer.

Concerns about the confidentiality of their counseling session was a particularly important issue for focus group members. Those who felt that their sessions would not remain confidential said that they did not seek assistance from their pastors. First, a statement from a man, followed by one from a woman:

> And then there is this other thing that I know things, and it's not the
> pastor herself, but I know things that have been shared that have kind
> of gradually gotten outside of the context.

> You have to be really careful because when you go to them and you
> got a personal problem and everybody in church knows about it. So
> you have to be really careful. You have to know the minister that you
> going to, know that that person is a person of integrity and that you're
> going to be able to tell that person something in confidence and not
> hear it the next day.

On the other hand, one man said that the reason that he talked to his pastor was because of the trust that is bestowed on a person of God.

> I was just gonna touch base on what he was saying about sometimes
> you can't talk to your best friend, you know. But, for me, sometimes

you can't really talk to family either. Sometimes there are things that you want to tell people but, you don't want it to be told to anyone else. And sometimes people that's really close to you like family or friends they have this tendency to sometimes accidentally say things that you tell them not to say, you know. I think in more in terms of the pastor its kind of like more sacred. You know, you can really trust him. Sometimes, you can really trust a pastor more than you can a best friend or a family member or . . . To me, that's, you know, I don't look at him as God, but that's like the closest thing to him because I am receiving what God wants me to have through him, and I just find that you know, that it really helps for this, if nothing else, there is this one person in the world that you can literally see that you can really trust.

Another man said that because his pastor was also a trained counselor, he was certain that there would not be a breach in confidentiality.

I think it's 'cause my pastor is a trained counselor, and I can just be overstating that point because other pastors may be the same way. But, there is a confidentiality factor that I know that my pastor just has. You know what I am saying, there's things that you discuss that just ain't leaving the room. So, I talked to him about just about everything. So, I don't have any issues that I would feel uncomfortable talking to him about. I haven't found one yet.

Participants also indicated that they would not seek assistance from their pastor because they had such a close bond with their pastor and that they were reluctant to reveal any negative information about themselves that might change their pastor's opinion of them.

I think it's because people aren't really comfortable in trusting of their pastor enough to know that you know when they get done with whatever session that they're having that this pastor will have a different outlook on them you know. A lot of people are concerned. When I get done with conversation, what views do you have of me? Are they the same as they were before?

You know there are certain things you won't open up because you're saying, "What's he going to think about me now?" You're thinking to yourself, "I respect this man, this man respects me." I want, I value his respect and see in your mind you're saying, and it may not be something that is going to affect him the way you think it's going to. If you perceive in your mind that this thing is too terrible. I can't tell him

this, you know. Because I don't want him to think ill of me, I mean,
I am respected here by this pastor, in this church community, in my
home, you know, and you're saying I can only take this to God. I need
to deal with this because I don't want to lose that respect and that's
just a personal thing that goes on within you.

Conversely, another man felt that rather than jeopardizing that relationship, seeking assistance from the pastor helps strengthen the connection
between church members and pastors:

So it's good to consult with your minister or pastor. And also it helps
build the relationship you have with your minister or pastor because a
lot of ministers and pastors in churches really don't know their
members. They know them by the offering or tithes or how often they
come to church, but they really don't know them as well as they
should.

Choosing to Disclose Difficult Problems

Focus group participants differed in their opinions as to whether one
should unconditionally seek assistance from one's pastor or minister for
personal problems. Much of this discussion was grounded in the notion
that there may be particular problems or issues that, because of their sensitive and personal nature, shouldn't be discussed with one's pastor. Evident
in the participants' comments were several concerns, such as preserving a
good relationship with the pastor and safeguarding a positive personal
image, distinguishing between those problems that should be addressed to
God instead of the minister, a sense of embarrassment and apprehension
about the issue, and concerns about the pastor's religious orientation and
qualifications to address the problem in question. First, however, we present the comments of several participants who said that they could discuss
any issue or concern with their pastor:

But, I don't see anything that I couldn't discuss with him you know
because I trust that whatever I go to him with, when I come out
of there it will be looking better.

My pastor know all our business.

Is there anything that I would not tell her. No, I would share with
her. And I have shared with her, because for the truth to come out for

me, if I am going to her for consultation, I mean I got to come clean.
I can't go with a hidden agenda, and I can't go, "Well, you know I am
sort of kind of OK." If I am really at the sincere and honest with myself
about getting to the root of the problem, I have to go there with it.
Because otherwise I am going to walk away feeling well, "OK, well I am
still struggling with this or I am still you know, searching."

So there's nothing, there's absolutely nothing I can't go to my pastor
and talk to him about. I don't like to go to him with real trivial things,
you know, but if there's something bothering me, something pressing
on me, I got family members who just declare that they won't be saved,
and I really don't know what to do. I really don't know what to do in
dealing with them. I have to go to him to talk to him on issues like that.
I love my wife to no end, but if there's something that she's doing and
I prayed on it and I prayed with her, and I still don't get any results,
and I've just fasted and I've stayed away from things and don't get
resolved, I'll take it to him.

Distinct from these opinions about clergy use for personal problems, an
equally vocal group of participants said that there are particular issues that
they would not discuss with their pastors. Although participants agreed
that they sought counseling from their minister, there were things that they
would not discuss with them. These comments are highlighted here because
they may reveal an area of unrecognized and unmet need with respect to
arenas of clergy assistance.

I think um … it's been my experience, but I'm not speaking for everybody,
I think that there are certain issues that you can discuss with a pastor
and certain issues you can just keep between you and the Lord.

One of the major areas of concern that participants were reluctant to discuss with their pastors concerned sexual relationships, sexual attraction,
sexual orientation, and women's medical problems. The following two
statements were made by men:

I say probably would be off limits is sexual issues you know, with your
pastor.

A coworker of mine was talking about um … he was going through a
time when he was questioning his sexuality and he wanted to go to his
pastor because his pastor had helped him out with a lot of his problems
in the past, but he felt uncomfortable talking about that particular subject
just because he knew the idea is wrong, that was wrong.

A woman also mentioned that she would be reluctant to discuss issues of her own sexuality and sexual attraction:

> Sexuality problems. My flesh rise up. I wish I didn't have this husband
> because that's how I feel and I know I gotta wait. I would be scared
> to share that with him, wouldn't feel comfortable.

Several women said they would not discuss female medical problems with their pastor.

> Um … or you know, I am a female with a female problem—medical
> problem—that the pastor doesn't need to know about, but you can let
> him know that I am sick and he can visit me, you know what I mean,
> but he doesn't need to know all of the details.

Finally, there were several interesting discussions on the issue of whether church members should discuss their problems with pastors and ministers. The comments of group participants are given here in their entirety to provide some notion of context and the progression of the discussion. The following example from the men's focus group discusses the question within the context of one's ongoing relationship with the pastor:

A   I won't go to my minister, because I don't know why, I feel like I don't want
him knowing my business, which is wrong. I mean, you know, if this is
wrong, I'll take it to God. But I have a fine minister, Reverend [X]. I mean, to
me he's all that.

B   Why can't you confide in him?

A   Because I'm ashamed of some of the things I do, that's why.

C   I think it's a macho thing. Men, macho.

B   We're conditioned not to talk to each other.

A   I didn't say macho, I said because I'm ashamed of some of the things that
I do, so the things that I say I know I shouldn't be doing.

D   Well you shouldn't be ashamed because we all have sinned and fallen short
of the glory of God, so you shouldn't be ashamed, you know, you shouldn't
be ashamed of what you do. Just talk to him if you have problems and not
be ashamed.

A   Well see, I stood in the church a couple of months ago and gave my
confession and said to the church people, "You all are going to get tired of

seeing me and I'm going to be here." Right after I said it, I just jumped right back in the streets, and I don't want him to feel like I'm some kind of a liar or I'm just some kind of a fake or I don't want him to feel like, "here we go again." To me that was just one time. And when I feel like I really don't want to confess my sins to him or my daily life, closer with God, things I do that, but at this point in time I don't want him to feel like…

D Well you're saying you don't confess to him, you confess to Christ.

Below are two additional examples of exchanges in the men's focus groups about topics that are appropriate to discuss with one's pastor. In the first discussion, Participant C is reluctant to talk with his pastor about his sexual activities. However, Participant B said that he did talk about sex with his pastor and the pastor provided assistance in preventing him from engaging in premarital sex.

A If you're out sinning, you don't want to go to the, "Hey Rev, you know, I did such and such thing last night," you know. You know, if you go out and stray off, you don't want to go and tell him, but you might tell him in a different way.

B But one thing, before I got married, I was, I talked to him about my sex life or whatever, and one of the things that my minister did, you know, my pastor, was, "Well, you know, you really shouldn't be doing this, you really should be doing that. I'm not trying to judge you, but the Bible says this and that." So he gives you the facts, but then he also said, "And now, since I'm here for you, if you can't find yourself staying away from that, come spend the night at my house." So he could be that help that you need. I mean, if we're talking about sex.

C I ain't going to talk to him about something like that because I know I ain't going to stop it. Honestly, I know I ain't going to stop it. So I wasn't going to talk to him about it, because to me, I read and I know what wrong and right is, I know what sin is and all that, I know fornication, I know all of this. So I couldn't find myself going and talking to him about something I already know. I know he'd know I'm lying. He can give me advice about things, but as to about sex, I wouldn't go to him to talk to him, "I need help, I need to know to learn how to fast myself with this," because I would be lying, I would be lying. I know as soon as I leave his face, I'm going to my girlfriend's house, which is wrong.

In the following exchange, two of the men noted that they would not discuss premarital sex (Participant A) or financial matters (Participant B) with their pastors, while the third man (Participant C) felt strongly that all issues should be discussed with their pastors.

A There are certain things that I can see being somewhat sensitive. You're talking about premarital sex, you're talking about things that you know preachers do not approve of. It's harder to take those things...

Facilitator: So that's an example of something you would not talk to your minister about?

A I don't know, I guess it depends. It would be more sensitive than me going talking about something like work or my faith or something else. I guess I would censor, I would go in with a script about what I was going to tell, he wouldn't get all the details. It would just be certain things. I would be somewhat apprehensive to take things to him I know, I know what's going to be said when I walk in the door.

Facilitator: Are there topics that you would just not go to your minister about? What are some examples of those?

B I don't think I'd, financially, personal problems, you know, but I don't think I would go to him about financial problems.

C Why not?

B I just, maybe because I think he's not trained in that field.

C Well, he's a steward, he's a good steward, and being a steward you have to be good, before you get kicked up to anything else, closer to the glories of God, you got to be a good steward in all things.

B Like business and financial deals, problems, I don't think I could take it to him. Personal problems or day-to-day living problems, yeah, but just because I think maybe he's not trained in that.

D You mean the stock market or something like that?

B He's a theologist, maybe, trained in that field.

C He's a priest over his household just like you.

B That's just my personal feeling.

Focus Group Summary

The quantitative and qualitative information provides a number of specific insights into beliefs, attitudes, and behaviors concerning the use of clergy for personal problems. First, with respect to descriptive information, the multiwave NSBA data indicate that somewhere between 25% and 32% of respondents consulted with ministers in response to a serious personal problem. Although rates for using clergy and private physicians were roughly comparable, respondents also used hospital emergency rooms and medical clinics to address problems, suggesting that medical and health resources are used primarily in response to serious personal problems. However, it should be noted that across all three waves of data, the rates for consulting clergy were slightly higher than the combined rates for the categories of private therapist, mental health clinic, and social services or welfare agency. Clearly, these data demonstrate that a sizable portion of respondents seek assistance from the clergy for personal problems.

Information from the focus group discussions addresses the particular reasons and circumstances of the use of clergy for personal problems. Of particular note is the range of responses and circumstances that are represented in the comments of the participants on these issues. First, the focus group information verifies that, overall, participants endorsed the view that clergy are a viable source of assistance in dealing with problems and provide a variety of types of assistance and advice on issues ranging from relatively mundane life issues (e.g., decisions about work or schooling) to essential questions of spiritual meaning and suffering (e.g., personal illness, bereavement). Second, the focus group information provides important insights into specific attitudes and beliefs about approaching clergy for help with personal problems. Of particular note were differences in attitudes regarding whether one should approach God directly without intercession by a minister or whether the minister serves as an important instrument through which relations with God are manifested. There were several perspectives on this question. Some responses conveyed the notion that direct communication with God was a sacred and authentic feature of an individual's religious life. As such, the relationship between God and the individual held primacy over other relationships (i.e., the individual and pastor) and considerations. Similar sentiments reflected the idea that final authority and power for addressing one's problems rested with God and not the minister. Conversely, others expressed the opinion that as God's instrument on earth, it was the sacred purpose and role of ministers to help individuals with their problems. Further, in talking with and listening to people about their problems, clergy provided an additional religious dimension that facilitated these discussions and that was missing with family and professional helpers. Importantly, clergy could counsel about the spiritual issues that were attendant on life difficulties. This apparent duality in how clergy were viewed was reflected in other statements made by participants that focused on basic issues of trust (e.g., confidentiality) and differences in how professionals versus clergy provide assistance. Finally, it is worth noting that use of ministers for problems may be a particular challenge for men who have been socialized to handle problems on their own and not reach out to others for assistance.

With respect to the circumstances under which participants sought assistance, it was clear from the focus group comments that there was considerable individual variability. Some individuals said that they rarely approached clergy, preferring instead to turn to family and friends for help, while others appeared to seek assistance from clergy more frequently. Of particular note in this regard were statements about whether men, in particular, are willing to disclose to someone else when they have problems. Participants cited accessibility and availability issues as being important with respect to receiving help from clergy, as well as the notion that speaking to one's minister about a problem was not stigmatized, as might be the case in talking with a mental health specialist. The presence of a long-term personal relationship with clergy was cited as a major reason why clergy were asked for help and an important part of their perceived effectiveness in helping others. However, as reflected in comments from other participants, familiarity with clergy often inhibited a frank and honest discussion about problems, particularly when they involved very personal problems (e.g., sexual relationship issues), and participants were concerned that their disclosures would have a negative impact on how clergy viewed them. In this regard, it appeared that issues of censure, stigma, and objectivity were important considerations in choosing which problems to take to clergy.

Information for the particular problems for which they are likely to ask for assistance revealed a number of interesting themes. For the most part, participants mentioned that they would be reluctant to discuss intimate personal matters involving sexuality, sexual orientation, and sexual health with their pastors. A number of these comments reflected the idea that the pastor would not condone their behavior in these areas. For women, issues of sexual and reproductive health (e.g., breast cancer, menstrual difficulties) may be particularly difficult to discuss with a male pastor, suggesting that the trend toward the ordination of women may open avenues of discussion for these concerns. Other comments focused on family relationships and economic situations as topics they would not bring up with pastors.

In discussing these issues, participants repeatedly cited a number of related concerns. First, participants felt that, because of their pastors' religious position on these matters, they could not engage in an open and objective conversation. In addition, an underlying theme focused on whether clergy possess specific expertise in either the substantive area in question or in their approach to counseling (i.e., objectivity). Second, there was concern that discussions with their pastor would not be confidential, and, in fact, many participants indicated that due to concerns about confidentiality, they would actively censor their own comments to the pastor. Third, participants were concerned that they would be viewed differently by their pastor if they were completely honest in their discussion of sensitive matters. Finally, with respect to the perceived efficacy of clergy assistance, it is clear that many individuals who have used clergy assistance have had very positive experiences and view the pastor's efforts as being effective. Other individuals, because they have had negative experiences with clergy, are less likely to view them as being an effective means to address personal problems.

Chapter Summary and Conclusion

African American pastors and ministers are a critical resource for the African American community. They provide services through the church, such as anti-poverty and material aid programs, youth programs, programs for the elderly and their caregivers, and health screening and awareness programs. Clergy also provide assistance to members of their congregations in the form of individual counseling and assistance in a range of personal issues, including marital and family issues, unemployment, legal problems, drug abuse, and mental health problems. However, we still know little about the process whereby individuals actively choose and seek out assistance from clergy. Overall, clergy confront problems of the same type and severity as seen by mental health professionals; many clergy, however, are unfamiliar with psychopathology and the symptoms of severe mental illness and tend to underestimate the severity of psychotic symptoms. Although only a few clergy are familiar with the mental health resources available in their communities, those with advanced education and liberal theologies are more likely to make referrals to mental health professionals.

The research of Harold Neighbors found that ministers were frequent sources of help to black Americans with serious personal problems. Individuals indicated that the type of assistance received from clergy included religious coping (i.e., prayer, reading the Bible), counseling advice (i.e., listening, giving advice, comfort), and specific and concrete actions (i.e., instrumental aid). Analysis of survey data indicates that when dealing with a serious personal problem, the most frequently sought out sources of assistance are the doctor's office and the minister, followed by other medical resources and mental health specialists. This pattern of findings is largely consistent across all of the waves of National Survey of Black Americans Panel Study.

The collection of responses from the focus group participants provides a somewhat different and enhanced perspective on the use of clergy for personal problems. The helping relationship between clergy and congregant has often been portrayed in the literature as one in which clergy are universally helpful and effective in addressing life problems. And indeed, the research literature suggests a number of reasons why clergy assistance could be expected to be useful and effective in handling life difficulties. The focus group responses highlight a number of these reasons, such as clergy accessibility and availability, the significance of an ongoing personal relationship, and the importance of a shared religious or spiritual framework in addressing life problems. However, it is also the case that not all individuals will actively seek assistance from clergy or view clergy's efforts as being particularly helpful. The responses provided here suggest that this may be the case because of reasons associated with particular beliefs and attitudes that the person has regarding clergy assistance in general, the specific nature of the problem in question, the traditional roles and orientations of ministers, and concerns about process issues in the helping relationship (e.g., confidentiality, objectivity). Taken together, this information provides us with a much fuller appreciation of both the dynamics and the individual circumstances of helping relationships that involve clergy. Continuing investigations of these issues can provide a more comprehensive understanding of the role of ministers in the delivery of health, mental health, and social services (Larson et al., 1988; Maton & Pargament, 1987; Mollica et al., 1986; *Report to the President's Commission on Mental Health*, 1978) and ways in which practitioners might collaborate with clergy in developing models of service delivery in the health and human services professions (Taylor et al., 2000; see also Chapter 10 in this volume, "Conclusion and Implications").

Chapter 6

Church Members as a Source of Social Support

O ne of the most notable and consistently documented features of the
Black Church is its involvement in providing for the spiritual and
physical well-being of African Americans (Frazier, 1974; Lincoln &
Mamiya, 1990; Nelsen & Nelsen, 1975). Black churches have fulfilled a
number of functions, including health and social welfare, educational,
political, and community and civic development (see Brown, 2003; Martin,
Younge, & Smith, 2003). A recent survey of African American congregations in the Northern United States (Billingsley, 1999; Caldwell, Chatters,
Billingsley, & Taylor, 1995; Thomas, Quinn, Billingsley, & Caldwell,
1994) finds more than 1,700 church-sponsored outreach programs.
Roughly two thirds of the churches in the sample sponsored at least one
community outreach program. A variety of services were provided, including basic needs assistance (e.g., food and clothing distribution, home care),
income maintenance programs (e.g., financial services and low-income
housing), counseling and intervention for community members (e.g., family
counseling, parenting/sexuality seminars, youth-at-risk programs), education and awareness programs (e.g., child care, life skill and academic tutoring), health-related activities (e.g., HIV/AIDS care, substance abuse
counseling), and recreation and fellowship for families and/or individuals.

Clearly, these church-sponsored initiatives and outreach efforts draw on
the traditions of mutual assistance and self-reliance within black churches
to improve the health and well-being of both congregation and community

139

members. In addition to these formal activities, however, black congregations constitute an important social network for their members that involve the exchange of various forms of social support. The research examined in this chapter focuses specifically on situations in which individuals indicate that they have exchanged (i.e., provided or received) various types of informal social support with members of their church. We begin this chapter with a brief discussion of literature that focuses on the nature of church-based social support, including what is known about the various kinds of aid provided and the social and personal correlates of receiving assistance. Following this, we discuss research that examines the ways in which support from family and church combine to produce particular patterns of assistance. Next, we consider research findings from several surveys on the frequency and type of support received from church members. Finally, information from the focus group study, "Appraisals of Religiosity, Coping and Church Support," provides specific insights from focus group participants on the types of informal social support they have received and given and the circumstances associated with these helping exchanges. The chapter ends with a summary and concluding remarks regarding the importance of church member support.

Church-Based Informal Social Support

Taylor, Thornton, and Chatters's (1987) study of black Americans' perceptions of the Black Church found that the overwhelming majority of respondents felt that the church had been helpful to the black community in a number of ways, particularly in providing various forms of social support (e.g., emotional, instrumental, affirmation). As noted previously, the Black Church, as an official and collective body, has been in the vanguard in sponsoring formal efforts and initiatives to improve the status of black individuals, families, and communities. However, individual exchanges of informal social support occurring between members of the church also constitute an important, if largely unrecognized, source of aid to individuals and families. Church-based support networks provide a unique opportunity to explore how social support operates within a defined social group and to understand what personal and social factors are associated with both receiving and providing assistance. Surprisingly, informal support from church members has received relatively little systematic attention and scrutiny.

Analyses among older (Taylor & Chatters, 1986a, 1986b) and adult blacks (Taylor & Chatters, 1988) show that church members are an important source of informal assistance, with two thirds of respondents in these studies reporting that church members provided some level of assistance to them. Persons who were official church members, attended church more frequently, and said that religion was important, were more likely to receive support from church members. These findings suggest that current assistance from church members is contingent upon one's level of tangible investment in the life of the church and past record of participation in church activities (Taylor & Chatters, 1988). Religious denomination differences in church support reveal that Catholics were less likely to receive assistance from church members than Baptists (Taylor & Chatters, 1988). This was likely due to differences between the groups with respect to church structure, congregational climate, and the nature of worship services. In particular, because the Catholic worship style and church structure is generally regarded as being more hierarchical and less communal, the exchange of informal assistance among church members may be impeded. Finally, men and younger black adults were more likely to receive assistance than were women and older persons, while divorced respondents were less likely to receive help from church members than were married persons.

In analyses focusing only on older adults, church attendance predicted both how often black elderly received assistance and the amount of aid provided (Taylor & Chatters, 1986a). In addition, the dynamics of support from church members was also dependent on one's age. Among elderly of very advanced years, those who had adult children were more likely than their childless counterparts to receive assistance from church members. For childless elderly, in other words, advanced age meant that they received support from church members less often. This finding suggests that adult children may act on behalf of their elderly parents to facilitate support exchanges from church members. In addition, Krause (2002a) found that older blacks were significantly more likely than older whites to report receiving emotional support and spiritual support from their church members.

Family and Church Support

African American churches and extended families are two of the most influential and established institutions within black communities (Berry & Blassigame, 1982; Billingsley, 1992, 1999; Hill, 1999; Lincoln & Mamiya, 1990; McAdoo, 1981; Staples & Johnson, 1993). Families and churches perform a number of important social support functions to address issues such as chronic poverty (Stack, 1974), under- and unemployment (Taylor & Sellers, 1997), coping with the loss of a loved one (Neighbors, Musick, & Williams, 1998), and providing assistance to those who are ill and disabled (Dilworth-Anderson, Williams, & Cooper, 1999). Further, individuals and families often maintain long-term bonds with religious congregations that may continue over a number of years or decades (Taylor & Chatters, 1988).

Lincoln and Mamiya (1990, p. 311) observe that black churches are closely associated with black family life and, through the church's teachings, belief systems, and rituals, the two institutions maintain a cooperative relationship with one another. Black churches constitute "quasi" family or fictive kin environments (i.e., one's church family) in which fellow congregants are referred to in kinship terms (e.g., brother, sister) and honorific titles are bestowed upon esteemed church elders (i.e., church mother). The concept of a church family or church kin symbolizes the special "family-like" quality of these relationships in which the rights and responsibilities of kinship are conferred on fellow church members (Lincoln & Mamiya, 1990). These include the development of long-term social and personal relationships and exchanges of informal social support (Chatters, Taylor, Lincoln, & Schroepfer, 2002).

Despite the importance of both family and church as sources of social support for African Americans, very little research investigates the nature and functions of these networks and the circumstances under which these two important sources of informal assistance operate concurrently. Walls and Zarit's (1991) study of enacted support from church and family among a small convenience sample (n = 98) of older black adults found that both family and church support were predictive of perceptions of well-being among the elderly. In a recent study, Taylor, Chatters, and Celious (2003) found that respondents who received support from church members were more likely to say that they had taken in a relative to live with them for at least a month. They argue that persons who receive assistance from church members are more likely to be engaged in reciprocal support networks, which may predispose them toward taking others into their home (i.e., household extension). Taylor and Chatters (1986b) investigated reports of receiving support from family, friends, and church members and the types of support each group provided to elderly black adults. Although family, friends, and church members each tended to provide a particular type of assistance, other groups might provide this type of support as well. For example, while respondents were more likely to state that they received "total support" or instrumental assistance (i.e., goods and services, financial assistance, transportation) from family members, friends and church members also provided relatively modest amounts of these types of support. Overall, church members provided help during sickness, prayer, and advice and encouragement, while friends provided companionship

(Taylor & Chatters, 1986b). The study findings show that, in addition to assistance from family, friends and church members are an important source of support to older black adults.

A recent article by Chatters and colleagues (2002) investigated the correlates of support from family and church members using data from the National Survey of Black Americans. Overall, slightly more than half of respondents received assistance from both family and church networks, one quarter reported assistance from family only, and roughly equal percentages (9%) received help either from church members only or did not receive help from either group. Among the approximately one third of respondents who reported only one source of support, family members, rather than church members, were more likely to be the group providing assistance (27% vs. 8%, respectively). This finding is consistent with research emphasizing the primacy of kinship bonds for supportive networks and relationships.

This analysis further revealed that there were important social correlates of receiving support from family and church members. Black Americans who said that their families were subjectively closer, who interacted with their families on a more frequent basis, and who participated in church activities more frequently, had a higher likelihood of receiving assistance from both groups. Conversely, respondents who were not involved with either family or church networks did not receive support from either group. These findings are consistent with research in the field of family relations that indicate that social integration in family networks is positively associated with receiving support from family members (Antonucci, 1985). Similarly, research on church support networks (Krause, Ellison, & Wulff, 1998; Maton, 1989; Pargament, Silverman, Johnson, & Echemendia, 1983) shows that involvement in church networks is associated with higher levels of received assistance. Persons who were involved with only one group (whether family or church) tended to receive assistance from that group only. For instance, respondents who had high levels of church participation but low levels of family integration received assistance exclusively from church members. Conversely, respondents who had low levels of church participation (or did not attend church) but had high levels of integration in their family network received assistance exclusively from their family members. Finally, only a few respondents were socially isolated and did not identify either extended family or church members as a source of support.

An analysis of Waves I and II of NSBA data (Taylor, Chatters, & Jackson, 1997) examined respondents' reports of support from church and family members across two points in time (1979/1980 and 1987). With regard to support from church members, more than half of respondents (55.3%) stated that they received support in both Waves of data, while

Table 6.1   Receipt of Support From Church Members Across Three
Generations

Church Support	Grandparent Generation	Parent Generation	Child Generation
How often do church members help?			
Often	19.9	19.7	24.4
Sometimes	25.2	22.5	31.4
Hardly ever	12.2	15.0	12.6
Never	25.5	21.0	17.4
Never needed help	17.2	21.8	14.2
TOTAL	100.0	100.0	100.0
N	658	744	443
Would church members help if it was needed?			
Yes	95.8	92.7	96.0
No	4.2	7.3	4.0
TOTAL	100.0	100.0	100.0
N	266	345	174

another 11.6% said that they received church member assistance in Wave I
but not in Wave II. Roughly 15% reported that they did not receive support from church members in Wave I but did receive support in Wave II.
Finally, 18% did not receive assistance from church members in either
Wave I or II. In contrast, support from family members was more consistent, with close to 80% of black adults reporting that they had received
support in both 1979–1980 and 1987.

Profile of the Receipt of Support From Church Members

Table 6.1 provides a profile of the receipt of support from church members
using data from the Three Generation Family Study (see study description in
Appendix A). Analysis of frequency of support shows that approximately
6 out of 10 respondents state that they receive help from church members.
Respondents in the Grandchild Generation were more likely to receive help
and to receive help on a frequent basis than those in the Grandparent
Generation. Those in the Grandchild Generation were also the least likely to
indicate that they never received help and that they never needed help (see

Table 6.2   Type of Help Provided by Church Members Across Three
Generations

How Are Church Members Most Helpful?	Grandparent Generation	Parent Generation	Child Generation
Advice	2.4	11.3	19.7
Companionship	14.0	18.8	17.2
Encouragement	4.1	9.1	13.4
Will do anything I need	2.7	5.2	3.8
Household general	2.7	0.3	1.3
Gifts or purchases of food	1.7	1.6	1.3
Gifts or purchases of clothes/furniture	0.3	0.7	0.4
Do me favors	2.4	0.3	2.1
Do things I'm physically unable to do	1.0	0.3	0.0
Repairs/maintenance	0.0	0.3	0.0
Gifts, presents	0.0	0.7	0.0
Do favors for each other	0.7	0.3	0.4
Financial aid	15.7	7.4	3.8
Provide housing	0.0	0.7	0.0
Baby-sitting	0.0	0.7	1.3
Transportation for children	0.0	0.7	0.4
Help if children are ill	0.3	0.7	0.4
Help if sickness or death in family	1.7	2.6	2.5
Help me informally	0.3	0.3	0.4
Transportation	8.2	3.6	3.4
Prayers, pray for me	14.3	17.2	17.2
Church activities	1.0	1.3	1.3
Help given when I'm sick	21.8	13.0	5.9
Help in general	2.1	1.6	3.9
Nothing, they need more help than I do	0.0	0.7	0.0
People don't help	2.1	1.0	0.0
Other	0.3	0.0	0.4
TOTAL	100.0	100.0	100.0
N	293	309	239

analysis of never needed help by Taylor & Chatters, 1988). Respondents who indicted that they "hardly ever received help," "never received help" or "never needed help" from church members were asked the follow-up question, "Would they help you if you needed help?" As shown in Table 6.1, roughly 95% of respondents who previously indicated little or no support from church members, subsequently stated that church members would help under these circumstances; this was the case across all family generations.

Table 6.2 presents information based on data from the Three Generation Family Study on the type of help that respondents received from church

Table 6.3   Receipt of Support From Church Members Across National Survey of Black Americans, Waves I-IV

Church Support	Wave I 1979–1980	Wave II 1987–1988	Wave III 1988–1989	Wave IV 1992–1993
How often do church members help?				
Often	25.4	23.6	18.7	21.3
Sometimes	27.3	24.9	21.2	24.0
Hardly ever	11.7	14.1	18.9	19.4
Never	17.6	18.5	23.6	23.9
Never needed help	18.0	18.9	17.6	11.5
TOTAL	100.0	100.0	100.0	100.0
N	1715	874	737	620
How much help are they to you?				
A lot of help	58.3	49.9	51.0	47.9
Some help	31.5	32.5	31.9	35.5
A little help	10.2	17.6	17.2	16.6
TOTAL	100.0	100.0	100.0	100.0
N	904	846	728	608

members. An examination of this table shows that a majority of black respondents received socioemotional support, and a significant number also received tangible assistance (e.g., financial assistance, transportation, services) and total support (comprehensive assistance). These data also reveal the most prevalent types of support across the three family generations. Companionship and prayers offered for the respondent were roughly comparable across the three family generations. Beyond that, however, respondents in the Grandparent Generation were more likely to receive financial assistance, help when sick, and transportation. Similarly, persons in the Child Generation were more likely to receive socioemotional assistance in the form of advice, encouragement, and baby-sitting. Also, a small percentage of respondents received comprehensive assistance: "They do anything I need." Church-based support of these types may have important health consequences. For example, socioemotional assistance in the forms of companionship, advice, and encouragement may be important in maintaining positive self-esteem, preventing loneliness, and ameliorating depression. Support that is provided by church members in times of illness may be critical in reducing the burden of care on family members, as well as countering the social isolation and loneliness that frequently accompany even short-term illnesses.

Table 6.4   Supportive Relationships With Church Members Across National Survey of Black Americans, Waves II-IV

Church Member Questions	Wave II 1987–1988	Wave III 1988–1989	Wave IV 1992–1993
How often do you see, write, or talk on the telephone with members of your church or place of worship?			
Nearly every day	25.0	20.9	23.2
At least once a week	34.0	31.3	33.0
A few times a month	11.9	16.9	12.6
At least once a month	7.4	6.9	6.4
A few times a year	6.8	6.9	7.1
Hardly ever	10.3	11.0	10.6
Never	4.8	6.2	7.1
TOTAL	100.0	100.0	100.0
N	883	745	624
How close are people in your church (in their feelings toward one another)?			
Very close	41.7	40.0	38.8
Fairly close	48.0	46.7	47.0
Not too close	9.3	10.6	12.0
Not close at all	1.1	2.7	2.3
TOTAL	100.0	100.0	100.0
N	852	730	613
Satisfaction with the quality of relationships with church members			
Very satisfied	48.6	48.3	47.5
Somewhat satisfied	43.1	44.0	43.6
Somewhat dissatisfied	6.2	6.0	7.0
Very dissatisfied	2.1	1.8	2.0
TOTAL	100.0	100.0	100.0
N	854	737	613
Think about the things you do for people in your church (or place of worship) and the things they do for you. Would you say you. . . .			
Give more	22.6	24.8	24.0
You get more	6.2	5.8	5.0
About the same	71.2	69.4	71.2
TOTAL	100.0	100.0	100.0
N	853	729	604

Table 6.3 provides information on support from church members, using data from the NSBA Panel Survey. According to Table 6.3, there is a slight decline in the percentage of blacks who received support from church members across the four waves of the panel survey. This pattern is consistent with the finding that older blacks are less likely to receive support from church members than are younger black adults (Taylor & Chatters, 1988). Respondents who said that they received help from their church members either "often" or "sometimes" are asked the follow-up question, "How much help are they to you?" The data in Table 6.3 show that half of these respondents report that church members are "a lot" of help.

Table 6.4 presents additional research on church member support networks. The questions in this table were available only in Waves II through IV of the survey. Across all of the waves of the survey, about 20% to 25% of respondents said that they see, write, or talk on the telephone with members of their place of worship nearly every day. Combining this category with "at least once a week" demonstrates that more than half of the respondents, across all waves of the survey, are in contact with their church members once a week or more. Overwhelmingly, respondents reported that their church members are close to each other and that they are satisfied with the quality of relationships that they have with their church members. Last, seven out of ten respondents maintain that, on balance, they receive as much support as they give to the members of the church support network.

Finally, data from the 1998 General Social Survey provide a profile of support from church members. Respondents were asked two questions on church support: "If you were ill, how much would the people in your congregation be willing to help out?" and "If you needed to know where to go to get help with a problem you were having, how much would the people in your congregation be willing to help out?" (response categories for both items were: a great deal, some, a little, and none). Forty-eight percent of black respondents said that congregation members would provide *a great deal* of help if they were ill, and 36% that congregation members would provide *some* help. Ten percent anticipated *a little* help from their congregation, and 6% believed that they would not receive help from their congregation if they were ill. With respect to help with a personal problem, close to 85% of the sample anticipated receiving either *a great deal* of help (58%) or *some* help (26.6%) with a personal problem. Eleven percent stated they would receive *a little* help, and 5% that they would not receive any help.

Taken together, the percentages presented in this chapter, in conjunction with the research findings from previous publications, suggest several conclusions. First, church members are an important source of support in the

African American community and may combine with assistance from other groups, such as family. Second, sociodemographic factors (e.g., age, marital status) affect the likelihood and amount of church support received. Third, one's level of involvement and investment in both church and family networks (e.g., church membership, amount of interaction, felt closeness) appear to be important in determining levels of assistance from these groups. Lastly, while there is some overlap, the supportive functions of church and family networks appear to be largely specialized and complementary.

Focus Group Findings

Next, we turn to a discussion of the focus group information from our study "Appraisals of Religiosity, Coping and Church Support" that addressed the question of support from church members. The following set of questions was used in the focus group sessions to assess participants' ideas about support from church members. Questions regarding church support asked: "Many people say that they get help and support from their church members. Have you ever received help from your church members? What types of help have you received? Have you ever given help to your church members? Tell me about that. How did that. make you feel? Is it important to give help to church members? Why is that?" In addition, a follow-up probe was used if necessary: "Are there other types of things that church members do for one another?" The transcripts from the focus groups were systematically reviewed for content relevant to questions of support from church members. Specific quotes that provide insight into the dimensions and process of support transactions within the church are highlighted and discussed in the following section. Given the volume of information provided, the comments are organized to address particular themes. The comments begin with a general description of types of social support provided by church members that includes a broad range of instrumental support, emotional support, companionship, and spiritual assistance. This is followed by a section focusing on how church members function as family and a discussion about the importance of reciprocity in church support. Comments then focus on the types of assistance participants themselves provide to others and the ways in which giving to others is personally significant. After this, participants discuss the difficulties involved in giving and receiving help from others. The comments conclude with a few remarks from participants who are not involved in receiving help from church members.

Church Members Provide
Instrumental and Emotional Support

As part of the focus group protocol, participants were asked to discuss various aspects of church support. Overall, the focus group participants said that church members provided various types of concrete and tangible assistance and behaved in a manner that was caring and supportive. Several individuals, in discussing specific examples of the types of assistance and situations (e.g., illness, birth of a child) in which church members provide support, touch upon both tangible assistance and services as well as emotional support. Of particular note, are several responses from the women's focus groups:

> If something goes wrong then, you know, they give you emotional support, they send you flowers, they send you cards, they call to check on you, they bring you food.

> But there's like—I mean, if there's people who need—I mean single parents who may need help, maybe emotional help, financial help, or just somebody to be there for them, to give them encouragement. And you—You know, you can kind of see people—I mean, you know, you see people when you see a need and you just try to fill it. I think that's what it's about and people do that for me.

> When women in our church have babies, we take food. You know, cook for maybe a week or two, you know, if they're just coming home or sick. We going over to clean the house, doing the laundry, that kind of thing.

> I had um, an operation last July. It was pretty traumatic for me. It was a hysterectomy and I was out of work for about eight weeks....I was there (in the hospital) for six days and someone was there the whole time, you know. They offered when I got home to come and do grocery shopping and, you know, and to me that's support, I mean that's when you really, really need it. I mean although I felt I didn't know what was up and what was down, they knew, it was like they were right on it.

> I've gotten assistance when I had two deaths in the family, um, it's you know, the monetary gifts were always there and even the support when I was bereaved and you need that support there, you know, from your spiritual sisters and brothers and definitely the pastor.

Several men gave examples of the type of assistance that their church members provided for them. The first response discusses receiving emotional support; it is followed by several examples of tangible assistance.

> And I remember just going in, a male would just look at me and say, "How are you doing?" And if there's trouble in my eye they always come over to me and say "It's going to be all right." A couple times a person from the choir's came back down, I was sitting down in the back, I was stressed out, I was upset, he just came by saying, "You're going to work it out."

> Church helps me a number of ways like everyone else, but part of the best way it helps me is when I walk in the building and I see other black men doing something, saying something positive.

> Other thing for me would be the accountability partners, you know, men coming together, supporting each other so that we can stay you know, as the old folks say, "We won't lose our religion." We can stay close to the Lord and try to get closer.

> The nurturing, there is a hug in the church every time I go. It's not only from the women, but from the men as well and that's probably the most strengthening thing.

> I mean, someone coming over to spend some time, that's encouraging, just stop by out of the blue or someone who's like "I was reading my Word and the Lord just placed you on my heart or in my spirit so I just thought to give you a call. What's going on?" If you have a relationship and a bond with someone and if you're both in the spirit, you're looking out for one another, so it's more than just financial. Like I said, it's like getting on the phone and calling them and seeing how they doing or praying with them or Bible study with them.

> Well, funerals, my father died and everyone, I mean, the church was there, was right there for us, and that's been quite a few years since he passed, but that's one of the things that stands strongest in my mind now when I look back at that. That meant so much to me and my family at the time.

> I had an accident about a little more than a year ago and I burnt my hand real bad and couldn't work and I wasn't able to drive, workmen's comp. So we didn't have anything coming in and my church looked out for me.

> When I first got the job that I got now, it's 50 miles away, I didn't have
> a car for two weeks, three weeks.... The first week one of my fellow
> brothers in the Lord drove me to work every day and he worked back
> here. So he would get up real early in the morning and drive me to
> work and come back, you know, every morning for the first week. The
> next week, someone gave me one of their, they had two cars, so they
> gave me one of their cars to drive until I found one.

> I didn't have money for a real suit and one of the brothers in the
> church, and I was an usher in the church, he approached me and said,
> Man, the Lord put it in my heart to bless you. I said, Yeah? He said,
> Yeah. I said alright. I'll receive that, you know. He said, I want you to
> come out to my car with me. And he pulled out a, and he was about,
> we are about the same size and he pulled out a suit that,
> that he gave me.

The same man went on to say that he has also received financial assistance and books from church members:

> And I was having problems with my rent. I said Lord, you know, it's going
> to be tight, you know, I don't know how I'm going to pull this through. I
> prayed, and the pastor had a day where he asked anyone who was going
> through financial, some financial struggles to come up front. And I went
> up front and he gave each of us a bucket and he asked the members, he
> said, If the Lord places on your heart to bless anybody in this line, bless
> them, you know, so I closed my eyes and started praying and the
> brothers started walking up front, you know, blessed me with financial
> aid. And so as far as books, you know, a person thought that I was, me
> being single, that there is a book regarding singleness, you know, which
> was by Dr. [X]. They thought it would be of value to me and gave it to me.
> I read it and it blessed me.

One man mentioned that he had received free dental care with the assistance of a church member.

> Even dentistry, you know, even dentistry, had some scaling done and
> everything completely free. I had to drive to Chicago three to four hours
> to get it, but, you know, I was there, you know.

The same man went on to discuss the manner in which he receives emotional support and the importance of both giving and receiving assistance.

> But I have had emotional assistance. But generally there is one
> particular person I go to a lot and where, whenever you go to them for

help they are putting you to work. So they're working, too, but you
work while you solve your problems. Like you need to do something
so come on. So one time I was cleaning the baptismal pool. And the
other time it was mowing the lawn, the church lawn, or planting seed
or whatever. So I have had really every major form of help from people
within the church body that you could think of, but I have also given
that same style of help. But it's that whole love piece. I ain't perfect at it,
but I'm trying to get there.

One man mentioned that the men of his church paid for his honeymoon
and that they are important sources of encouragement.

And the church men just sent us off, man, like we went off like seven
days off to Jamaica and it was like so much money that was gave to us
and so much gifts. So after we came back from the honeymoon, the
church like, you're on your own now, but it was a blessing. They was
there for me and a lot of times we, the church is there for us, but we
don't realize it, that, you know, I don't care if you just praying and
encouraging. It's like the main thing, a lot of times encouragement
means a lot. It's just encourage a brother like you say, if someone in
the church said, "brother I'm praying for you" and that means a lot.

Several respondents said interaction and fellowship with church
members was important and that it often extended beyond church-related
activities and contexts. Here are what two women stated:

In addition to being part of groups like working with the youth group
in the church or working with the usher board or things like that, you
kind of establish a relationship with those people, and you kind of do
things with them outside of the church, too in addition to going out
and praying with people, sometimes you do things together. Just go
out for a walk, you need a friend to walk with so you kind of establish
that kind of rapport too.

One of the things some of the women at our church started was
walking Monday, Wednesday, and Friday. So that is kinda like a
support when you are walking, you're talking and in that things just
come up, and start sharing. So that's been pretty good.

Two men said:

I think the major type of support for me has been good counsel, good
folks, good friends. It reminds me of the old pictures in your mind, you
see two old fellows playing checkers sitting up talking, that's the kind

of thing that has really done the most for me, just having a support system.

I think of the church family, I think of the students in the church. By being able to interact with them, I guess it helps to keep me away from things I shouldn't be doing.

A female college student noted:

So, one of the greatest things that I, that we do, is simply fellowship. We hang out with each other...like, one of us will be like, ya know, party at my house. During that time of fellowship, we don't just listen to [black gospel recording artist] and just cook and eat to our hearts' content with our two dollars everybody done chipped in...but we also talk about ya know, how we are doing, ya know. And, you'll see people in corners, everybody else being all loud, playing Taboo, but you will see a few people in the corner ya know, kicking it with each other and letting each other know what is going on in their lives and helping each other how to figure out or how to overcome challenges.

Importance of Building Relationships With Church Members

One man mentioned that the strong relationships that are formed among church members are strengthened through outside activities.

I mean meeting your brothers and sisters at church is nice, but true relationship is not built, is not necessarily built in the four walls of our church. But you find out that if you are trying to find, to knit a relationship based upon most churches worship services, it's not likely going to happen. Because most people come to church, they are there to hear the word or worship the Lord, whatever they are there for, but we talking about you know a one-on-one relationship, that's going to have to take place over lunch or help the person move or mowing their grass or helping them clean their house or something like that. That's where true relationships are formed. It's not formed, I mean I'm not saying that you couldn't buddy up with someone in church, but if you are talking about a true meaningful relationship, it's not gonna take place more than just on Sunday worship service.

In contrast, a man who felt less integrated in his church mentioned that he interacted with church members only on Sunday.

We don't call one another, especially men. We say, "I love you, brother,"
on Sunday morning, but we don't call each other during the week, we
don't stay in contact with one another. But then when their old buddies
come by and say, "Let's go out and drink," they go with them. The
church folks don't stay in contact enough with one another.

One man mentioned that he went on a vacation with the members of his
church, which is not uncommon in many black churches.

I also went on a cruise two years ago and 60 of our church members
were on that same boat. We just kind of picked a time to go together
and when we took the picture, it was amazing cause we were all up the
stairway and we were all over the place. Many brought kids and
everybody along, and those are some of the types of things that we
have kind of gotten into. As well as, a lot of my church members are
my co-workers and professional folks that I see, you know, every day
and around town. There is a community that is established not only
inside the church, but also outside the church and I think that
relationship kind of permeates from within the church.

Another female college student noted how even though her church is in
another state, the church members still maintain an important role in her life.

Well, I am originally from [another state] so, the church that I belong,
that I go to is like my family church. My grandmother, my godmothers,
and a lot of people in the church have kind of known me all of my life.
They've supported me even while I've been away at school just by
praying for me and just kind of thinking about me and sometimes,
they will like send me money or cards or little things just to let me
know that they are thinking about me. They just keep me in prayer so
they haven't like, really forgotten about me, which is great.

Importance of Having Church Members Provide Support

Other respondents noted the importance of having church members
provide support.

I've received a lot, not cards because something happened, but little
note cards people send in the mail. They come on a Tuesday when
nothing had happened, but you just needed. And so, I think that that's
something I have started doing. It's just a card, just when you think
about somebody, you know.

It does mean so much to get something that has been handwritten, that may say, I'm thinking about you. I love you. God bless you.

It's good to know that you have your church members, members of your church, there to be kind of like that network to kind of help you through things. You have to remember that every church member, they bring strengths and people can help each other with different things, in different ways. You might be able to help somebody move their stuff when they need it, or they might need, they may need many things and it may not always be about money.

For someone say, you know, "Brother I get up at 4:00 in the morning. Before I get up um...and after I get up and walk out the door I'm going to call your name out in prayer." How uplifting that is, is two or three together in his name say, "Brother I'm praying for you." And that's, I mean, a lot of times we there spiritually.

Several other women who commented about the importance of having church members around during times of need, focused on the ready availability of support in the form of prayer. Their comments show that shared prayer on behalf of others is a means of strengthening the personal, social, and spiritual bonds among participants.

If something goes down, she jump on that phone in a minute and call the prayer partners. And this is how we bond, we bond. But, that's where I have found, you know, the support through one another. We have to be caring about one another and that's for different things that I need.

A couple of people in my church, after a while, you kind of know what is going on in each other's lives. And you have a feeling about somebody and you know, you pick up the phone and you're touching base, and invariably, somebody in the circle is like, well I need prayer, and, I need this kind of help. So, I think just knowing that you've got these people there that are standing right with you or standing right by your side.

When we first got saved, there was a group of us that grew up together and we had such a bonding. And if one was in trouble, then we all was in trouble. And we all came together and we would pray. Sometimes we would go to different one's house and we would just pray. Or if I am going through something, I would just jump on the phone and make a call and they were there.

Similarity Between Church Members and Family Members

Similar to research on the church as a family, focus group participants discussed the similarity between church members and family members with respect to the conditions and circumstances of giving and receiving assistance. The focus group protocol itself inquired only about assistance from church members; any references to family or the family-like functions of the church were volunteered by focus group participants. One man stated:

> I think that the church has just become an extension of the families. Really, in a lot of ways, like H [another focus group participant] mentioned, better than your families. Thank God for the opportunity to give to others in my church, you know...that's what I would do for family.

One man mentioned an example of a serious problem that happened to his mother in which both family members and church members provided a considerable amount of assistance. In his comments, he said that he anticipated that his family would provide assistance to his mother. However, he expresses amazement and appreciation at the support provided by church members:

> Well, I think I got a beautiful church. When my mother got burned, she had a house that caught on fire and she got third-degree burns, she had to have a skin grafts and stuff. And besides the family, church people—not just from our church—they was there, you know, helping clean up, there for you at the hospital, I mean they was there for her. That's why I knew there are people that care. People that care are in the church.

There were several instances in which focus group participants said that church members are a much more important source of informal support than extended family members.

> I think that many times I would like to say members of my church have been a great help. You know, at time of need and I think it's important to know, especially me not growing up with the traditional nuclear family, that I have a family to go to. The church has kind of like been my family. This coming weekend, I'll finally see my father for the first time in 30 years, and so me not having a father, I looked to some of the older men, the seasoned men in the church, as mentors and as a

network for counseling, for help with simple things like, "Brother can you help me with five dollars so I can, you know, so I can get to work this week, you know. I'll make sure I get this back to you on Friday."

I think sometimes when you go to church, you really feel that sense of family because sometimes your real family might act in terms of you know, nothing of what a family is really like. You know, you might have a whole lot of relatives, and not really a family you know there's not togetherness and unity you know. They just might be people that you are related to, versus when you go to church, you feel that sense of family, togetherness, unity, you know, and you can call on this person and you know, know that you can depend on them you know cause sometimes you can depend more on you know, your church family versus you know, your other family, you know. And, I really think that helps a lot of people you know, realize that they are loved, that they are cared about, you know, that they are important you know and that they do have somebody.

For me it's been an extended family. One of the primary reasons that I didn't relocate when I was offered a position to relocate was because I never had any other type of family so this, this church thing is just not, you know, a group of people I can do without. This is my family and I know them better than I know my own mother and father. So support from members is definitely, its big, I think is bigger than support from the pastor because I always got their number.

Formal Programs in the Church

In other comments on the subject, these women concurred with other focus group participants that church members were generally supportive of one another. In their particular circumstances, however, they had chosen not to seek monetary assistance or general support from church members. Several respondents mentioned formal programs or groups of individuals in the church that perform various services for other church members.

We have people who go ya know, do housework, cut the grass you know, things like that.

We work with a group that goes around and houses the homeless for a week at a time, and the young people go to, they go and sing, ya know, for the residents there.

Some people financially, you know, they have a problem with their rent or their light bill, churches have helped out and will help out food, schools, scholarships, you know.

> There's some women that come with the kids and they need help. And
> the deacons can set aside, they got a fund set aside to help people.

> We have, at our church, we have a benevolence fund where people
> who are in need, whether its for some short-term problem or
> something, you can go and get benevolence support and that's been a
> help. I can remember a time where there was a couple in our church,
> they were in school, and we had this Christmas program where we
> would go to social services and get a list, a list of people that need
> help and lo and behold, somebody in our own church was on that list.
> And I know that had to hurt our pastor, because all they had to do
> was ask, you know. But out of that the church ended up taking them in
> and blessing them with food and things like that. And they testified
> and talked about that, to us, to other folks in the church.

One woman felt that although the informal services provided by the
church are important, there should be a limit on the type of services that are
provided:

> They have, a member in our church, her husband has Alzheimer's and
> he is getting to the stage where he will leave the house. So the nursing
> guild set up people that would be with the wife and the husband
> 24 hours a day. I didn't too much agree with it and was, think well it
> wasn't no nursing skill, but, I thought, that's something, you know.

Later in a focus group session she said:

> There was nothing I could do or nothing that I could say to anybody,
> but I thought that that was a bit much for the pastor to ask for them to
> have 24 hour nursing service. I thought that was a bit much.... I know
> there are services that are provided to people who can't afford it... and
> if they could afford it, then they should be paying for it.

Reciprocal Relationships

As shown in previous statements by focus group members, many people
talked about being involved in reciprocal relationships with their church
members. One man said this about his reciprocal relationship:

> Like I said, we went through a tumultuous time last year and just rains
> of support. And, any of those folks know that they can call us at any
> time and expect the same. And, I think that, at least in our church, it's
> permeated the relationships that are formed inside the church.

Two other men mentioned that because of the reciprocal relationships that have developed in the church, they feel obligated to provide help to others when it is needed.

> In the sense that if someone has extended whatever help, financial or whatever that they did, you almost feel a responsibility to when someone else is in need. It is not like twisting your arm, but it's a way of showing your love for that person. And if there is something that you can do that is reasonable, and I like I said earlier, it could be as simple as helping somebody move their stuff. I have done it many times for my church, but you know I realize that by doing it, I know that if I needed something, that's the person that I can say, you know, I need something.

> But, I think that is, you know, that's part of that whole community and family. That you can, if somebody else is in need, God forbid that they gotta go outside the church to get help, if they can avoid it, you know, because we ought to be able to take care of each other.

Giving Help to Church Members

Several men gave examples of the types of assistance they have given other church members.

> I know an individual who was sick and he didn't have any food. I took food literally myself to his house. So care about people, you have to show you care. It's one thing to say "I love you." Well, you're trying to preach the gospel to somebody and tell them to be saved and they say "I'm hungry," and you say "I'll pray for you." It don't work that way. You know, you gotta feed them first.

> I help, I help them paint, cut the grass and stuff, didn't charge them.

> When I offer people money, if I give them money, I don't expect it back, because I'm giving it to them, it's not a loan. I mean, if you feel like you should pay me back, then I'll take it back, let's be clear! But when I set that money aside to give to somebody it's because I know I'm helping them. Like there's this one person said they can't wear dresses to church because they can't afford stockings. But they didn't ask for money, but you know, we're going to take some time and some money to give them a donation to help them do the things they really want to do.

Several men mentioned how important it was to give to church members and how good it made them feel to give.

> I mean, to me it just, it just makes, it makes me feel good to know that I can help someone. I mean it make me feel like I made a Godly decision when I can do something to put a smile on someone's face, or stop a bad thing from happening to them. It just makes me feel like I really, you know, took whatever God has given me and, you know, shared it like I should have.

> Like this food program that we do every Thursday, I get a great enjoyment out of doing that. Because there is some people out there that's hungry, and there's some people come by and take advantage of it. But we have so much food there that anybody comes there can eat, if we have leftovers we give it to them.

> I think for me too, it, it's a good feeling. However when me and my wife typically give stuff we give it in secret and private cause we are not looking for man's accolades, but it does give you a good feeling to know that you can help out a brother or a sister. It's different from being at the gas station and giving somebody a couple of dollars for washing your window, and they are then probably going to go drink it up. It's a different kind of feeling that you know you are helping somebody out that *really* needs help and is really trying to get over a certain point in there lives. So, I think it definitely gives a good feeling.

> Yeah, I do my kind of in relation to the Glory of God and pleasing God and I think that's where my feeling come from. It's fine to help others, and I try to go out of my way to do that. I try to mentor to several kids. I try to mentor to several people period.

> It's good to be able to do things for people and that's what the Lord wants us to do. And that's why he says it's more blessed to give, in other words blessing means happiness. You will be made happy by enriching somebody else's life.

> I just think for me, the greatest expression of loving is to give. So, when you give you are just expressing the love of Christ. So that for me, at least, that's about it, that's the main thing.

Difficulty in Giving and Receiving Help

A number of comments from focus group members indicated that giving and receiving support from church members was not always an easy process, due to the difficulty in asking for help from others. In some instances, focus group members admitted that they were unable to ask for help from church members.

> 'Cause the one time I got caught up my flesh, I think is when my husband had stole my van. Sold it to the people, the people!!! And I was like, I withdraw, too ashamed. Here I am trying to walk with God. He's the one steals the van after doing his thing or whatever, and I am too ashamed to let the saints know I need a ride to church or whatever. Couldn't even humble myself to ask for a ride or whatever, I was so ashamed. It's like I withdrew from the church for like a month or whatever.

Another respondent noted that sometimes it is hard to give help to some church members because they do not want to be a burden or because of past negative experiences.

> You know I'm finding some people are hard for you to do. You can go and see them and offer them help. You want to do something to help, you know. To ease some of their loneliness if they been in the house sick. But, I am finding that a lot of people now that really don't want you to. I do not know if it is their pride or what. And I'm finally getting to know some, sometime I just say, look, mother so and so, I hear what you are saying, but I am fitten to clean right now for you. And then they say, Oh, baby I am so glad. They don't want to be a burden or whatever. And I find that some people feel like you're coming to be nosey or you hear them say that somebody had taken something back or talked about them or whatever. So, they got their bricks up.

In contrast, another participant said that although he knows that some church members do not want to receive assistance, he felt very comfortable asking for help, in part, because he has been a contributing member in the church.

> I don't have a fear about going when I have a problem, because when I don't have a problem I pay my tithes and my offering and I try to do the things that I know is, right to do. Not to say that I feel like they owe me because I have been doing what I'm supposed to be. But if I'm a good member in standing there and they do something for me, certainly I would accept it if I'm in need. A lot of people probably say, I wouldn't take from the church, I wouldn't accept that or whatever, but if you're in need you can miss your blessing because you don't know when God is actually speaking. God is saying learn to receive.

> Especially for people who are givers, they have a hard time receiving and I'm certainly a giver and for me receiving has really never been a real problem. A lot of people say well, I'm a giver and I don't like to receive or I have a problem receiving.

Another man said that church members are obligated to help each other and should not be ashamed of seeking help from each other.

> If I walk up to you and say, Man, I'm a brother in the Lord, and you are able to discern through the Holy Spirit that I'm telling the truth and I need your help, whether you know my name or not or ever see me again, you should feel obligated to help me. Because it says in the Bible that we are to love each other as Christ loved us and that was one of the Great Commandments, Love the Lord thy God with thy heart and mind and, to love each other, to love your neighbor as thy self. You know, you got to get to that point. And so we can no longer continue to do the, well, I'm not going to go to anybody. You know, that's pride. That's nonsense.

One man said that he had to learn how to ask for help from church members:

> And you find out that helps build relationships because you are able to help someone and then you know at some point you are going to need the help of someone else. And at one time I was afraid, because being a man, I don't want nobody to know my business. So, I have had to learn that there are certain things that when you need help, there is nothing wrong with asking because if you never ask, you never know where your help will come from if you don't ask.

In the same focus group, another man responded that he might not ask for help from church members, but it is not because of pride.

> Well you know I don't know how much of it is pride. Oftentimes I won't ask if I don't think I need. Not so much because of pride as it is realization that others have greater needs.... I've never thought about it as being pride and it may be, I mean, you may be right and if that is the case, that's something I have to work on. But often times I would think, well, is this a selfish request? Is this something that I can do without? Or by me asking does that mean that someone else who might be in greater need won't be able to have. I mean, I don't know. I guess I'd like to think one way, but I really don't know which one is the truth.

The same man goes on to say that he has received a considerable amount of assistance from his church members without necessarily seeking out assistance.

> So I think, I have gotten a lot from my church without necessarily asking. There were times when I was down because of work and I might help someone else and get more out of the interaction than I had actually given. So I would say that I have probably gotten a lot. Originally when he asked the question, I would probably say, yeah I've gotten a lot, mostly emotional or mental, moral support, but then talking, I realize, and I guess it has probably been revealed by some of my other responses, that I often don't ask a lot.

In a similar vein, another man feels fortunate that he does not have to seek help on a frequent basis and wants to be sure that his problems do not take away from other church members who may have more problems.

> But you know, for the most part I think I have been somewhat fortunate, been blessed and so I haven't been in situations where I perceived my need to be extremely great, though there are needs that I do have. But when I have these needs, I ask myself, well, are they great enough to, you know, ask someone or trouble someone else with, when that means it might take their time or their resources away from others who might be in greater need.

Finally, there are a few instances in which respondents indicate that they have not requested support (or particular types of assistance) from church members. Men focus group participants provided these statements.

> I don't ask for money.

> I don't ask anybody at church.

Focus Group Summary

The statements expressed by the focus group participants clearly illustrate that church members constitute a valuable source of tangible, emotional, and spiritual support. Focus group members reported that their fellow church members were emotionally warm, compassionate, and caring and provided a variety of types of assistance, on both an ongoing basis as well as during critical times of need. Focus group participants expressed a number of sentiments that indicated that church members were emotionally supportive and accessible. Further, their comments about church support reinforced a general portrayal of relations among church members as being warm and welcoming. Nevertheless, a few group members said that they would not seek monetary assistance or any type of material aid from church members. This is in contrast to the majority of participants who stated that exchanges of small amounts of money ($15-$25) as loans or gifts were relatively common. Other forms of material aid included gifts of relatively expensive late model used cars, as well as more substantial amounts of monetary assistance.

Focus group members also discussed issues related to the dynamics of support exchanges in terms of questions of reciprocity and the difficulties that are inherent to social support (e.g., a sense of being obligated to someone, issues of personal pride). Participants discussed issues of church support within the context of religious teachings about giving to others and viewed such behaviors as an expected part of being a member of the church and a religious person.

It is important to emphasize that although focus group participants were positive in their comments, they did not idealize their relations with church members. When asked about potential problems and negative social interactions involving church members, they candidly discussed the problems associated with the development of cliques and factions and often disruptive interpersonal disagreements and interactions involving church members. These comments and perceptions are consistent with emerging research (Krause, Chatters, Morgan, & Meltzer, 2000a) on negative interactions and problematic social relationships among church members. The issue of negative interactions between church members is discussed in detail in the next chapter.

Chapter Summary and Conclusion

Although the research literature examining the nature and functioning of church-based social support is still modest in size, overall it is developing greater depth and sophistication. Available work shows that a variety of types of informal social support are exchanged within church networks. Further, assistance from church members is not trivial and appears to be especially important for particular groups, such as the elderly. Personal and social characteristics such as age, marital status, and gender appear to be related to receiving support from church members. In addition, a past record of involvement and connection to the church is associated with receiving greater amounts of aid from church members. Finally, several investigations have begun to explore how support from both church members and family may combine to shape distinctive patterns of assistance.

Analysis of several surveys indicates that many black Americans are actively involved in church support networks. Findings from the Three Generation Family Study indicate that approximately six out of ten respondents receive help from church members. Respondents in the Grandchild Generation were more likely to receive help (and to receive help on a frequent basis) than were those in the Grandparent Generation. Members of the Grandparent generation were more likely to ask for financial assistance, help when sick, and transportation. Individuals in the Child Generation were more likely to receive socioemotional assistance in the form of advice, encouragement, and babysitting. Analysis from the National Survey of Black Americans Panel Study revealed that black Americans frequently interact with their church members, feel that their church members are close to each other, and are satisfied with the quality of relationships that they have with their church members. Last, data from the General Social Survey reveals that black Americans believe that their church members would provide assistance to them if they were ill or if they had a personal problem.

In keeping with the model of stress and coping discussed previously (see Chapter 4), social support from church members represents an important coping resource (i.e., social resources) that individuals can draw upon to assist them in dealing with a problem. The variety of types of social support provides clear evidence that assistance from church members is useful as a coping resource. In particular, the focus group information revealed that church members provided tangible forms of assistance (e.g., money, food) and services (e.g., transportation), emotional aid, companionship and fellowship, and spiritual support. Further, several responses from focus group members underscored the importance of church members providing supportive encouragement for the individual and fostering a sense of belonging in the church. A number of life circumstances and situations appear to be important for receiving support; in particular, illness, bereavement, financial difficulties, and family transitions such as childbirth. However, focus group participants also said that support from church members was ongoing and offered on a regular basis and not just in response to particular events.

Finally, used together, the survey data and the focus group information provide a fascinating picture of the nature of social support from church members. The focus group information indicated that there was a wide range of services, goods, activities, and helping behaviors that were exchanged among church members. Information with this level of detail is not typically available in surveys of church support. In addition, the focus group illuminated a number of issues related to social support exchanges (e.g., reciprocity, the benefits of providing support to others) that are rarely examined in surveys.

Chapter 7

Negative Interaction
Among Church Members

Over the past 10 years, research on the nature of interpersonal relationships has focused increasingly on the role and impact of negative interaction in social relations. Negative interactions can best be described as actions by members of one's social network that cause distress, resentment, shame, or sadness. These include behaviors such as negative comments, criticism, discouraging the expression of emotions, or interfering in one's affairs. A variety of terms are used in the research literature that correspond with the concept of negative interaction, such as problematic relationships, problematic support, negative social exchange, negative social support, and social undermining (see Lincoln, 2000). To date, the majority of research on negative social interaction has focused on family and friend networks.

This chapter focuses on the issue of negative interaction among church members. We begin with discussions of previous research on the general topic of negative interaction and then turn to studies of negative interaction involving church members. Following this, we examine negative interaction among church members using data from the 1998 General Social Survey. The remainder of the chapter is devoted to a discussion of information from the focus group study, "Appraisals of Religiosity, Coping and Church Support," in which participants share their experiences with negative interaction in their churches. The chapter ends with concluding remarks concerning the significance of negative interaction among church members.

Research on Negative Interaction

According to a vast collection of research findings, social support is conducive to better physical and mental health and psychological well-being (see Lincoln, 2000). Conversely, accumulating research finds that negative social interactions may lead to lower levels of happiness and life satisfaction and other indicators of psychological well-being. In addition, there is some debate regarding how positive (i.e., emotional support) and negative aspects of social interaction with others operate jointly and their overall impact on health and well-being. That is, it is not clear whether negative interaction involving family and friends offsets the positive impact of emotional support. Research findings in this area are equivocal; some findings show stronger effects for negative interaction, while other research finds that emotional support is more important for outcomes. Finally, other work indicates that negative interaction and emotional support are roughly equivalent in their impact on outcomes (see Lincoln, 2000).

There are several reasons why negative interactions such as criticisms and unfavorable comments are potentially harmful to psychological well-being. Family, friends, and co-workers represent important reference groups with whom we share a number of common values and beliefs and meaningful emotional and social attachments. The relationships and the quality of social interactions within these social reference groups are important in terms of how we come to view and define ourselves. Consequently, negative comments from friends, family, and co-workers about our behaviors or attitudes have the potential to cause negative feelings such as embarrassment, sadness, or shame. Negative comments from family, friends, and co-workers may be particularly disturbing and salient because they are unexpected and uncharacteristic of customary social interactions.

Negative Interaction Among African Americans

To date, very little research has examined negative interaction among African Americans. Available research is typically based on small, nonprobability samples, which have limited generalizability to the African American population as a whole. In a study of HIV-positive African American men, Gant and Ostrow (1995) found that negative interaction had a greater impact on measures of mental health than did emotional support. Social conflict with social network members (e.g., feeling misunderstood) was highly correlated with tension/anxiety, depression, anger/hostility, and loneliness. Davis and colleagues have conducted a series of studies investigating the relationships between African American adolescent mothers and their parents, with a particular focus on the impact of negative interaction (Davis & Rhodes, 1994; Davis, Rhodes, & Hamilton-Leaks, 1997; Rhodes, Ebert, & Meyers, 1994). In general, pregnant and parenting adolescents who receive more parental (i.e., mother and father) support have lower levels of depression (Davis et al., 1997). In contrast, adolescents who reported relationship problems with their parents (i.e., negative interaction, conflict) such as disappointment, intrusiveness, and criticism, reported psychological distress (Davis & Rhodes, 1994; Rhodes et al., 1994) and social adjustment problems (Davis & Rhodes, 1994). Further, adolescents who received less parental support and reported more negative interaction with fathers had higher levels of depression compared with their counterparts (Davis et al., 1997). Although these study samples are small and specialized, the findings are consistent with the literature on the effects of negative interaction.

Two recent studies by Lincoln and colleagues investigate negative interaction using national samples that include a large number of black respondents. Lincoln, Taylor, and Chatters (in press) examined the correlates of negative interaction using the older African American subsample of the American Changing Lives data set. They found that older African Americans with more education were more likely to report negative interaction with relatives and friends, whereas older African Americans who were married and those who had children experienced fewer negative interactions with members of their social network than did their counterparts. In another study, Lincoln, Chatters, and Taylor (in press) investigated the impact of negative interaction on psychological distress for black and white adults using data from the National Co-morbidity Study. Their analysis found that, among whites, negative interaction increased psychological distress. Among blacks, however, there was no significant impact of negative interaction on psychological distress.

Negative Interaction Among Church Members

Research on negative interaction has typically examined family, friendship, and work-based networks, while relatively little research on this topic focused on church members. Krause, Chatters, Meltzer, and Morgan (2000b) note that there is some limited research on conflicts within churches that center on particular issues, such as the ordination of women as ministers. Further, anecdotal evidence indicates that disagreements that arise within the church (e.g., the competency of the pastor in performing his or her duties, differences in church doctrine and practice, conflicts over the issue of tithing, decisions about how church funds are spent) can be a source of significant conflict and strife. In certain cases, conflicts between opposing groups of church members can be so disruptive and divisive that church factions eventually leave the congregation permanently, either to join a different church or to establish a new church.

As noted in the previous chapter, church members share close emotional bonds and provide a high degree of support and guidance to one another. However, in addition to these positive aspects of social relationships, church-based networks may also be a source of negative interaction. As noted by Ellison (1994), church congregations are especially important and powerful environments with respect to exercising negative social sanctions (e.g., criticism, shunning, public censure) for church member behavior that is deemed inappropriate. In addition, participation and membership in church-based networks may entail problems related to individual privacy and autonomy (i.e., social intrusiveness). Church members who diverge from accepted behavioral standards in terms of lifestyle and moral conduct or who hold divergent beliefs regarding church doctrine and practice may be subject to open criticism, gossip, and ostracism. Finally, because involvement in church congregations may put heavy demands on time and financial resources for individual members, there may be conflicts between members about perceived differences in these contributions, as well as the anticipated social benefits that derive from church involvement. Given the special circumstances of church networks, we expect that negative interactions involving church members of the type described would be an important issue in black churches. These concerns may be particularly salient for black as opposed to white churches because of higher levels of attendance at religious services and other church-related activities (see Chapter 2). Consequently, there is more opportunity for both positive emotional assistance and negative interaction.

Krause's work on negative interaction among church members has found that, consistent with research on negative interaction among family and friends, negative interaction from church members has an adverse impact on psychological well-being (Krause, Ellison, & Wulff, 1998). In a focus group study of white and black elderly, Krause and colleagues identified three major areas of conflict among church members: (a) conflict between church members, (b) conflict between church members and their pastors, and (c) conflict over church doctrine (Krause et al., 2000b). Negative interaction between church members took the form of gossip and the formation of church cliques. Examples of conflict over religious doctrine centered around four primary issues: abortion, religious teachings involving the role of women in the family, the use of alcohol, and whether homosexuals should be welcome in the church. The work of Krause and colleagues provides important insights into the nature and consequences of negative interaction within religious settings. For the purposes of the present chapter, we focus exclusively on negative interactions among church members, as opposed to conflict because of doctrine or conflict with pastors.

Survey Findings on Negative Interaction Among Church Members

As previously discussed, very little research has examined negative interaction among church members and, to date, there has been no research on this issue among the adult black population. The 1998 General Social Survey contains two questions that assess negative interaction among church members: "How often do congregation members make too many demands on you?" and "How often are the congregation members critical of you and the things you do?" (the response categories are: a great deal, some, a little, and none). As shown in Table 7.1, negative interaction among congregation members does not occur very often. Only a few respondents felt that church members made too many demands (3.3%) or criticized (4.0%) them on a frequent basis (the response category "a great deal"). In contrast, 57% of respondents said that church members never made too many demands, while a full 70% felt that congregation members were never critical of them.

Analysis of the National Survey of American Life also shows relatively low levels of negative interaction among church members. Close to 80% of black adults say that church members never take advantage of them, roughly 70% say that they are never criticized by church members, and about half report that church members never make too many demands on them. Within both the 1998 GSS and the NSAL, slightly more respondents indicated that they felt that, at some level, church members made too many demands on them (40%–50%) than were critical of them (30%). This difference is consistent with Ellison's (1994) observations that for some highly involved individuals churches are "greedy institutions" that often require significant investments in time and financial resources. This may be particularly evident for the types of informal duties that may be expected of church members (e.g., cooking meals, running errands, providing transportation).

As evident in the GSS and NSAL data, negative interaction with church members is a relatively rare event for black Americans. Comparing these

Table 7.1   Negative Interaction Among Church Members, From the 1998 General Social Survey

Negative Interaction Items	Percentage
How often do congregation members make too many demands?	
Very often	3.3
Fairly often	7.3
Once in a while	32.5
Never	57.0
TOTAL	100.0
N	151
How often are congregation members critical of the things you do?	
Very often	4.0
Fairly often	6.7
Once in a while	19.3
Never	70.0
TOTAL	100.0
N	150

frequencies with the figures in the previous chapter on church-based social support clearly demonstrates that black adults received emotional support from church members much more frequently than they experienced negative interaction. These findings are consistent with previous research on emotional support and negative interaction from family and friends (Lincoln, Chatters, & Taylor, in press; Lincoln, Taylor, & Chatters, in press). However, as discussed previously, even infrequent negative interaction may have a major impact on psychological well-being. Negative interactions, because they are unexpected and uncharacteristic, may be particularly salient and harmful to psychological well-being.

The finding that, overall, negative interaction with church members is a very infrequent occurrence was not totally unexpected. The data presented in Chapter 5 indicate that black adults generally feel that church members are very supportive and, further, they feel close to church members and satisfied with these relationships. Additionally, we can assume that if negative interaction with church members were a frequent occurrence, individuals would likely leave the church to join another congregation. The option of choosing another social network (i.e., "voting with one's feet") is typically not available when it comes to negative interaction in family networks. In extreme cases of family conflict, however, members may choose to limit interactions or become estranged from family networks. Similarly, in the case of negative interactions with co-workers, individuals are usually constrained in their choices to seeking new employment, although there may be options for seeking redress for problematic interactions in the workplace. In the situation of negative interaction with church members, individuals have the option of limiting their interactions to a select group of congregants or leaving a congregation in which relations are strained and conflictual.

However, it is important not to minimize the potential gravity of the decision to leave one's church. Anecdotal evidence suggests that linkages to churches may involve a number of years and several generations of a family. The social and personal associations that are developed within a church often assume the status of kinship relationships, with comparable rights and obligations. Further, given a significant investment in the development of the church, individuals may be very hesitant to relinquish their moral claim to ownership of the church. Given these and other circumstances and dynamics, the decision to leave a church is often fraught with distress and ambivalence.

Focus Group Findings

We now turn to a discussion of information from the focus groups in which participants were asked to reflect on instances of conflict between church members. Focus group discussions on negative interaction between church members is likely to be particularly informative, given the prominence placed on the nature of relationships within the church in New Testament texts (i.e., church members are warned against a whole host of negative interpersonal behaviors including quarreling, jealousy, outbursts of anger, factions, slander, gossip, arrogance, and disorder).

One of the first themes to emerge from the focus group information was the recognition of the dual nature of religious institutions and the people who inhabit them. In particular, the focus group participants were aware that the church represents a special and sacred community that comes together to worship God in word and deed. On the other hand, they were also clearly aware that churches, as human organizations, sometimes fall short of this ideal. Focus group members were clearly divergent in their assessments and tolerance of conflictual situations and relationships between church members. In addition, a number of explanations were offered for why it was the case that relationships in churches were not always harmonious.

Church Members, Like Family Members, Have Conflict

Several of the focus group participants noted that problems among church members weren't unexpected or unusual. They thought that it should not be surprising that church members, like families and any other group of people, experience conflict with one another. For instance, the following responses from two men indicate that, just as in other groups of individuals, some level of conflict is to be expected among church members:

> Well, I think with churches, with family, you are always going to have conflict. I think, in our church, some of the things we've seen are probably not unnatural.

> Like I mentioned, it's the same things that go on anyplace else. I mean, you going to have jealousy, you go have envying, you go have strife, you know, these things exist in the church, you know. Because the church is just a body of believers, you know, people who are seeking to grow in grace, you know.

Gossip

When focus group participants were asked about the conflicts that church members have with one another, one of the major issues was the problem of gossip. Several responses from the men illustrate this point:

> Just flat out gossip.

> Gossip, man, just killing folks.

> But I do believe that, that issue right there would probably be one of the largest issues for churches that there is the gossip of the tongue and what people have to say and rumors and what's going on with somebody else's life. You know, it's just like the big soap opera thing that goes on in churches.

> They talk about people and they get into other people's business. They do what human people do, you know, and it's normal.

> It's so easy to fall into gossip. But, I tell you this, more often than not, we have spoken evil of people and have hurt people and have killed them with our tongue. And I believe by far that is maybe the biggest problem that I have run into in my church.

So there have been times when you share problems that people
brought to you and you were completely pure at heart. You were trying
to seek advice and trying to get some other people to come
communicate with you in prayer and other times just flat out gossip.

And I really thought about this while I was sitting in a wedding last
weekend and there were little quirks that didn't happen. Some of the
people, you can hear them just groaning and complaining about, oh
they didn't do that right or you know, they forgot to do this and all this
other stuff. I thought about some of the quirks at my wedding and
everything else and how upset people were at the time and now when
you go back and look at the video, we kind of laugh about it.

Several women also noted that gossip was a problem among church
members.

If you getting the Word, you will change, but if you busy gossiping,
you worrying more about me or sister or brother so and so than you
are about your own soul.

You got so much gossiping here and gossiping there and people
getting caught up in this and caught up in that. If I was going to
church and worrying about what everybody else is doing, you never
hear the Word of God and never get the understanding of
the Word of God.

Several of the focus group participants provided examples of how gossip
negatively impacts church members. One man noted that, in some instances,
he might unintentionally behave differently with someone because of things
that he has heard about them.

You'll treat people differently because of it. It may not be something
that is intentional, but you tend to treat people differently from what
you hear, matter, matter it be true or, you know, something,
a rumor or whatever.

Another man noted that persistent gossip makes it impossible for those
who are the target of gossip to grow and change from mistakes that they
may have made in the past:

You know, so and so, he went to jail. Yeah, that was 20 years ago, but
he's a convict and he's still a convict. Now this person has founded a
multimillion dollar business, helping the community, you know, but

when it's all said and done, it rolls down to him being a convict, you know. And so, the thing is we put people in positions where we don't even allow Christ to change them, you know, because it's more comfortable for us to just think we're better than them because of what we know about them and we want to always hold that over their head.

A woman noted a similar sentiment:

And I think a lot of it is murmurs or some of it may not even be factual, but it's something someone told someone else, like cats whispering and just story changes and it gets bigger and sometimes out of proportion....If you repented on it and you're constantly hearing what you did, what you did, you were wrong and God ain't going to forgive you and, you know, just the murmurs in the wind. It kind of hinders the person from being a changed person and who knows that might be the way that they either become more aware of their shortcomings or either to change their ways.

Avoiding Gossip

Focus group participants recognized that gossip is a major problem in churches and also indicated that they are committed to refraining from this practice. Several men mentioned various ways they try to avoid gossiping.

I don't want to, I really don't like to take in a lot of negative things and I stay away from people that feed a lot of negative stuff, because, you know, that stuff, it gets into your spirit.

I came here to praise and worship God. I didn't come for, to know who's pregnant or who's doing this and doing that.

I don't want to know. I don't want to know who did this and who done that and why they did what they did. I tell my wife the same thing all the time, you know. Why you want to hear something if it ain't going to benefit you, me, our family, it's not going to do anything for us?

Where we have to be is at a place that we can sort of try our best to tame our tongues. When they come to you, you just tell them. You say look, I ain't into that, you know, or whatever. Or even sometimes I don't even tell them nothing. They talking and go on with your talk. I don't comment. I don't get involved in it. It's not my conversation. It's not my thing. I don't know nobody's business too much in the church either, because I had got enough problems of my own.

This brother talks about taming the tongue and it's a deadly force and something that is very difficult to do and something we should all work at, I work at. And, we like to sit in the seat of the scornful and judge, you know, which is not good and sometimes our words come out against people quite often that shouldn't. But taming the tongue, we really should try to work at.

Generational Differences

In addition to gossip, generational differences could be a source of conflict between individuals who are older and have been church members for several years and those who have only recently joined the church. These comments by two women reflect conflicts over differences in the direction of the church and role expectations for church elders.

> And I think other problems that occur is longevity. Somebody been in the church for 25 years that, you know, they don't want to see things change. I've been here and I'm going to stay here and this is how we're going to do stuff and we're going to be doing it for years and we're going to continue. And when you got new people coming in with new ideas, they don't want to hear.

> And it's hard … you know and I know that for me, because I have always been taught to respect my elders. You know, old folks is old folks. My grandmamma say, "You keep on living baby, you gonna get old, too." But it's hard for me sometimes you know, sometimes I have to catch myself. I really do because there are some seniors that belong to the church that I attend that sometimes I feel as though they don't walk in the senior calling. And I really have to catch myself, and it's offensive to me, it really is its because, now how am I supposed to respect these individuals if they are not walking in senior calling. Not doing the things that seniors are supposed to be doing, not showing me the way as seniors. And it's like, me and God, I know my arms are too short to box with God. But sometimes, we go round and around, because it's like, I have issues with that. I really have serious issues with that. So, I am like, "God, now I know I am supposed to respect my elders, but how am I supposed to get past this?"

Conflict Over Special Programs and Board Meetings

Another women mentioned that she has seen a lot of conflict in her experiences involving special church programs such as Women's Day.

> Women's Day, they ought to abolish that. Hey, hey, they ought to abolish that. I do not know how it goes in other places, but I have been to a number of the Baptist churches where we have Women's Day, and Women's Day may turn out to be fine, but all the bickering about who is going to be the chair of this? Who is going to march in first? What colors we going to wear? All that kinda mess. They ought to abolish that mess cause it ain't scripture at all and so many hurt feelings have happened at the end of such as that. And it may not be Women's Day. It may be any particular program.

Another woman mentioned that she has experienced conflict between church members at board meetings.

> I was just going to say um…you want to see conflict, go to a church board meeting. I don't mean the business meeting, those can get ugly, too. But, you know, sometimes you just have to stop and pray and remember that, yes, this is God's business and we have to remember that we are his instruments. Because I have walked out on church board meetings because I couldn't stay.

There were a few instances where focus group respondents mentioned some very serious disagreements among church members. According to one woman:

> I mean I've literally seen church members argue and fight. They look like they're about to scrap.

Losing Church Members Because of Conflict

Two women participants felt that they were losing potential church members because of the conflict in churches.

> Maybe they just joined the church or they're new to Christ and then they see all this, and they're gone. Because they're like, "If this is what this is about, bye."

> I am finding a lot of people are sour with churches. When you go out to witness now, you hear a person say, "I don't go to church. I know too many hypocrites. I know too many of this and too many of that."

Avoiding Conflict

Although focus group participants recognized that there was a considerable amount of conflict between church members, they said that they personally tried to avoid conflict. One woman stated:

We are Christians, we are supposed to be thinking about the common good and justice and love and helpfulness, and I am upset because Sister Sarah got on the same Gucci suit that I got on. Please, can we regroup here?

One woman said that her minister does an effective job of reducing conflict in her church by focusing on spiritual beliefs and convictions.

And one thing I think my minister does a very good job with in getting us to honor the Christ-spirit in each of us, and if there is say, a disagreement or a conflict, often times, someone will stop and will pray about it and that just has such a calming effect. And again, I think she has done a very good job in instilling that honor and respect that we have for each other in the church, cause again, personally, I couldn't go to a church where there is a lot of conflict. I hear about stuff, I hear about people fighting in church, walking out during the message, and we just don't have that. Because I think for me, the church is a haven, that is one place where I am assured that I can go and there isn't any conflict there. It's very serene, it's very peaceful. The people, I can embrace them as my brothers and sisters, so again, a church that...I'm not going to say rooted in conflict or has some very, some major personality clashes, personally I could not go there.

Feeling Unwelcome

Focus group participants also indicated that, at times, churches make people feel unwelcome. That is, people may not feel welcomed into the church for a number of reasons, including their style of clothing or the way they wear their hair. For example, two focus group members noted that:

I know a lot of people from my neighborhood that won't go to church because they worried about they ain't got church clothes. Because they know when you going to church people will be talking about them, what he doing in here, I mean. It shouldn't even be like that. It should be, when you come to church, you should be welcome no matter who you are, no matter what you are. So, it's a lot of people that don't welcome people in the church.

In the Bible it say, "Come as you are." That means come as you are. And in the Bible days when they was going to church, they weren't coming in suits and gators and driving up in Cadillacs. So how can you tell me that if I come to church with braids in my hair or just regular jean hookup, then I'm not coming, I know you want to look presentable when you go to church, but if I'm coming to church and if it's in my heart, it's what's in my heart, not in my outside appearance.

Several participants also noted that, in many instances, churches can be unwelcoming because of class differences or lifestyle differences.

> I look at the church as like being a hospital. Instead of a natural hospital, it's a spiritual hospital where people come for spiritual healing. And I agree with B [another focus group member] that when people come in that we are not comfortable with, or they are not the same lifestyles that we have or that we are accustomed to, or they are not on the same educational level that we are on, we tend to shun them. If they do not have the right kind of clothing on that we think that they should wear...the hair isn't combed, or the way we think it should be combed they are taboo. And God forbid they have a stench to them...you know, they are really hit and it's like, and I think that we fall short and we lose a lot of souls that way, that leave and never return.

The focus group members realized that not making people feel welcome is a problem, and many felt that this was an issue that churches would have to overcome. For instance, one woman indicated how important it is to make gang members feel welcome within the church.

> We have to realize that when people come from that world, there is a bond in that world. It is just like the little group says, the gangs, they got each other's back. They got love and since they got love for each other and if you were going down, they there for you. And when a person walk from that world and leave everything they were doing to come over here in the church, you need to have some kind of support or some kind of somebody there. I think it's what happens to a lot of people. They get there and nobody pick them up and nobody minister to them, and they kind of left alone with everybody. You know, they need somebody to talk to or some contact or something. And you find them drifting straight out back there in the world. So, I think there is very much need for support groups or just somebody. I don't like to see people coming in and nobody talk to them or visit with them or whatever. Usually, I try to make people feel quite comfortable because it means a lot you know to feel like you are a part of something.

A man said that church members have also left the church because they could not establish relationships.

> In my church there's been people who have left and that was one of their reasons for leaving, because they couldn't establish relationships. And it's kind of disheartening for me because when I hear it, because I

know if anyone can talk to me and at least you know, shake my hand and give me a hug, in the kind of person that I am, and I can be difficult at times, I know there is *somebody* in our church that you can talk to or something.

Helping People Feel Welcome

Conversely, one man related how two older men went out of their way to ensure that he felt welcome in his church.

> All my clothes was totally outdated, totally outdated. I came up in there. I had beads on, earrings on, my hair was braided. There was a lot of people saw me coming, you know, and they were turned off automatically. Who is this brother coming up in the church looking like this, rings, earrings and hair all with braids, beads hanging off his neck? These two brothers came up, shook my hand and it was like they didn't see any of that. It was just like they didn't even see it. These two men became like spiritual fathers to me. And they mentored me in my relationship all the way into the pool, through the pool, you know. And they're still some of my closest friends, you know. And one is old enough to be my father, the other my grandfather. But they saw beyond my appearance. They didn't let that turn them off, you know. They came forward shook my hand. "How you doing young man? Good to see you here."

One woman noted that her church has established a mentor or sponsor program to address some of these issues. This type of program helped new people in the church establish relationships, and it also indirectly helped the mentors themselves.

> In our church, when new members join they are kinda assigned a, I forget what the reverend calling this now, but a mentor kind of. And my mentee, she's been in the church now for several years, but she still comes to me and asks things. And sometimes I know and sometimes I don't. But, it made me grow more. It also kept me on my Ps & Qs 'cause I don't want her to see me 'cause she thinks so much of me, I don't want her to see me in the wrong place, you know. How will that affect her?

Other Concerns

In addition to the issues previously noted, a few men mentioned a number of other concerns that could be disruptive to a church.

But the other thing I think is egos, getting in our way and I've seen egos really impair relationships in the church, start coalitions and everything else.

It's also a lot of argument about a church. You know, like some churches they have a white Jesus, some churches have a black Jesus.

Don't date nobody in the church.

Problems in Church Do Not Inhibit Attendance and Participation

Finally, two men indicated that their religious faith had evolved so that even though there were problems in their churches, that did not keep them from attending religious services or being a part of the church.

I mean, you know, I was more concerned about what everyone thought and I saw people doing things that I thought they shouldn't be doing, so I stopped going to church. And then I came to the realization that it's not about them, as well. It's about my relationship with God that's important. And if these people want to act like fools or whatever, want to clown, so be it. I can't control that, you know, all I need to worry about is me.

And then I used to look around the church and look at all the people jealous, I mean, like you say people talking about each other and some people worrying about what you wearing to church and this and that. I mean, I used to think like, you supposed to be so saved and so religious, you over here gossiping about me, talking about this and that and all that. And then as I got older, I started learning for myself that it ain't about none of them, it's all about going to church for yourself, you know what I'm saying. Everybody in the church ain't right, just like everybody in the world ain't right, so it's all about yourself. They can talk and do what they want to do, you ain't got to worry about them, it's all about you.

Focus Group Summary

Focus group participants provided important information concerning the nature and extent of negative interaction between church members. Although participants clearly did not condone negative behaviors between church members, there seemed to be some recognition that this was an unfortunate but common occurrence within churches. Accordingly, some level of forbearance was evident and a recognition that churches are no different from other social organizations in experiencing problems of this sort. Indeed, several comments reflected the idea that the express purpose of the church is to minister to individuals who are in the process of developing spiritual maturity. As one participant put it, "Because the church is just a body of believers, you know, people who are seeking to grow in grace, you know."

Nevertheless, problematic interactions in the church were viewed as serious concerns; number one among them was the issue of gossip among church members. Focus group participants clearly understood the potential harm that gossip posed, both to the target individual and to the church as a collectivity. In addition, participants' efforts to refrain from gossiping indicated that they felt that there was real potential for harm to the person who engages in gossip as well. This was reflected in statements that gossiping prevented one from growing spiritually and achieving the benefits of religious worship (i.e., not hearing the Word).

Another problem that was discussed by focus group members was that of churches being "unwelcoming" in their attitude toward others. Participants said that people new to the church were sometimes ignored or subtly shunned because of differences in appearance and perceived social class. Participants voiced the fear that treatment of this type effectively dissuaded new individuals from joining and staying in the church. Focus group members spoke of various measures that could be used to provide a more welcoming church atmosphere and ensure the continued participation of newcomers.

Finally, an important theme underlying comments about negative interactions between church members was the notion that these behaviors were particularly unsettling given the context in which they occurred; that is, a religious institution. The paradox of these negative behaviors being committed by members of the church was not lost on the focus group members and was a source of obvious consternation and genuine concern. Again, while participants expressed disquiet about these situations, they also demonstrated considerable forbearance and an attitude of understanding as individuals within the church attempt to grow in spiritual maturity.

Chapter Summary and Conclusion

Negative interaction, and particularly negative interaction among church members, is an issue that has received very little systematic attention from researchers. The issue of negative interaction is an important one because previous research has shown that negative interaction can have a harmful impact on psychological well-being. With the exception of recent articles by Lincoln and colleagues, the majority of previous research on negative interaction among black Americans is based on small, nonprobability samples. Although these studies are important in providing information on specialized samples, they have limited generalizability to the black population overall.

The discussion of the survey data and the focus group information presented in this chapter is the first published research on negative interaction among church members on the adult black population (18 years of age and older). The descriptive profile from the two national surveys show that negative interaction (i.e., criticism, too many demands) from church members is not a frequent occurrence. The participants in the focus group study noted that negative interaction among church members does occur and takes the forms of gossiping about others, people being made to feel unwelcome in the church, and differences between church members based on generational status. Focus group members recognized that these were serious problems, but they also discussed different ways that they were trying to rectify these issues.

The seeming discrepancy between accounts of negative interaction from the survey data and the focus group information may be attributable to several reasons. First, the question formats used to assess negative interaction are very different. The survey questions asked about the respondents' personal accounts of the frequency of the three distinct types of negative interaction. In contrast, the focus group question format inquired more generally about whether there were instances in which church members had negative interactions with one another. Participants in the focus groups were free to discuss a variety of situations that involved negative interaction, and, further, the information was not specifically focused on their own personal experiences with other church members. The survey questions about the frequency of the respondents' own experiences of being criticized and having too many demands placed on them by church members were more directed in their content and reference to the respondent. Further, focus group members may have been reluctant to discuss specific instances in which they experienced negative interactions with church members, preferring instead to discuss various issues and dynamics affecting the church membership more broadly.

These two sources of information should not be viewed as being essentially discrepant with one another and therefore assume that one portrayal of negative interaction is accurate and the other incorrect. Instead, it may be useful to see them as different aspects of negative interaction that suggest further areas of inquiry as to the nature of negative interaction among church members. In particular, future survey questions may want to inquire about the prevalence of gossip and feelings of being unwelcome in one's church, while focus group inquiries could examine issues of being criticized, being burdened, and being taken advantage of. In this way, both survey data and focus group information may be used to provide a fuller appreciation of the nature of negative interaction among church members.

Part III

Effects of Religion

After describing patterns and functions of religion in Parts I and II of the book, we turn our attention to tangible impacts of religion on the daily lives of African Americans. Our emphasis specifically is on several key outcomes that have served as the focus of our own empirical research over the past couple of decades. The strongly positive influence of religion in African American life is most apparent through its documented impact on health and psychological well-being. Both individually and collectively, religious African Americans and black churches have been a force for good in the lives of people as expressed in individual-level indicators (e.g., lower rates of depressive symptoms in churchgoers) and in population-level indicators (e.g., mortality and morbidity profiles) of health and well-being.

Part III differs from the previous sections of this book in that it reports on the results of the many empirical research studies conducted by the authors, their colleagues, and other researchers that are focused on health and well-being outcomes of religious involvement, overall, and in relation to the black population. Current explanatory models of the mechanisms and pathways responsible for religion's effects on health are presented. Information about religious effects on physical health is presented in Chapter 8, and Chapter 9 is devoted to research on mental health and psychological well-being.

Chapter 8

Impact of Religion on Physical Health

A small but growing body of research has explored the impact of religion on the physical health of African Americans. Measures of religious participation and affiliation, as well as subjective self-assessments of religiousness, have been investigated in relation to various health outcomes, including global self-ratings of health, indicators of physical functioning, chronic disease morbidity, and even longevity. Results are not conclusive, but growing evidence supports a generally beneficial influence of religiousness on physical health.

This chapter begins with a brief overview of existing research on religion and health, including reference to key epidemiologic, social-scientific, and geronto-logical reviews. Results of notable religion and health studies using data collected from African American respondents are then documented in detail. Studies of morbidity (illness) and mortality (death) are reviewed separately. Special attention is given to findings from several large, ongoing national or regional probability surveys, including the National Survey of Black Americans (NSBA). Finally, the implications of existing findings are discussed and a variety of psychosocial mechanisms are proposed to help explain a protective effect of religious involvement on physical health among African Americans.

Research on Religion and Health

Over the past century, the impact of religion on physical health and illness has constituted a popular, if somewhat obscure, topic of empirical research in epidemiology and medicine. Hundreds of published studies have identified religious differences in a wide range of physical health outcomes and have examined the effects of religiousness on health status indicators and measures of disease states (Jarvis & Northcutt, 1987; Koenig, Larson, & McCullough, 2001; Levin & Schiller, 1987). Nearly every major disease entity and cancer site has been studied in relation to religion, and especially large bodies of published data exist for morbidity due to coronary heart disease, hypertension and stroke, and cancer, and for overall and cause-specific mortality. This research literature, which has come to be known as the epidemiology of religion (Levin & Vanderpool, 1987), is part of a larger body of findings also linking expressions of religiousness to mental health, psychological well-being, healthy lifestyle behaviors, health care utilization, and other health-related outcomes (Chatters, 2000; Levin, Chatters, Ellison, & Taylor, 1996).

Until recently, this literature has not been very well known, perhaps because few of these studies were designed specifically to study the effects of religion on health. Rather, in typical epidemiologic fashion, investigators directing these studies of atherosclerosis, cervical cancer, respiratory disease, life expectancy, colitis, and other outcomes collected data on scores of social, psychological, and biological variables, among which were one or more religious indicators. As a result, a statistical finding bearing on the impact of these religious variables on the health outcome or disease being studied often ended up buried in a table in a published report. More often than not, such results were not discussed in these papers, mentioned in the abstract, or indexed as a key word. Only after several years of exhaustive bibliographic researching, reading, and collation did the full scope of this literature emerge (see Levin, 1994a, 1994b).

Results from these studies have presented a fairly consistent pattern. These studies, for the most part, show a salutary relationship between religious involvement and health status. This is expressed in two ways. First, observable differences in rates of morbidity and overall and cause-specific mortality exist across major categories of religious affiliation, with lower rates typically found among members of religions or denominations that make strict behavioral demands; for example, Seventh-day Adventists and Latter-day Saints. Second, higher levels of active religious participation or observance are associated, on average, with less illness and with better health across a variety of scales or indices.

Until recently, however, most of the studies in this literature were not designed solely and explicitly to investigate this issue. Coupled with the paucity of true experimental evidence, no one study is ideally designed to "prove" that religion exerts a positive influence on health (Levin, 1996).

Across this literature, however, the consistency of findings in the face of diverse samples, designs, methodologies, religious measures, health outcomes, and population characteristics actually serves to strengthen the inference of a positive association between religion and health. This finding has been observed in studies of old, middle-aged, and young respondents; in men and women; in respondents from the United States, Europe, Africa, and Asia; in research conducted in the 1930s and in the current century; in retrospective case control, prospective cohort, cross-sectional, and longitudinal panel studies; in Protestants, Catholics, Jews, Muslims, Buddhists, and Parsis; in studies operationalizing religiousness as any of more than a dozen variables (religious attendance, affiliation, private prayer, Bible reading, church membership, subjective religiosity, etc.); in research limited to t tests or bivariate correlations and in research testing structural-equation models with LISREL or using Cox proportional hazards models; and in U.S. studies among Anglo whites, Hispanics, Asian Americans, and African Americans (Levin, 1994c).

Within the past decade and a half, comprehensive specialized reviews have been undertaken of the religion and health literature. These include several systematic reviews and meta-analyses of published empirical studies within epidemiology, the social sciences, and gerontology. Each of these reviews has identified a moderate and statistically significant impact of dimensions of religiousness on health outcomes of various types.

The religion and health literature in the fields of gerontology and geriatrics has been especially well summarized. A generally positive association between religious participation and overall health status or physical well-being was the conclusion reached by a traditional review of the literature (Levin, 1989), a systematic review of clinical studies in selected gerontology journals (Sherrill, Larson, & Greenwold, 1993), and an NIH-funded systematic review of 15 years of aging research (Levin, 1997). More recently, similar conclusions have been reached in an annotated bibliography of clinical research on religion and health (Koenig, 1995), a comprehensive textbook summarizing results of more than 1,200 studies of religious effects on a variety of quality-of-life–related outcomes (Koenig, Larson, & McCullough, 2001), and a meta-analysis of selected empirical studies of religion and mortality rates (McCullough, Hoyt, Larson, Koenig, & Thoresen, 2000).

Religion and Health in African Americans

As with biomedical research in general, early reviews found that religion and health research among African Americans was mostly scant and superficial

(Levin & Schiller, 1987). Even today, research on health, as in other topical domains, has yet to address and account adequately for the uniqueness, and diversity, of African American religious experience in the diaspora (Lincoln & Mamiya, 1990). Studies currently under way at the Program for Research on Black Americans (PRBA) have been instrumental in providing empirical verification of the unique patterns of religious expression among African Americans. Research using the four waves of the NSBA, for example, has centered on investigating the correlates of organized religious participation and the role of church members as sources of informal social support. These forms of religious expression, in turn, have been investigated in relation to a variety of physical-health- and well-being-related outcomes.

Research from PRBA, much of it documented throughout this book, points to the pervasive and generally positive influence of religion on the welfare of African Americans. Studies have shown that African Americans describe the church as having a generally beneficial impact on their lives (Taylor, Thornton, & Chatters, 1987) and that very few African Americans, even those reporting no current religious preference and no religious attendance since entering adulthood, exhibit a complete absence of all overt religious involvement (Taylor, 1988a). Further, close to two thirds of African Americans say that church members are integral members of their social support networks (Taylor & Chatters, 1988). This salience of religion in the lives of African Americans is distinctive and not characteristic of the general population. Results from four national probability surveys show that African Americans report higher levels of religious involvement than white respondents according to more than a dozen varied indicators of organizational, non-organizational, and subjective religiosity (Levin, Taylor, & Chatters, 1994; see Chapter 2 in this volume, "African American Religious Participation").

These findings underscore the central role of religion and churches in the lives of African Americans, and they should encourage researchers studying the influence of religious involvement on health to make special note of racial and ethnic differences. More often than not, however, this does not occur. As noted in several data sources, the health profile of African Americans, on average, differs for the worse from that of U.S. whites (Braithwaite & Taylor, 1992; Dressler, 1993). Coupled with this, racial differences have been shown to exist in patterns of religious involvement and in important indicators of socioeconomic status. As a consequence, studies of religion and health require investigators to be sensitive to the religious contexts of the populations under study and to the complex interplay among religion, race, and social class (Ellison & Levin, 1998). Further, patterns of both religiousness and health status, especially mortality rates, vary by age and gender. Taking into account demographic issues such as black-white differences both in the age structure of the population and in the gender ratio of specific age cohorts, as well as the long-observed racial crossover in mortality rates at advanced age (Markides, 1983a, 1983b; Markides & Machalek, 1984), adds further theoretical and methodological complexity to the requirements for religious research in this area among African Americans.

Some of the best and most programmatic research on religion and health among African Americans has emphasized older adults or changes in the religion-health dynamic across the life course. Some of this work has focused explicitly on African Americans; other research based on general populations has taken a racial-comparative approach, such as through stratification by race or through use of black-white dummy variables. This latter approach has been sharply critiqued as simplistic in that it masks considerable diversity among African Americans, may tend to suppress significant health disparities, and is not entirely useful for informing health policy (LaVeist, 1994). These points are noted, but research in this vein constitutes some of the best evidence of connections among religion, health, aging, and race.

Religion and Morbidity in Study Samples of Whites and Blacks

The authors of the first comprehensive review of epidemiologic studies of religion made a special note of the fact that most large-scale investigations chose not to investigate racial differences, not just in religion-health associations but in rates of morbidity or mortality in general (Levin & Schiller, 1987). Three approaches to race seemed to predominate: (a) an all-white study population was sampled; (b) a general population sample was used, but race was not explored in any analyses; or (c) a population of unknown racial composition was sampled and no descriptive data on numbers of African Americans were provided. Likewise, in the aforementioned systematic review of gerontological research (Levin, 1997), it was noted that while half of all studies used an all-black or multi-ethnic study sample, explicit racial comparisons in religious effects on health outcomes were very rare.

Over the past couple of decades, with the rise of gerontological research on a potential religion-health connection, racial comparisons have begun to appear sporadically. These data offer a limited, but interesting, glimpse of black-white differences in the relationship between religion and health. Most of these studies have made use of data from large, ongoing national or regional probability surveys, such as the NORC General Social Survey (GSS), the Americans' Changing Lives (ACL) Study, the NIMH Epidemiologic

Catchment Area (ECA) Program, and the Established Populations for the Epidemiologic Study of the Elderly (EPESE). These large-scale surveys are anchors of respective multiyear programs of data collection, and all have multi-racial samples. Therefore, while religion and health studies using these data are few in number, they are of mostly recent vintage, include large numbers of African American respondents, and their representative samples allow widespread population-based inferences to be drawn.

An early effort to explore racial differences in religion and health used GSS data on older adults 65 years of age and above ($N = 1,493$) collected as a part of the 1972–1977 surveys (Steinitz, 1980). Frequent attendance at religious services was associated with both higher self-ratings of health and satisfaction with health among white respondents only, and strength of denominational affiliation was also associated with greater health satisfaction among whites only. Among older African Americans, neither religious measure was a significant correlate of health.

A later study using GSS data on 25- to 54-year-olds pooled from the 1972–1982 surveys (St. George & McNamara, 1984) provided the opportunity for a more detailed look at the relationships explored in the earlier study (Steinitz, 1980). The investigators found distinct racial differences in two measures of religiousness. Frequency of religious attendance was unrelated to either subjective health or satisfaction with health in both white men (Ns ranged from 1,353 to 1,853, depending upon analysis) and white women (Ns from 1,570–2,024), whereas in both African American men (Ns from 144–205) and women (Ns from 188–244) attendance was strongly and significantly associated with both health measures. Strength of religious affiliation was mildly associated with health satisfaction in white men and women but was very strongly related to both measures of health in African American men. The results of these two studies taken together provided early evidence of an effect-modifying influence of age or cohort on the relationships among religion, race, and health.

A more recent study (Drevenstedt, 1998) pooled a dozen years of GSS data, from 1974 through 1991, to ensure sizable numbers of ethnic minority respondents, including non-Latino African Americans ($N = 1,803$). Simultaneous stratification by age, gender, and ethnicity provided an excellent opportunity to explore the nuances of the associations of religious attendance and subjective religiousness with subjective health. Positive and significant associations were found in whites and in younger (18–39 years old) African Americans and Latinos. Among younger African American men, controlling for the effects of social support or socioeconomic status reduced the association between religious attendance and health to non-significance; this effect was not seen in women. In both genders, however, controlling for the effect of subjective religiosity reduced the health effect of attendance.

Data from the African American and 60-and-older oversamples of the first wave of the ACL, conducted in 1986, were used to construct a sample ($N = 448$) for structurally modeling associations among two religious indicters: a composite measure of physical health problems and a variety of well-being-related outcomes (Krause, 1992). It was hypothesized that health problems and family deaths precipitated religious responses, such as greater religious attendance and increased subjective religiousness, that, in turn, would directly and indirectly reduce psychological distress. Findings mostly confirmed these expectations, in that religiousness served to counterbalance or offset the otherwise deleterious effects of poor personal and family health by heightening feelings of self-esteem.

The full first wave of the Americans' Changing Lives (ACL) survey was used to explore racial differences in the relationship between several dimensions of religious expression and a three-item index of health status that combined subjective health, prevalence of chronic conditions, and functional limitations (Ferraro & Koch, 1994). The African American oversample was incorporated into analyses ($N = 2,550$), and black-white differences were examined in the results of models regressing the health index onto a wide variety of religious, psychosocial, and sociodemographic indicators. Religious practice (comprising religious attendance, reading religious books, and watching or listening to religious television or radio) was a significant predictor of health among African Americans but not among whites. Also among African Americans, but not among whites, receiving comfort and consolation from religion was associated with poorer health, which probably reflects a likeliness to turn to religion as a coping response to illness.

Using data collected from 1982 to 1984 as a part of the Piedmont Health Survey ($N = 2,894$), one of the five sites of the Epidemiologic Catchment Area (ECA), racial differences were examined in effects of religious attendance and devotion on depressive symptoms (Ellison, 1995). The analytic strategy used in this study allowed investigation of the potentially moderating effects of chronic illness prevalence on a religion-depression association. Among whites, greater religious attendance was associated with fewer depressive symptoms; controlling for the effects of chronic illness only slightly reduced the magnitude of this effect. Among African Americans, attendance and depression were not related. In both racial groups, religious devotion (i.e., prayer and Bible study) was associated with greater depression; chronic illness slightly moderated this effect in whites, but the effect was independent of health in African Americans.

Data from the first and fourth waves of the Duke Established Populations for the Epidemiologic Study of the Elderly (EPESE) study ($N = 2,623$; ages 64 and older), conducted from 1986 to 1989, were used to examine racial differences in a series of hierarchical models of religious and other effects on subjective health (Musick, 1996). Frequent religious attendance was a significant predictor of health in both African Americans and whites and withstood controlling for effects of health-related behaviors and social ties in both groups. Religious devotion, by contrast, was not associated with health bivariately, but significant associations emerged after controlling for effects of objective measures of health. Specifically, a suppressor effect was observed for functional health in both racial groups. Additional analyses showed that African Americans with the highest levels of functional impairment engaged in more private devotional activities than less-impaired African Americans, to the greater benefit of their self-assessments of health.

A study using data from the New Haven EPESE study ($N = 2,812$; ages 65 and older), conducted from 1982 to 1994, examined differences between African American and white Protestants in several physical-health–related outcomes. In one study (Idler & Kasl, 1997), the racial identity of Protestants was not a statistically significant source of variation in physical activity, body mass index, or self-rated health. This is an interesting finding, as African American Protestants exceeded their white counterparts in religious attendance and subjective religiousness, variables that have been found to be associated with health in other studies.

The best study to date of racial differences in religion's impact on physical health was a recently published investigation of 1,500 noninstitutionalized Christian adults aged 66 years or older (Krause, 2002a). This study used a sophisticated multistage probability sampling technique to obtain a nationally representative data set derived from the Health Care Finance Administration (HCFA) Medicare Beneficiary Eligibility List in 2001. The health effects of several religious indicators were structurally modeled, with emotional support and optimism posited as potential mediators. Results revealed generally higher levels of religiousness among African Americans; that frequent church attendance and an index of congregational cohesiveness were significant predictors of a global self-rating of health status; and that cohesiveness influenced health by way of heightening optimistic expectations. Structural-invariance analyses showed that this set of relationships was stronger among African Americans than among whites, especially the mediating effect of optimism. The author concluded that, "older Black people may derive greater health-related benefits from religion because they are more involved in it" (p. S341), and that the role of optimism as a salient mediator was consistent with theoretical writing on the Black Church.

Religion and Morbidity
in African American Study Samples

Since the late 1980s, two well-developed programs of empirical research on religion, health, and well-being have been based on data collected from samples of African American populations. The NIA-funded collaborative research of Taylor, Chatters, and Levin, based primarily on analyses of NSBA data, has focused on patterns, predictors, and outcomes of religious involvement in African Americans, with an emphasis on religious determinants of physical health and psychological well-being. The NIMH-funded research of Diane Brown and associates has resulted in a number of interesting studies of the impact of religion on patterns of psychological distress and well-being in African Americans.

One of these studies (Brown & Gary, 1987) used data collected from African American adults ($N = 451$) living in Richmond, Virginia. The authors found an interesting and statistically significant gender difference in the stress-buffering effects of religious activity on physical health. Among men, no relationship was present, whereas for women, a significant interaction was found between religious activity and stressful life events. Specifically, for those women reporting high or moderate levels of religiousness, greater amounts of life stress were associated with poorer physical health. For women reporting low religiousness, stress and health were unrelated. The authors explained this seemingly counterintuitive finding as a reflection of African American women increasing their participation in religious activities as a means of coping with stressful circumstances and concomitant personal and family health challenges.

A later study by the same research team (Brown & Gary, 1994) examined associations between physical health status indicators and selected measures of religious involvement using data from a community survey of African American men ($N = 537$) conducted in a major U.S. urban area. Interestingly, there were no significant associations between any of three religious measures (religious attendance, a scale of overall religiosity, and presence of a denominational affiliation) and either a self-rating of health status or hypertension prevalence. Additional analyses, however, revealed strong preventive effects of all religious measures with respect to both current smoking and daily drinking, known risk factors for a variety of chronic diseases. Moreover, low levels of all three religious measures also increased the probability of experiencing depressive symptoms. It could be, the authors speculated, that religious effects on health in this population are more likely to show up in the long run in reductions of morbidity and mortality rather than in current assessments of health in a generally young (mean age = 42.6, $SD = 18.0$) sample.

Ongoing research at the Program for Research on Black Americans since the late 1980s has systematically investigated religious effects on a variety of measures of physical health status. A special emphasis has been on examining religious effects on both subjective self-ratings of health and on "harder" health status indicators, such as indices of chronic disease prevalence and functional disability. Another principal objective has been to advance the methodological sophistication of research in this area through use of multifactorial theoretical models; multidimensional measurement models of religion, health, and well-being; multivariable and multivariate analytic procedures such as structural-equation modeling and two-way ANCOVA with factorial design; and a strategy of replicated secondary data analysis (see Chatters & Taylor, 1994).

Initial studies of religion using the first wave of the NSBA were focused more on exploring patterns of religious participation and use of religious support, research that is documented throughout this book. In a few of these studies, using the older-adult subsample ($N = 581$; ages 55 and older), a measure of health was used as a predictor of a respective religious indicator, rather than the other way around. Since this work was cross-sectional, the directionality of results from these analyses is somewhat ambiguous, and positive findings may actually imply an effect of religiousness on health. In point of fact, these associations were uneven and few positive findings were identified. In one study (Taylor, 1986), a summary index of health disability was unrelated to frequency of religious attendance; in another study (Taylor & Chatters, 1986a), the same index was unrelated to either the frequency or amount of church support received. In a third study (Taylor & Chatters, 1991a), disability was positively associated with watching religious programs, as might be expected of elderly shut-ins.

Following this earlier work, a more comprehensive program of research was initiated with two emphases, neither of which involved health. These were to determine patterns of African American religious participation (Levin & Taylor, 1993), as well as black-white differences in participation (Levin, Taylor, & Chatters, 1994), and to validate multidimensional measures of religiousness for use with the full NSBA (Chatters, Levin, & Taylor, 1992) and with the older-adult subsample (Levin, Taylor, & Chatters, 1995). This groundwork culminated in a comprehensive, age-comparative investigation of religion, health, and well-being published in the *Journal of Gerontology: Social Sciences* (Levin, Chatters, & Taylor, 1995). A theoretically based structural-equation model was used to examine the effects of three dimensions of religiousness on indices of both physical health and psychological well-being in the first wave of the NSBA ($N = 1,848$). Multiple multi-item measures were used to assess religiousness, health, and well-being.

Data were analyzed using maximum-likelihood estimation in LISREL, the structural-invariance of the model was assessed across three age cohorts (≤ 30, 31–54, and ≥ 55), and a strategy of split sample replication was used. Findings from this study revealed that organizational religiosity (a composite of religious attendance, church membership, involvement in church organizations and other church activities, and holding church office) exhibited a strong, statistically significant effect on well-being even after controlling for the effects of health and of sociodemographic factors typically associated with religiousness, health, and well-being. Moreover, analyses showed that the overall model tested in this study was age-invariant; that is, the tested model of these relationships was equivalent across the three age cohorts.

These provocative findings suggested that the impact of religiousness on well-being is not solely due to the confounding of religious attendance and functional health among older, disabled adults, as has been suggested (Levin & Vanderpool, 1987). The effect of religion is also apparently not due to religion and well-being having common predictors, such as age, gender, and socioeconomic status (see Levin & Tobin, 1995). This study offered strong and convincing evidence that religiousness, specifically participation in organized religious activities, is a salient determinant of physical and psychological well-being in African Americans.

A follow-up study sought to replicate the above findings among older adults in three multiracial national probability surveys (Levin & Chatters, 1998a). Data were from a combination of older adult and African American oversamples or subsamples from the 1974 Myth and Reality of Aging (MRA) survey ($N = 2,183$; ages 65 and older); the second Quality of American Life (QAL) survey ($N =1,056$; ages 55 and older), conducted in 1978; and the first wave of the ACL ($N = 1,553$; ages 60 and older). This study provided an opportunity to see if associations were present nationally regardless of the study sample used, the time period in which data were collected, and the specific variables used to assess each major construct (i.e., religiousness, health, well-being). It also offered a chance to see how race affected estimates of structural parameters in the model. Findings from this study revealed that the same theoretical model tested in the NSBA study fit well with each of the three data sets. Statistically significant religious effects were found in all three samples, notably consistently positive effects of organizational religiosity (e.g., religious attendance) controlling for other factors. In both the ACL and MRA samples, organizational religiosity was associated with better health, even after controlling for all other study constructs. In the QAL, subjective religiosity was associated with better health, again after controlling for other measures of religiousness and for all sociodemographic variables. In all three data sets, African American respondents were significantly more religious across all religious constructs. Nevertheless, controlling for the effects of a race, in concert with several other exogenous variables, did not diminish the statistical significance of these religion-health associations. These results provided strong evidence that the findings observed in the NSBA study were not unique to African Americans.

Religion and Mortality in African Americans

Since the early 1990s, a steady stream of investigations has begun focusing on whether religious participation serves to protect against premature mortality and to increase longevity (see McCullough, Hoyt et al., 2000). Most of this research has been conducted by epidemiologists, demographers, or physicians; typically has made use of population-based probability samples; and has employed analyses, usually of adjusted rates (e.g., Cox proportional hazards modeling). Throughout these studies, the religion-mortality relationship has been expressed in various ways, such as relative hazards, odds ratios, graphed survival curves, or life expectancy estimates. Unfortunately, another distinguishing feature of these studies has been a lack of attention to both black-white differences in a potential religion-mortality association and the nature of this association in African American populations. In most religion-mortality studies, data on race (a) were not collected, (b) were collected but unreported, or (c) were reported but not used in analyses. A couple of studies have reported relative hazards rates for religion adjusted for race, one has reported racial differences in rates, and only two large-scale national surveys have reported on mortality using exclusively African American samples.

Survival data from the Duke EPESE study ($N = 3,968$) reported a relative hazard (i.e., likelihood of mortality) of 46% less among frequent church attenders over a period of 6.3 years (1986–1992). Controlling for effects of race, along with age, gender, and education, reduced the protective effect only slightly, to 41% (Koenig et al., 1999). Follow-up data from 28 years (1965–1994) of the Alameda County Study ($N = 5,286$) found a 36% lower relative hazard among frequent religious attenders when controlling for effects of race, along with age, sex, education, and religious affiliation (Strawbridge, Cohen, Shema, & Kaplan, 1997).

An important advance in religion-mortality research was achieved in a study conducted at the Population Research Center of the University of Texas (Hummer, Rogers, Nam, & Ellison, 1999). Data on U.S. adults

($N = 21,204$) were compiled from the National Center for Health Statistics (NCHS) Multiple Cause of Death Public Use Data File, a data source that matched respondents from the 1987 National Health Interview Survey's Cancer Risk Factor Supplement to the National Death Index list of deaths through the end of 1995. Cox proportional hazards models were estimated, with an added improvement over previous studies—a potentially graded pattern of protective effects was investigated by differentiating between religious service nonattenders and those who attended church less than once per week, once per week, and more than once per week. In addition, effects of hypothesized mediating factors, such as health practices and social ties, were controlled for in a series of seven hierarchical models. These models also adjusted for effects of socioeconomic status and three measures of baseline subjective and functional health status.

A highlight of this study's findings was identification of a significant racial difference in the survival advantage for frequent religious attenders. The life expectancy estimate at age 20 for religious nonattenders in the total sample was 55.3 years; for more–than–weekly attenders, it was 62.9 years. This advantage is about 7 years, and it exhibited graded characteristics across the four response categories. For non-African Americans, the respective life expectancy estimates were 56.1 and 63.4 years—a similar 7-year advantage. For African Americans, however, results were striking: nonattenders had an estimated life expectancy at age 20 of 46.4 years; for more–than–weekly attenders, the estimate was 60.1 years. This translates to a nearly 14-year survival advantage for frequent religious attenders. Significantly, this level of religious attendance closes the racial gap in life expectancy from nearly 9 years in nonattenders to less than 3 years.

The first religion-mortality study of an exclusively African American sample was conducted at Brown University. Data from the 1984–1988 Longitudinal Survey of Aging (LSOA) were used to investigate the determinants of mortality among older African Americans (Bryant & Rakowski, 1992). Baseline data for the LSOA were collected as part of the Supplement on Aging to the 1984 National Health Interview Survey. In this study, African American adults ages 70 and older were included ($N = 473$) and were tracked for mortality occurring through the end of 1988. Data were analyzed through logistic regression, and results were reported as odds ratios adjusted for age, gender, education, living arrangements, numerous health indicators, and composite indices of friend and family networks. Despite these comprehensive controls, frequent church attendance was strongly and significantly associated with survival. Respondents who did not attend church services or church-based meetings had 1.77 times the odds of dying within the 4-year follow-up period than did church attenders.

For women, the adjusted odds ratio was 1.63 and for men was 2.72. These results are striking and underscore the considerable survival advantage attributable to church attendance in older African Americans in as brief an interval as 4 years. Even more striking is the finding that this advantage is not due to the presumably salutary benefits of social support that result from church involvement nor to the observation that regularly church-attending older adults are healthier than nonattenders. The effect of religious participation on longevity in this population must be due to other functions or characteristics of religiousness.

The finest study to date of religion and mortality in African Americans built upon the best elements of both the Hummer and associates (1999) and Bryant and Rakowski (1992) studies. Data from African American respondents ($N = 3,002$) were selected from the NCHS Multiple Cause of Death Public Use Data File by the same University of Texas research team (Ellison, Hummer, Cormier, & Rogers, 2000) in order to investigate survival patterns over the identical 8-year follow-up period (1987–1995). Cox proportional hazards models were again estimated, this time with an added twist—within-group variation was examined through stratifying the sample by age (18–54, ≥ 55), region (South, non-South), and gender. As before, graded effects of religious attendance were investigated, and potentially mediating effects of health practices and social ties were controlled for in hierarchical analyses that also adjusted for socioeconomic status and health.

Results confirmed a "strong effect of nonattendance on mortality risk [that] is robust, pervasive, and remarkably strong across all subgroups of the population" (Ellison et al., 2000, p. 630). The hazards ratio for nonattenders in the overall sample was 2.23; in the final model, controlling for effects of every variable in the study, the ratio was 2.22. In other words, church nonattenders experienced more than twice the risk of dying in the 8 years of study follow-up compared to frequent attenders, a result unable to be explained away by controlling for effects of 14 additional variables. Even for those who attended church as much as weekly, compared to more frequent attenders, the hazards ratio was 1.47 in the final model, indicating nearly one and a half times the risk of death. Unadjusted ratios from subgroup analyses painted a similar picture. In younger African Americans, the relative mortality risk associated with nonattendance was 3.76; for older African Americans, it was 1.96. For African American women, it was 2.54; for men, it was 2.42. For African Americans from the South, the hazards ratio was 2.11; for non-Southerners, it was 2.08. Adjusting for effects of health, socioeconomic status, health behaviors, and social ties altered these findings only minimally; in some instances, suppressor effects emerged and hazards ratios actually increased.

Religion, Race, and Health:
Theoretical Considerations

To summarize, prior empirical research provides evidence that measures of religiousness are significantly associated with physical health outcomes in African Americans. This is true for both morbidity and mortality—for indicators of health and illness and for rates of death or survival. Evidence for racial differences in a religion-health relationship are mixed—some studies show black-white differences, others do not. In large part, this seems to depend upon the health outcomes being studied, the age of respondents, and the study design used. In general, age appears to have an inverse moderating effect on the relationships among religion, race, and health—that is, among older adults, religion's salutary effect among African Americans is most observed.

It is important to stress that neither physical health status nor religiousness are unitary constructs. It is imperative that researchers interested in these issues specify which aspects or dimensions of religion are hypothesized to impact which dimensions of health. The religion and health field long ago moved beyond the point where atheoretical exploratory research could be justified. Findings linking various expressions of religiousness to a variety of health outcomes are now commonplace, and increasing attention is being paid to a religion-health connection among African Americans. The next step for researchers in this field is to move beyond investigations of what, who, where, and when—the foci of descriptive epidemiology—and begin to explore questions that ask how and why (Levin, in press-b). In other words, research should seek to identify those functions, characteristics, or expressions of being religious or practicing religion that are known to or would be expected to impact on health in this population (Levin, 1996).

Starting in the late 1980s, scientists began to propose explanations or hypotheses for observed effects of religious involvement on health. A set of sociological explanations was offered by Idler (1987), who proposed that religion's impact on health was mediated by the social cohesiveness, belief in theodicy, fostering of coherence, and healthy behavior ideally engendered by regular religious participation. Additional psychological explanations were proposed by McIntosh and Spilka (1990), who contended that religion can be a positive resource for health by promoting internal locus of control beliefs and a strong faith in God.

A comprehensive effort to outline possible explanations for religion-health associations was offered by Levin and Vanderpool (1989), combining insights from epidemiology, biomedicine, psychiatry, the social sciences, and other fields. The product of this work was a list of a dozen alternative explanations based on a variety of proposed biological, behavioral, sociomedical, and psychodynamic pathways and mechanisms, and a few other possibilities. Three explanations were proposed based on possible methodological artifacts—that is, that positive findings were the result of conceptual, psychometric, or analytical errors or biases—although the weight of current evidence appears to rule these out (Levin, 1994c). In addition, the reviewers added that, hypothetically, "superempirical" (i.e., parapsychological) or supernatural forces might be at work but noted the barriers to scientific investigation of such influences at the present time. This work has subsequently been expanded both in a lengthy article in *Social Science and Medicine* (Levin, 1996) and in the book *God, Faith, and Health* (Levin, 2001).

The biobehavioral and psychosocial explanations for significant religion-health associations proposed by Levin and Vanderpool (1989) can be applied specifically to findings derived from study samples consisting of African Americans. These alternative hypotheses offer a useful context for interpreting the meaning and implications of these findings in the lives of African Americans and for understanding potential black-white differences in religious effects on physical health. One possible explanation for significant religion-health associations in African Americans is that strong commitment to a religious system of beliefs may lead people to adopt *healthy behaviors* that are known to reduce the risk of morbidity due to chronic illness. Religions typically prescribe and proscribe certain behaviors, such as those related to smoking, drinking, substance abuse, diet, sexuality, and hygiene (Spector, 1979). Conservative, evangelical, and Pentecostal denominations especially may sanction belief systems that place a premium on holiness and on personal behavior aligned with strict interpretations of scripture. Themes such as judgment, fear of God, obedience to God's word, sanctification, justification, and maintaining the body as a "temple of the Holy Spirit within you" (I Corinthians 6:19) may be salient cues to refrain from activities that serve to place believers at risk. The correspondence between those behaviors most discouraged through religious proscriptions and those behaviors identified as risk factors is another serendipitous connection between religion and epidemiology. Modest but steady movement by African Americans to affiliate with conservative Protestant groups (Ellison & Sherkat, 1990), including Pentecostal and Holiness churches, suggests the continuing salience of this explanation for the salutary impact of religion in this population.

A second explanation is that regular religious participation may serve to strengthen connections to the most historically successful network of *supportive resources* in most African American communities (Bryant, 1980).

The Black Church, as described by Frazier (1974), Lincoln (1974a), Quarles (1964), and others, has operated as an informal social support network without peer, providing tangible and emotional support as well as a strong sense of group identity and cohesiveness through maintenance of primary-group relationships (Chatters, Taylor, Lincoln, & Schroepfer, 2002). Black churches deliver a wide array of services to congregants, including information and referrals related to employment, housing, finances, and health care, and direct delivery of counseling, transportation, and other services (Taylor, Luckey, & Smith, 1990). These types of church-based resources represent the largest source of support received by older African Americans (Taylor & Chatters, 1986b). Considerable research in epidemiology has demonstrated the value of strong social ties for lowering the risk of morbidity and mortality in both African Americans and whites (House, Landis, & Umberson, 1988). No surprise, then, that the Black Church, the primary voluntary association of African Americans (Taylor, Thornton, & Chatters, 1987), has also been described, explicitly, as a "therapeutic community" (Gilkes, 1980). Active participation in church offers African American churchgoers not only spiritual sustenance but access to personal and social resources that can provide help in coping during times of need, moderate the deleterious effects of chronic life stressors, reduce the risk of depressive symptoms, and cultivate healthy relationships that strengthen ties to a supportive community of like-minded people (Ellison, 1994).

The psychodynamics of religious expression among African Americans may also influence perceptions of health through a variety of channels. Regular devotional activity, such as group worship and prayer, may (a) serve to buffer the stress of daily life, (b) provide a sense of purpose and meaning to life and discourage both hopelessness and the belief that things happen only by chance (i.e., external locus of control), (c) engender an expectation of good health in keeping with scriptural promises to that effect, and (d) provide a means or framework for experiencing forgiveness and hope and for recontextualizing disability and suffering (Koenig, 1994) (see Chapter 4 in this volume, "Prayer as a Source of Coping"). These cognitive and affective features and sequelae of religiousness suggest several additional explanations for religion-health associations among African Americans—explanations that posit mediating or effect-modifying roles for religiously motivated emotions, beliefs, and thoughts and attitudes.

A third explanation for a religion-health connection among African Americans is that religious worship may engender *positive feelings* that impact upon the susceptibility to, course of, or recovery from illness. How people internally process the experience of private devotion and public worship both reflects and effects a range of emotional states that are, ideally (but not always), positive. Prayer can be motivated by and can instill feelings of gratitude, forgiveness, comfort, peace, joy, trust, ecstasy, and love (see Chapters 2 and 3). Religious worship can provide an opportunity for catharsis, relieving the weight of accumulated stressors, and for renewal of body, mind, and spirit. This psychological function of religion is no less salient a theme in African American churches, historically, than the more well-known sociological function (Lincoln, 1974b) just described. The former may also contribute to the latter. According to Wach (1944), prayer and other rituals of worship "not only serve to articulate the experiences of those taking part but contribute in no small measure to the shaping and determining of the organization and spirit of the group" (p. 40).

Besides a salutary effect on health through fostering social integration, worship's emotional sequelae may even more directly affect physical well-being. This can be understood through the well-documented interactions of the nervous, endocrine, and immune systems that help the body adapt to infection, inflammation, and tissue injury (Reichlin, 1993). The field of psychoneuroimmunology describes homeostatic mechanisms by which particular affects or mood states may translate into observable alterations in physiological parameters, for better or for worse. Affective disturbances and physical disorders may influence each other bidirectionally through biological, behavioral, or cognitive pathways (Cohen & Rodriguez, 1995). Likewise, positive psychological events may exhibit an immune-modulating effect that can mitigate pathophysiological responses (Maier, Watkins, & Fleshner, 1994). A recent investigation of the impact of religious factors and ethnicity on blood pressure (Steffen, Hinderliter, Blumenthal, & Sherwood, 2001) found that religious coping (e.g., trust in God, seek God's help, find comfort in religion) was associated with both lower ambulatory and clinic blood pressure among African Americans but not whites. The authors suggest that this may be one of the pathways through which religiosity and cardiovascular health are related.

A fourth explanation is that particular *beliefs or personality styles* believed to be salutary are consonant with or encouraged by certain religious beliefs or worldviews. Studies of constructs such as Type A and internal locus of control, among others, have demonstrated that personality factors or specific beliefs about life may respectively increase or decrease risk or morbidity (see Levin, 2001). Personality may also serve to modify the effects of stressful life changes on symptomatology (Ormel, Stewart, & Sanderman, 1989). Health-impacting psychosocial constructs, in turn, appear to have meaningful religious correlates or antecedents. For example, researchers have identified the interconnections between Type A and the Protestant work ethic (Furnham, 1990) and among Type A, religion, and health outcomes (Levin, Jenkins, & Rose, 1988). Another construct, John Henryism, developed as a means of capturing a particular style of active coping specifically among African Americans (James, Hartnett, & Kalsbeek, 1983; James & Thomas, 2000), has exhibited inconsistent and conditional effects on morbidity, though it is not clear how it interacts with religion. This fourth explanation for significant religion-health associations among African Americans is thus more speculative than the previous three and awaits systematic investigation.

A fifth and final hypothetical explanation is that the *attitude of faith* that drives and is fueled by religious participation is a significant resource for maintaining health and recovering from illness. Affirmation of a "faith that heals" was proposed nearly a century ago by no less a figure than William Osler (1910), a founding father of Western biomedicine, in a famous article in the *British Medical Journal*. This same theme was revisited three quarters of a century later by Jerome D. Frank (1975), preeminent psychiatrist, writing in the *Johns Hopkins Medical Journal*. Since then, health psychologists, clinicians, and others have begun systematically to explore constructs such as hope, optimism, and positive expectations in relation to physical and psychological well-being and the course of illness (e.g., Snyder, 2000). Empirical and theoretical work is accumulating that continues to validate the impact of mental outlook and other psychological factors on physiological parameters, biomolecular activity, and responses at the cellular level (Myers & Benson, 1992). Studies such as the HCFA analysis reviewed earlier (Krause, 2002a) demonstrate the potential of optimism as a mediating link between religion and health among older African Americans. As this line of research expands to include more in-depth consideration of patterns of faith expression unique to particular religio-ethnic communities, much may be learned about how the relationship between mind and body is influenced by social, environmental, and spiritual characteristics of human populations.

Each of these hypothesized explanations for religion-health associations in African Americans suggests that regular religious participation may influence one's self-perceptions of health. Religious involvement may also affect the actual biological parameters or markers of one's physical health by way of the complex pathways believed to link behavior and beliefs with the neurological, endocrine, and immune systems (see Sternberg, 2000). The emerging field of mind-body research and the continuing rapprochement between the physical sciences and religion suggest that study of the impact of religious involvement on physical and mental health will represent a cutting edge for medical research in the current century. The next generation of research into the influence of religious involvement on the health of African Americans would be wise to take a more explicitly multidisciplinary approach, incorporating findings and theories from the social, behavioral, and biological sciences with epidemiologic concepts such as host resistance, salutogenesis, and the natural history of disease (Levin, 1996) in order to understand the provocative relationship between religion and health.

Chapter 9

Impact of Religion on Mental Health and Well-Being

Similar to the growing number of studies that examine a potential connection between religion and physical health in African Americans, there has been a growing empirical research literature investigating the effects of religious factors on indicators of mental health and psychological well-being in this population. High-quality research by psychiatrists, geriatricians, medical sociologists, social psychologists, and epidemiologists has focused on the disease-preventive impact of religious participation on depression and other psychiatric outcomes, indicators of positive well-being (i.e., life satisfaction and happiness), and other psychosocial constructs. Research findings from this body of work, based on a number of excellent studies involving both black and white and exclusively African American samples, show both the presence of a beneficial effect of religion on mental health and well-being among African Americans as well as interesting black-white differences in patterns of association.

This chapter begins with an overview of two traditions of work on religion and mental health and well-being. We begin with a discussion of clinical and population-based research on religion and mental health, which is followed by an overview of research addressing the impact of religiousness on dimensions of psychological well-being (primarily from the field of gerontology). Results are then presented from key studies of religion, mental health, and well-being using data collected from African American respondents. These include studies of depressive symptoms, life satisfaction, and happiness, and other psychiatric and psychosocial outcomes. Finally, implications of these findings for clinicians and researchers are discussed.

Religion and Mental Health: Clinical and Population-Based Research

Empirical research on religious correlates and determinants of mental illness dates back several decades (see Levin & Chatters, 1998b). More than 40 years ago, the seminal Midtown Manhattan Study (Srole & Langner, 1962) compared the prevalence of mental illness among active and currently unchurched Catholics, Protestants, and Jews. The investigators found that the nonaffiliated had higher levels of mental illness than actively religious respondents. Throughout the 1960s, investigators explored associations between a variety of religious constructs and measures and a wide range of mental-health–related outcomes in order to identify whether religious participation, broadly defined, had preventive effects on subsequent rates of mental illness. Efforts to summarize trends across studies found that research evidence was "at best sketchy and often inclusive" (Becker, 1971, p. 391), with the relationship between religiousness and mental health being described as largely negative (Sanua, 1969), or just the opposite—that religious commitment is protective against psychopathology (Stark, 1971). The 1970s witnessed explosive growth in the literature on religion and mental health, prompting its characterization as "huge and unwieldy" (Pattison, 1978, p. 121). The National Institute of Mental Health (NIMH) annotated bibliography of empirical and theoretical publications on religion and mental health published between 1970 and 1980 listed 1,836 entries, including citations of more than 1,500 scholarly journal articles, chapters, books, and reports (Summerlin, 1980).

As programmatic research began to accumulate, a series of more sophisticated reviews of religion and mental health studies appeared in the 1980s that noted a consistently positive relationship between religion and mental health, including a meta-analysis of 24 studies of religion and psychopathology (Bergin, 1983) and a systematic review of more than 200 studies of religion in relation to outcomes as disparate as suicide, drug use, alcohol abuse, delinquent behavior, marital satisfaction, psychological distress, functional psychiatric diagnoses, and depression (Gartner, Larson, & Allen, 1991). Further, a quantitative review by Larson and associates found that two thirds of studies of religion published throughout the decade in *American Journal of Psychiatry* and *Archives of General Psychiatry* identified a positive effect of religious commitment regardless of the specific mental health indicator under study (Larson, Sherrill, Lyons, Craigie, Thielman, Greenwold, & Larson, 1992).

Since 1990, studies of religion and mental health have flourished, and based on these research findings the positive impact of religious commitment, on average, is by now well accepted (see Koenig, McCullough, & Larson, 2001). Sophisticated programs of research have been developed, such as the work of Koenig at Duke University Medical Center, editor of the authoritative *Handbook of Religion and Mental Health* (Koenig, 1998). This research has focused on religion as a resource across the natural history of disease that is important for primary prevention of mental illness in the community, as an ally in the therapeutic process for hospitalized patients, and as an important factor facilitating recovery from depression and other psychiatric illnesses (Koenig, 1999). The important role of religion in mental health was formally recognized by the inclusion in the *DSM-IV* (*Diagnostic and Statistical Manual of Mental Disorders*) of a new category acknowledging religious and spiritual problems as potential sources of psychological distress (Turner, Lukoff, Barnhouse, & Lu, 1995).

Religion, Aging, and Psychological Well-Being

In a theoretical overview published several years ago, we concisely summarized the current state of research on religion and well-being conducted by gerontologists and contrasted it with research on religion and mental health published by psychiatrists: "Within social gerontology, religious research has never been mainstream, but, unlike in psychiatry, published studies have given considerable if sporadic and unsystematic attention to mental health and psychological well-being" (Levin & Chatters, 1998b, p. 37). This summary comparison is still mostly valid, except that in recent years gerontological research on religion and well-being has become increasingly programmatic and mainstream. The volume of research produced in this area has spawned literature reviews (Levin, 1989; Koenig, 1990), meta-analyses (Witter, Stock, Okun, & Haring, 1985), and systematic reviews (Sherrill, Larson, & Greenwold, 1993), including a National Institutes of Health (NIH)-sponsored quantitative summary of empirical studies through the middle 1990s (Levin, 1997). Chapters reviewing gerontological research on religion and well-being have been included in the authoritative *Handbook of the Psychology of Aging* (McFadden, 1996b), in the edited book *Religion in Aging and Health: Theoretical Foundations and Methodological Frontiers* (Levin, 1994c), and in several comprehensive encyclopedias of gerontology (Levin, 1995, 2002; McFadden, 1996a). These reviews are unanimous in their conclusion: religion exerts, on average, a moderate, statistically significant, and mostly positive influence on dimensions of psychological well-being.

Religion, Mental Health, and Well-Being in African Americans

Throughout the empirical literatures on religion and mental health and on religion and psychological well-being, a subset of studies has sought to explore their connection within samples of African American respondents and patients or to investigate racial differences in these associations (see Ellison, 1998). Unfortunately, most of the otherwise excellent early summaries and reviews of this literature paid little or no attention to the racial composition of study samples (e.g., Becker, 1971; Bergin, 1983; Gartner et al., 1991; Koenig, 1990; Larson, Pattison, Blazer, Omran, & Kaplan, 1986; Sanua, 1969; Sherrill et al., 1993; Summerlin, 1980), perhaps because of the tendency of clinical researchers to disregard sociodemographic correlates of health and illness. To be fair, even those summaries of gerontological studies reviewed by social scientists (e.g., Witter et al., 1985; Levin, 1989; Moberg, 1990) have had little to say about race or ethnicity. It is an unfortunate fact that a large proportion of studies in this area have so ignored the potential influence of race on quality-of-life outcomes that the racial or ethnic composition of study samples has not even been reported. As one of the present authors has noted, racial and multiethnic comparative research "will not fulfill its promise if it simultaneously blurs the heterogeneity of populations" (Levin, 1997, p. 21).

The presence of an overlooked body of data on religion, mental health, and well-being among African Americans has only recently been identified through more systematic overviews of existing research published within the past couple of decades. The NIH-funded quantitative review mentioned earlier (Levin, 1997) identified 73 empirical studies from a sample of aging and social science journals between 1980 and 1994 in which one or more religious variables were included. Most of these studies were investigations of one or another dimensions of well-being, such as life satisfaction. Of these 73 studies, 47 (nearly two thirds) reported on the race or ethnicity of their study sample. Among this group, 11 studies were of African American respondents only, while 26 studies comprised multiethnic samples; of these, 13 noted the inclusion of African Americans. In total, 24 studies reported the presence of African American respondents in their study samples. However, not all of these studies focused on racial differences in religion–well-being associations nor on the presence of such an association among African Americans. In many instances, race was reported but then not used in subsequent analyses, while, in other cases, race was used solely as a sociodemographic control variable without reporting enough information about its association with other study variables to be able to discern its full effects (e.g., Strawbridge, Shema, Cohen, Roberts, & Kaplan, 1998). Even where this was not the case and where racial differences were explicitly reported or where an African American sample was used, probability sampling has been rare, outcome variables have been mostly single-item measures, and analyses have tended to be low-order and unsophisticated. Two notable exceptions, just as for research on physical health described in the previous chapter, have been the NIMH-funded programmatic work of Brown and colleagues and those studies conducted at the University of Michigan and elsewhere that have made use of data from waves of the National Survey of Black Americans (NSBA) and other large national probability surveys.

In general, research studies on religion, race, and mental health and well-being have tackled the issue of race in one of three different ways. First, there are those studies in which a binary race variable (i.e., black vs. white) has been introduced in statistical models, ostensibly in order to control for the effects of race on a presumed religion–mental-health or religion–well-being association. As discussed in the previous chapter, this is a less-than-ideal way to investigate the role or function of racial identity on a respective outcome or association (LaVeist, 1994). Many more studies of religion, mental health, and well-being have taken this approach than can be meaningfully reviewed in this chapter. Only those in which specific racial effects are reported (e.g., bivariate correlations, standardized or unstandardized regression coefficients) are cited here and discussed.

Two other types of study approaches offer a more direct means of evaluating the role of race. A second set of studies has made explicit racial comparisons in associations between respective religious variables and mental health or well-being indicators. In these studies, investigators stratified their analyses by race (i.e., black vs. white) in order to compare and contrast structural relationships across race. A third group of studies has used African American study samples exclusively. These investigations constitute much of the work produced by those of us using NSBA data and by Brown's team, and many of these studies focus on older adults or on age differences across the life course.

Studies in Which Effects of Race Are Controlled

About a dozen studies of religion, mental health, and well-being published from the 1970s through 2002 included a race variable whose effects were controlled in subsequent analyses. While this is not an ideal approach for investigating the impact of race, as noted earlier, this is not meant as a criticism of these studies, none of which was designed explicitly as a study of the effects of race. Rather, these studies were set up to investigate determinants of particular psychiatric or psychosocial outcomes, and the respective investigators, sensitive to the potential importance of race as a likely correlate of both religious participation and the outcome under study, commendably ensured that its effects were controlled in multivariable models.

Religion and Mental-Health Outcomes

Several of these studies investigated the association between measures of religiousness and clinical mental-health outcomes such as depression and anxiety. All were based on large national or regional probability samples. Most revealed statistically significant protective or buffering effects of religion. The role of race in these findings, though, is less clear. The earliest study in this category, and the only one focusing on anxiety, was an investigation of 318 randomly sampled adults from Memphis, Tennessee (Petersen & Roy, 1985). A three-item anxiety scale, developed for this study, was regressed separately onto each of five religious variables, only one of which (church attendance), was found to have a significant inverse association with anxiety. After controlling for effects of several sociodemographic variables, including a binary race variable, the moderate protective effect of church attendance actually increased somewhat. Earlier bivariate analyses had shown both greater church attendance and greater anxiety among African Americans. Two conclusions can be inferred from these findings: Race is not a critical factor in shaping the association between religion and anxiety, and other factors besides religion must mediate a race-anxiety association.

Three studies that examined religious effects on indices of depressive symptoms showed mixed race effects. Further, because of differences in analyses, how the race variable was used, and the results that were reported in these studies, it was not an easy task to tease out the impact of race and to decipher precisely how it affected the larger religion-depression relationship. In a study using data from a 1984 probability sample ($N = 401$) of metropolitan Chicago adults (Ross, 1990), strength of religious beliefs exhibited a significant protective effect on an eight-item depression measure based on the Langner scale. This finding resulted from an analysis that controlled for effects of six sociodemographic variables, including race, that had no net effect on depression. These results suggested a minimal impact of race on the association between religion and depression.

A study using data from the 1998 General Social Survey (GSS) topic module on religion ($N = 337$) found significant direct and indirect effects of several religious variables and scales on a six-item depression index comprising items similar to the CES-D. In a multivariate structural model, fundamentalism was found to be a moderate predictor of depression, while protective effects of religious attendance and prayer were mediated respectively by church-based social support and religious coping. This model controlled for effects of race, which preliminary analyses found to be unrelated to depression but strongly associated with prayer, religious coping, fundamentalism, and religious attendance, such that higher scores were found among African Americans (Nooney & Woodrum, 2002). These results suggest that racial status may have antecedent effects that condition both higher and lower depression, depending upon whether one endorses fundamentalist views.

A third study used data collected in 1987–1989 as part of the Durham (North Carolina) Veterans Administration Mental Health Survey (Koenig et al., 1992). This investigation included both cross-sectional ($N = 850$) and longitudinal ($N = 202$) components and focused on a probability sample of men aged 65 and older, 28.3% of whom were African Americans and 22.2% of whom were classified as black Protestants. Through various analyses, African American race was determined to be protective against depression, as measured by the 30-item self-rated General Depression Scale (GDS), specifically because of a strong association with religious coping. In bivariate analyses, religious coping was used more by African Americans and black Protestants; religious coping was inversely related to depression; and there was less depression among both African Americans in general and black Protestants. A variety of cross-sectional and longitudinal models elucidated these relationships further.

Religion and Psychological Well-Being

Half a dozen studies in this category investigated religious effects on indicators of positive well-being, typically life satisfaction or happiness. All of these were based on data collected from large national or regional probability surveys, mostly various waves of the General Social Survey (GSS).

The same caveats as for the previous group of studies hold here as well: Variations in the construction of analyses and the reporting of associations with race-related variables limits the interpretation of racial effects. Four of these studies used data from GSS samples collected in the 1970s and 1980s. Throughout these studies, life satisfaction was measured through a summary index drawing on a pool of longtime GSS items assessing domain-specific appraisals, and each study used a different number of these items. Religion was operationalized in a variety of ways: religious attendance, devotional intensity, religious affiliation, strength of religious affiliation, closeness to God, images of the divine, existential certainty, and divine interaction. Not all of these variables were analyzed in conjunction with race, but general information on religion, race, and well-being can be derived from these studies.

Data from the 1973 GSS sample of adult Americans ($N = 1,347$) was used to model predictors of life satisfaction, including religious attendance (Clemente & Sauer, 1976). Frequent attendance, a significant bivariate correlate of life satisfaction, was also a significant predictor of life satisfaction after controlling for the effects of several sociodemographic variables including race, itself a strong correlate of life satisfaction (with higher scores among whites). The religious effect on well-being in this study thus did not appear to be reduced to a significant extent by race. The 1983 GSS was used to model effects of a variety of religious and secular constructs on life satisfaction (Ellison, Gay, & Glass, 1989). Using a strategy of hierarchical ordinary least squares regression, measures of religious attendance and devotional intensity exhibited strong and significant effects on life satisfaction after controlling for effects of numerous sociodemographic and sociological variables and constructs, including race. In this study, non-white racial status was associated with significantly lower life satisfaction in the baseline model, yet controlling for its effects did not prevent the appearance of religion–life-satisfaction effects. These findings thus mirror the results of the 1973 study.

Pooled data from the 1983 and 1984 GSS samples were used to explore whether several religious measures significantly predicted scores on four well-being indicators (Pollner, 1989). Race (higher scores denoting whites) was strongly associated with global happiness, life satisfaction, and marital happiness, but not with life excitement. Despite controlling for effects of race and several other sociodemographic variables, two religious measures exhibited statistically significant net effects on well-being. Religious attendance was a significant predictor of global happiness and marital happiness, and divine relations (a questionable composite of closeness to God, prayer, and history of an out-of-body experience) was a significant predictor of all four well-being indicators. Once again, even after controlling for racial effects, religion–well-being associations remained. A later GSS-based study used data from the 1988 sample to investigate religious predictors of indicators of life satisfaction and personal happiness (Ellison, 1991b). After a series of hierarchical ordinary least squares regressions that controlled for several sociodemographic and sociological variables, including race, religious attendance was not a significant predictor for either outcome. However, a measure of existential certainty was strongly predictive of both life satisfaction and personal happiness. Life satisfaction was significantly associated with denominational status for individuals who were a nondenominational Protestant, a liberal Protestant, or a Mormon or Jehovah's Witness, while Catholic affiliation was associated with lower personal happiness. In no analysis of either well-being measure did race exhibit any significant effects in any model. As in the other GSS studies, race was not a significant factor in the relationship between religion and well-being.

Two additional studies have explored this issue in samples other than the GSS. Data from the Akron Area Survey of 1985 were used to examine the association between religious measures and several original measures of well-being in a sample of 560 adults (Poloma & Pendleton, 1990). Bivariate analyses revealed that race was not significantly associated with religious satisfaction, life satisfaction, or happiness, but that whites had less existential well-being and less negative affect. Religious satisfaction, in turn, was strongly associated with life satisfaction, existential well-being, and happiness, but not with negative affect. The absence of a full set of associations among race, religious satisfaction, and well-being effectively precluded an interpretation of their interrelationships in this study.

The most sophisticated study in this category is a structural-equation analysis of older-adult respondents from three national probability surveys (Levin & Chatters, 1998a). Data were from a combination of older-adult and African American oversamples or subsamples from the 1974 Myth and Reality of Aging (MRA) survey ($N = 2,183$; ages 65 and older); the second Quality of American Life (QAL) survey ($N = 1,056$; ages 55 and older), conducted in 1978; and the first wave of the Americans' Changing Lives (ACL) survey ($N = 1,553$; ages 60 and older), from 1986. More details of this study are provided in the previous chapter. Findings revealed statistically significant religious effects on psychological well-being in two of the samples, specifically a significant net effect of organizational religiosity on items taken from the Affect Balance Scale in the QAL and a significant net effect of subjective religiosity on a composite of selected Life Satisfaction Index-A and Center for Epidemiologic Studies Depression (CES-D) items in the ACL. In both data sets, African American respondents were significantly more religious according to all religious constructs; they also had a lower level of well-being in the ACL. Similar to most of the other studies reviewed in this section, controlling for the effects of a binary race variable, in concert with several other sociodemographic variables, did not affect the presence of significant religion–well-being associations.

Studies That Investigate Racial Differences

A smaller group of studies has provided a more explicit and comprehensive look at potential racial differences in the effects of religiousness on mental health and well-being. The previous groups of studies simply controlled for effects of a binary race variable (i.e., black-white), thus limiting the race-related inferences able to be drawn. However, the present studies took a different approach by examining religion–well-being associations separately by race, thus enabling a comparison of the direction and magnitude of effects in African Americans and whites. With one exception, these studies made use of large, well-known probability samples consisting of standard measures of religiousness and validated indices of depressive symptoms, positive well-being, or similar outcome measures. The most methodologically limited study used data collected from a convenience sample of 144 undergraduate psychology students at SUNY-Buffalo, 46% of whom were African Americans and 41% of whom were whites (Blaine & Crocker, 1995). This study sought to identify racial differences in religion and well-being associations, as assessed by several measures of religion (religious attendance, salience of religious beliefs, and three scales assessing types of religious attributions) and well-being (self-esteem, life satisfaction, hopelessness, a composite well-being scale, and the short form of the Beck Depression Inventory). Based principally on analyses of correlation coefficients, the authors found that neither religious attendance nor salience of religious beliefs were related to any well-being measure among whites. In contrast, among African Americans, frequent religious attendance was associated with greater life satisfaction, and salient beliefs were associated with greater life satisfaction, less depression, less hopelessness, and greater overall well-being. Further, meaning-enhancing religious attributions were significantly associated with overall well-being among African Americans but not among whites.

The remaining studies in this section were based upon large multistage probability surveys; several had longitudinal designs, and all but one employed a strategy of multivariable modeling. Two of these studies were early investigations using data from the GSS. Four of these studies were more recent investigations using data from the two most notable multisite psychiatric-epidemiologic studies conducted to date, the NIMH Epidemiologic Catchment Area (ECA) Program and the Established Populations for the Epidemiologic Study of the Elderly (EPESE).

Data on older adults aged 65 years and older pooled from the 1973–1977 GSS samples ($N = 1,493$) were used to examine racial differences in the relationship between several religious variables and several measures of well-being (Steinitz, 1980). Frequent religious attendance was significantly associated with all four well-being measures (happiness, life exciting, family satisfaction, satisfaction with where you live) only among whites; there were no significant effects among African Americans. Likewise, for belief in life after death, only among whites was this associated with an exciting life and satisfaction with where you live. Confidence in organized religion, however, was strongly associated with family satisfaction among African Americans only.

A second GSS study using data on 25- to 54-year-olds pooled from the 1972–1982 surveys (St. George & McNamara, 1984) found that strength of religious affiliation was a significant net predictor of global happiness in both genders and both races but was much more salient among African Americans. This same variable also significantly predicted a measure of excitement in life, but only among whites. The same pattern of associations was found for religious attendance: Much stronger impact on global happiness in African American men and women and an effect on life excitement only among whites. Using data collected from 1982 to 1983 for the Durham (North Carolina) ECA study ($N = 2,894$), effects of religious affiliation, attendance, and devotion were modeled hierarchically on the Diagnostic Interview Schedule measure of depressive symptoms (Ellison, 1995). Among whites only, frequent religious attendance was associated with fewer symptoms net of the effects of other factors. Among African Americans only, absence of a religious affiliation was strongly associated with more depressive symptoms. In both racial groups, religious devotion (i.e., prayer) was associated with more symptoms with little evidence of a racial difference.

In another study conducted in the Durham area—the Duke EPESE ($N = 3,007$), using data collected from 1986 to 1989—striking racial differences were found in the longitudinal protective effects of frequent religious attendance on depression in community-dwelling older adults aged 64 and over with cancer (Musick, Koenig, Hays, & Cohen, 1998). Among whites, religious attendance exhibited no gross or net effects on any of the four dimensions of the CES-D scale (depressed affect, positive affect, somatic-retarded activities, interpersonal relations). Among African Americans, however, strong and significant religious attendance effects were found for positive affect at the bivariate level, after controlling for the effects of baseline positive affect and the other religious measures, and after adjusting for several sociodemographic, sociological, and health-related variables. These findings contrast with those from the New Haven EPESE study ($N = 2,812$), which used data on adults aged 65 and older collected from 1982 to 1985 (Idler & Kasl, 1992). The investigators sought to identify whether measures of religiousness exhibited protective effects on a variety of health-related outcomes, including depressive symptoms. When baseline depression was included in the model, neither public nor private religiousness had any effect on depression. These analyses were rerun separately for African American and white Protestants, but still no effects emerged.

The most recent study of racial differences in religion and mental health also made use of data from the New Haven EPESE, including follow-up data from 1988 (Van Ness & Kasl, 2003). In contrast to other studies in this area, the investigators focused on a cognitive rather than affective outcome: cognitive dysfunction as assessed by scores on the Short Portable Mental Status Questionnaire. Dichotomizing the outcome as intact versus any dysfunction yielded a significant protective effect for at least weekly religious attendance on cognitive dysfunction in 1985, three years after baseline. This protective effect was no longer evident in 1988. Logistic regression analyses were then repeated after racial stratification. Religious attendance was found to be a strong protective factor only among whites.

African American Study Samples

The ideal way to study effects of religion on psychological distress or well-being in African Americans, naturally, is to use samples of African American respondents. This is much easier said than done, as few large probability surveys of African Americans exist that simultaneously include measures of both religious involvement and mental health or well-being (unless one is fortunate enough to obtain funding for a more sophisticated study involving original data collection in an African American population). By default, then, one must rely upon small community or clinical samples of convenience or the proportionately small subset of African American respondents in most health surveys. Accordingly, nearly all of the best research in this category, which is reviewed in this section, falls into one of two groups: five mostly clinical studies of depressive symptoms, all the work of Diane Brown and her colleagues; and eight studies of mostly positive well-being outcomes such as life satisfaction, five of which used data from the NSBA or other population-based data sources from the University of Michigan.

Religion and Depressive Symptoms

Five studies of religion and depression by Diane Brown and Lawrence Gary and their colleagues have been based on data from exclusively African American probability samples. Together these studies make a strong case for a protective effect of religious involvement on depression in this population. An early study used data from a sample of noninstitutionalized African American adult men ($N = 142$) from a large northeastern U.S. city (Gary, 1985). Through analysis of variance, differences in mean CES-D scores were examined across a measure of participation in personal, group, or institutional religious activities (ranked into three groups of high, medium, and low religiosity). The mean CES-D score in this sample was 12.11. A very clear protective trend was apparent in the findings, such that low, medium, and high religiosity were associated with decreasing CES-D scores (12.78, 12.08, and 11.30, respectively). These results did not quite attain statistical significance, however, due principally to the small numbers of respondents in each category. Data from a community survey of African American adults from Richmond, Virginia ($N = 451$) were used to investigate the relationship between several measures of religiousness and scores on the CES-D (Brown, Ndubuisi, & Gary, 1990). In this study, a 10-item summary index of religiosity was constructed from several items assessing institutional and nongroup religious activities, as well as attitudes about religion. Analyses revealed a significant inverse association between religiosity and depressive symptoms. As in the prior study, religiosity was divided into three categories; for both men and women, CES-D scores were lower in successively higher categories of religiousness. Comparison of slopes revealed that this protective association was stronger in men than in women. Further analyses of religiosity-stress interactions provided evidence of an additional stress-buffering effect of religion on depression. Specifically, religion buffered the effect of stress on depression for men who had a personal injury, but not women.

The absence of a stress-buffering effect for other types of stress and in women was borne out in an earlier analysis using this sample (Brown & Gary, 1987). They speculated that the lack of a significant interaction between religiosity and stress may be attributable to (a) consistently high levels of religiosity maintained by this population on a daily basis that limited the variance of this construct, and (b) religiosity being directly protective against depressive symptoms in a way that was not conditioned by the presence of other stressors or crises (Brown et al., 1990).

Another study of religion and depression by these investigators that was based on a sample of 537 African American adult men from an eastern U.S.

city (Brown & Gary, 1994) again used the CES-D to assess depressive symptoms. Regression analysis results revealed significant protective effects for both religiosity and presence of a denominational affiliation. After controlling for effects of a variety of sociodemographic variables, denominational affiliation maintained a significant protective effect against depression. A subsequent investigation (Brown, Ahmed, Gary, & Milburn, 1995), with a more explicitly clinical and epidemiologic focus, used data from a sample of 865 African American adult men from Norfolk, Virginia. In this study, the past-year prevalence of depressive symptoms was assessed using the DIS instrument for diagnosing major depressive episodes. Based on results of their previous studies, a measure of religious affiliation was included in a list of potential protective factors. The investigators found that the one-year prevalence rate of major depression among respondents without a religious affiliation was 6.4%, the highest for any category of any exposure variable in the study except for poor health status (6.9%). For respondents with a religious affiliation, the prevalence rate was only 2.8%. After adjusting for effects of variables measuring sociodemographic and household characteristics, health, stress, and family history of mental illness, the prevalence odds associated with lack of a religious affiliation was no longer statistically significant.

Religion and Positive Well-Being

Eight studies have examined religious effects on measures of positive well-being, such as life satisfaction or happiness, among African Americans. Three of the early studies in this area were based on nonprobability samples of small numbers of respondents recruited from local populations on the east coast. Although the findings from these less representative samples are not generalizable to the population as a whole because each of these studies focused specifically on older adults, their findings underscore the generally salutary influence of religion within this life-course stage. The earliest study (Heisel & Faulkner, 1982) examined how religiosity and changes in religiosity with age affected well-being in a sample of 122 adults aged 51 and older from New Jersey. Overall religiosity was significantly associated with life satisfaction and, accordingly, declines in religiosity were associated with less satisfaction and less happiness. A study of 98 elderly churchgoers from Central Pennsylvania (Walls & Zarit, 1991) found that well-being, as assessed by the PGC, was predicted by receipt of church-based support. This finding pointed out that religion may impact on well-being in this population in multifaceted ways, and not just as a result of the positive affect or satisfaction resulting from a perception that one is personally religious. Finally, a study of 166

New Yorkers aged 65 and over (Coke, 1992) identified significant bivariate associations between both subjective religiosity and frequency of religious attendance and life satisfaction as assessed by the Diener measure. Interestingly, multiple regression analyses controlling for effects of other variables revealed that subjective religiosity was the strongest predictor of life satisfaction in the overall sample. Moreover, among men, it was the only predictor, explaining an enormous 27% of the variance in life satisfaction, and, in women, was a stronger determinant of well-being than even health.

The other five studies in this category were the work of social scientists using the NSBA or data from other national surveys based at the University of Michigan. Results from these studies underscore a salutary role of religion for psychological well-being in this population, nicely complementing the studies reviewed in the previous section that identified a protective effect of religion for psychological distress. The beneficial mental-health impact of religion for African Americans, then, appears to span a couple of the early stages of the natural history of disease: from primary prevention of psychiatric illness in clinical and community populations to promotion of well-being among samples of the general population. Two studies directed by Krause identified positive effects of dimensions of religiousness on psychosocial characteristics that often serve as personal resources used to cope with life stress. Using data on African Americans aged 60 years and older ($N = 448$) oversampled from the Americans' Changing Lives survey, Krause (1992) tested a sophisticated, multifactorial model positing links among religion and a variety of other psychosocial and health-related constructs. Results identified a strong, statistically significant effect of subjective religiosity on self-esteem, which, in turn, strongly protected against depression. In data on a similar age cohort taken from the NSBA ($N = 511$), a multi-item index of organizational religiosity was also strongly predictive of self-esteem, and a measure of non-organizational religiosity (including a self-assessment of religiousness) was a significant predictor of mastery or personal control (Krause & Tran, 1989).

Three studies of religion and life satisfaction in African Americans have been conducted using waves of the NSBA. Each study introduced a different innovation in empirical research on this topic, mainly involving age-related or temporal effects. These include the examination of hypothesized moderating effects for several variables, including age; investigation of the age-invariance of a model of relationships between religion and life satisfaction; and a longitudinal examination of these relationships across four waves of data collected over a 13-year period. One study presented results of analyses that tested effects of several religious variables on life satisfaction controlling for the effects of numerous sociodemographic factors, family-related variables, and stress (Ellison & Gay, 1990). A key feature of these analyses was examination of both the main effects of age and effects of interactions between age and religious participation, all while stratifying data by region of residence (i.e., southern vs. non-southern). Among southern African Americans, life satisfaction, which was strongly conditioned by age, was predicted by Catholic affiliation even after controlling for age effects. Among non-southern respondents, religious predictors of life satisfaction included Baptist affiliation and religious attendance. These findings emerged even after accounting for the effects of significant interactions between age and attendance and age and subjective religiosity. Regardless of region, then, there were significant religious predictors of life satisfaction in African Americans, and these were not completely explained by the tendency of both life satisfaction and some expressions of religiousness to be higher in successively older age cohorts.

A subsequent study (Levin, Chatters, & Taylor, 1995), discussed in detail in the previous chapter, used NSBA data to test a structural model positing effects of three religious dimensions on a three-item measure of life satisfaction, mediated by effects of physical health. Findings revealed that organizational religiosity, a composite measure including religious attendance, was a significant determinant of life satisfaction even after controlling for effects of health and every other religious and sociodemographic construct in the study. Especially remarkable was that this net effect of organized religious participation on well-being was about as large as, or larger than, the gross (i.e., uncontrolled) effect of health on life satisfaction. Moreover, this pattern of effects was found to be invariant when assessed separately in three age cohorts (≤ 30, 31–54, and ≥ 55). These results were quite groundbreaking, as they challenged the conventional belief that health status and socioeconomic status were the primary determinants of general well-being in adults (see Levin & Tobin, 1995), regardless of age or race.

The most recent study of religion and positive well-being using data from the NSBA was a comprehensive investigation of longitudinal effects of eight different religious indicators over a 13-year period (Levin & Taylor, 1998). Results revealed both contemporaneous and longitudinal effects of religion on well-being. At the baseline wave of data collection, in 1979 and 1980, whether bivariately, controlling for effects of health only, or controlling for effects of health and seven sociodemographic variables ($N = 1,988$), all eight religious variables were statistically significant predictors of both life satisfaction and happiness in all analyses: 48 significant findings out of 48 tested. At the fourth data wave, in 1992, the same analyses were rerun, this time including the RAND Mental Health Inventory (MHI) psychological distress scale ($N = 601$). All eight religious variables had significant effects on one or more of the outcome measures, controlling for other factors. Finally, a two-wave panel analysis was constructed that examined effects of baseline religious measures on wave-4 well-being measures. Bivariately, all eight religious variables predicted life satisfaction and/or happiness 13 years later. After comprehensive controls for effects of baseline well-being and wave-4 religion and health, however, these effects were minimized.

To summarize, considerable empirical research conducted over a period of at least 20 years points to a significant influence of dimensions of religiousness on indicators of mental health and psychological well-being that seems to vary by, but is not explained away by, race. This is expressed in several ways: (a) by studies of psychiatric outcomes such as depressive symptoms in which religiousness exhibited protective effects even after controlling for effects of race; (b) by studies of positive well-being outcomes, typically life satisfaction, in which positive religious effects also were not explained away by controlling for racial effects; (c) by studies using samples in which black-white differences were found in the presence and magnitude of religious effects on mental health or well-being; (d) by studies of African Americans, especially older adults, in which religiousness was a salient protective factor against depression; and (e) by studies of African Americans in which various expressions of religious involvement were correlates or predictors of positive well-being or other psychosocial outcomes. Whether or not religion is more salient a preventive resource among African Americans than among whites is still an open question. But its importance as a generally protective factor for psychological distress and well-being among African Americans is strongly supported.

Religion, Race, and Mental Health: Directions for Future Research

The findings reviewed in this chapter show clearly that religion, broadly defined, represents a salient force for mental health among African Americans. Religion exhibits its influence both directly—as a protective factor that serves to prevent subsequent mental illness and psychological distress—and as a moderating or buffering factor that serves to alleviate the otherwise deleterious impact of life stress and physical challenges on subsequent mental health and well-being. Moreover, religion seems to exert both disease-preventive and health-promotive influences in this population. These conclusions suggest several important future directions for research.

Several next steps can be identified that can advance research on religion, mental health, and well-being in African Americans beyond the stage of simple epidemiologic analysis where it has remained for the past couple of decades. By now, it is well established that rates of depression and scores on well-being scales vary, on average, by levels of religiousness such that more religious survey respondents or patients are less depressed and have greater life satisfaction and happiness. This we know with increasing certainty. Other more substantively interesting questions, however, have gone largely unaddressed while researchers continue to investigate the same relationships as always, in the same way, varying only the study samples.

One important issue is to identify specifically what kinds of religious expression are most salutary for well-being among African Americans and what kinds are less so. Saying that religion is good for you is a lot like saying that eating food is good for you. No doubt, an epidemiologic study following people who eat and those who do not eat for several years would find a considerably higher rate of morbidity and mortality in those who starved. But such a study would tell us nothing about what particular foods are good for what people, in what amount, in what circumstances, and why this is so in terms of specific nutrients, and for whom certain foods cause harm. There is a danger that research on religious factors in mental health and well-being is starting to fall into the same trap. A recent effort to develop and validate a wide variety of religious measures for use in health-related research (Fetzer Institute/National Institute on Aging, 1999) is an important step in broadening the kinds of questions that researchers in this field might consider.

A second important issue for researchers is to differentiate between the epidemiologic and clinical roles of religion. More specifically, there is a need to distinguish between religion's protective or preventive function and its ostensible healing function, including its role in recovery from illness. The natural history of disease is a variable too often overlooked in epidemiologic and medical studies (Levin & Chatters, 1998b; Levin, in press-a, in press-b), regardless of topic, and is especially important here in light of the controversy surrounding purported evidence of a healing effect of certain religious activities such as prayer (see Levin, in press-a, in press-b). Findings from sociological or epidemiologic surveys identifying significant associations between religious measures and mental-health outcomes do not, of course, in any way imply that religion heals disease, but unfortunately this distinction is typically lost in portrayals of this research in both the popular media and among groups of uninformed skeptics.

A third important focus of further study should be issues related to the diversity of the African American population. Studies whose sole approach to race is to control for effects of a binary race variable serve to reinforce the erroneous view that African American racial status is a monolithic entity. The African American category, as does every other broad ethnic label, masks considerable heterogeneity—socioeconomically and culturally—and no more so than with respect to religion. The African American religious experience in the diaspora is characterized by probably a wider mix of affiliations, institutions, normative practices, beliefs, and sanctioned values and experiences than for any other North American social group identified by ethnic or national origin (see, e.g., Lincoln, 1974a). It is hard to fathom how the main features of the religious life of members of southern holiness sects; urban Muslims; middle-class mainline Protestants; young, upwardly mobile, suburban Pentecostal converts; and Gulf-Coast Roman Catholics could have a lot in common, much less exhibit an identical pattern of effects on indicators of well-being or quality of life.

A fourth important issue that needs to be studied is how patterns or trajectories of religiousness evolve over the life course. Mapping these patterns among African Americans, especially in relation to potentially concomitant patterns of psychological well-being, would be an exciting challenge, both methodologically and theoretically. This kind of dynamic modeling of transitions and trajectories has already been proposed for health (Clipp, Pavalko, & Elder, 1992), and its application to religion–well-being relationships will be a major frontier for religious gerontology in the coming years.

Finally, historical and phenomenological studies are needed of African American expressions of spirituality and modes of health-related behavior in the context of a longstanding history of "therapeutic pluralism" (Raboteau, 1986). Scholars have documented the coexistence of respective professional, folk, and religious systems of etiology, diagnosis, and treatment that have existed side by side, and hand in hand, since African Americans first arrived in North America. Just as syncretisms of Christian and West African religion continue to survive in rural and urban Afro-Caribbean communities (e.g., *vodun, pukkumina, shango, cumfa, santeria*), so, too, do synergistic combinations of allopathic and religious perspectives on disease and healing continue to evolve both in the Western hemisphere (e.g., Brown, 1989; Griffith, 1982) and in Africa (see Appiah-Kubi, 1989; Janzen, 1989). Two additional observations: This commingling of scientific and traditional orientations is especially visible in relation to psychiatric illness, and it is by no means unique among African Americans (Kiev, 1964).

In closing, ever since the formative years of psychology and psychiatry, religion has been the focus of considerable scholarly writing by many of the leading minds in these fields. Beginning in the late 19th Century, when the psychology of religion emerged as a field of study, and continuing into the 1920s, noted figures such as Pratt, Hall, Leuba, Starbuck, James, and Freud devoted their attention to religion (Beit-Hallahmi, 1989). This interest did not last, however, and the study of religion and mental health soon fell dormant. Renewed scientific and scholarly consideration of the interface of religion and mental health has by now been solicited for more than four decades (see Academy of Religion and Mental Health, 1959). Yet the same general, descriptive sorts of questions posed in studies in the 1960s are still being emphasized. For African Americans, much of this descriptive analysis has made its point: Religion is a potentially important factor for mental health and well-being. It is now time to probe deeper into African American religious life in order to answer some of the more sophisticated questions that can be posed regarding how religion influences mental health and well-being.

Chapter 10

Conclusions and Implications

O ver the past 20 years, social and behavioral science research on the role of religion in the lives of African Americans has grown in both amount and quality. Overall, there has been marked development and improvement in conceptual and methodological approaches to studying religion within the African American, as well as the general, population. Current programs of research, which are based in solid theoretical and conceptual frameworks, use sophisticated analysis models and strive toward understanding the linkages between religion and relevant social, behavioral, and health factors, have made important contributions to research and scholarship on this topic. This book reviewed research on the role of religion in the lives of African Americans in several key areas: religious activities, prayer and its role in coping, use of ministers, support from church members, negative interaction within churches, and religion's effects on physical health and mental health and well-being. In addition, narratives from a focus group study involving African American men and women provided important and detailed information about the lived experience of religion in relation to a number of these topic areas.

The introductory chapter to this volume articulated a number of specific goals that we had in mind in writing this book. We were interested in developing a book that would provide an overview of current research linking religion to the social behaviors and health status of African Americans. Further, we felt it important and vital to highlight those research efforts that were based in current theory and conceptual models of these relationships, thus contributing more broadly to the development of knowledge in these areas and addressing a noticeable lack of adequate theoretical development in early research. Along with this, research efforts that reflected important innovations in the conceptualization of various forms of religious participation, and that used appropriate study methodologies (e.g., sampling, measurement, study designs) and data analysis strategies, were given particular attention. Our overall goal was to provide an overview of religious involvement that emphasized the diversity and variability of these orientations and behaviors in the African American population, as well as an appreciation for the dynamic and continuing influences of historical, societal, economic, and community contexts in patterning these phenomena.

Finally, we wanted the book to be of interest and practical use to a wide audience of health and social welfare practitioners, members of the clergy, and students in these and related fields. Increasingly, clinicians and practitioners in social work, public health, nursing, psychology, and medicine are asked to address questions of religion as they relate to their clients and patients. The development of specialized courses and programs of study in religion and spirituality in professional schools is a testament to the growing importance of these issues for health and social welfare practice. Further, many theological seminaries and schools of divinity recognize the importance of addressing the social welfare and physical and mental health needs of their congregations. This interest is reflected in graduate training in areas such as pastoral counseling that combine education in both divinity studies and clinical counseling and the growth of programs that offer joint MSW (Master of Social Work) and Master of Divinity degrees (e.g., University of Chicago, Boston College). The growing rapprochement between religious and clerical training, pastoral studies, and the health and social welfare professions signals a need for the wider accessibility and use of social and behavioral science research and knowledge on religion.

Both health and social welfare practitioners and professional clergy should be cognizant of the multifaceted role of religion in shaping a variety of health and social behaviors. Secular helping professionals (e.g., social workers, public health educators, psychologists, nurses, physicians) need to be aware of the nature and meaning of religion for their clients and patients and to be able to evaluate and employ research findings critically in the development of individual interventions, treatment plans, and programs. Members of the clergy and those in the religious helping professions need to understand the methods and practices of the social behavioral sciences and the relevance of research findings for the health and social and psychological well-being of congregation members and the functioning of the church. Unfortunately, all too often social and behavioral science research on religion is of little practical use to practitioners and clergy because the crucial step in translating research findings and developing implications for practice and ministry is missing or incomplete (exceptions to this are Pargament, 1997; Koenig, 1998; Koenig, McCullough, & Larson, 2001). In this, the last chapter of the book, we turn our attention to considering concluding remarks, suggestions regarding the practical implications of this work as a whole, and a discussion of current data collection efforts.

Chapter Review and Implications

A considerable amount of research verifies that religion and religious concerns are of particular importance to the African American population. The overall profile of religious involvement includes indicators of formal religious participation, as well as personal devotional activities and subjective assessments of religiosity. The collection of research findings provides a broader appreciation of the independent effects of sociodemographic factors on religious involvement across discrete samples of African American adults. Collectively, these findings demonstrate a general consistency across independent samples of respondents that were collected at various points in time, thus providing greater confidence in the unique contributions of select factors such as gender, age, and region for understanding differences in religious participation.

Overall, these findings suggest that the various statuses and roles that people occupy may be important in patterning levels of religious involvement, and, further, these differences may, in turn, relate to disparities in access to the resources (e.g., social support) that are available in religious organizations. Women, older adults, and Southerners are highly invested in religious pursuits and, thus, may be particularly advantaged in terms of church resources and experience greater benefit from such involvement. Conversely, there may be groups of individuals who are potentially overlooked with respect to the types of informal and formal services and access to social networks and interaction in churches. Religion and religious participation is a particularly important factor in the lives of the elderly. Noted declines in health among the elderly are frequently associated with decreases in formal religious activities such as church attendance. Church attendance is a crucial indicator for this group as it provides access to social resources in the church and important opportunities for social interaction and contact. Although older individuals who are restricted in attending church may use other religious outlets (e.g., print and electronic religious media), the social losses attendant to ill health may exacerbate existing health problems. Similarly, persons whose circumstances or statuses are stigmatized by the church (e.g., divorced persons, persons with HIV/AIDS) may, by choice, be less inclined to attend church and thus receive less assistance from these networks. Finally, although there is relatively little systematic information on religious involvement among adolescents, they represent a special group that has traditionally been the focus of formal church programming (e.g., youth and young adult ministries). The involvement of adolescents in churches provides a prime opportunity for primary intervention with youth around the broad issues of physical and mental health and personal and social relationships.

Turning to a consideration of prayer and its uses in coping with life problems, the research literature suggests that prayer is a vital and integral part of religious life that fulfills a number of functions for black Americans. Prayer, when used as a strategy for positive coping, may be particularly beneficial to those experiencing life difficulties. For example, at least one of the functions of prayer in coping with difficult life problems centers on its role in regulating emotions and reducing stress and worry. However, prayer as a means to cope with problems may also involve negative forms of religious coping that are detrimental to coping outcomes and adjustment. Nominal assessments of whether or not an individual prays when coping with a problem, without consideration of the specific substance of prayer, may mask its negative content (e.g., being punished by God) as a form of negative coping. In these instances, prayer would be paradoxically associated with greater depression and psychological symptoms, poorer life quality, and less sociability.

Finally, beyond the fact that people often turn first to clergy and religious resources when responding to problematic situations, we have little information about how and when individuals enlist different sources of support and engage in different types of help-seeking strategies. If prayer is used early in the coping process to reduce perceived threat of a problem, it may forestall other efforts and result in significant delays in seeking formal assistance for problems. For example, upon detecting a suspicious physical symptom that may be an indicator of serious disease, a person may decide to pray about the problem. In and of itself, this initial step may be important in reducing worry and stress associated with the problem. Without adequate follow-up, however, the use of prayer in isolation from other actions may be potentially detrimental to health. These and other examples suggest that there is considerably more that we need to know about the personal and social circumstances that are associated with the use of prayer in coping.

Clergy, and particularly senior ministers, are pivotal in determining the church's mission, interpreting and applying church doctrine to life issues, and in defining and forging relationships with outside groups and organizations, including social service and health agencies (Caldwell, Chatters, Billingsley, & Taylor, 1995; Lincoln & Mamiya, 1990). Given the prominence of clergy in these matters, we would like to entertain a number of broader implications and suggestions about how collaborative partnerships between clergy and health and social service providers and practitioners can be fostered (see Taylor, Ellison, Chatters, Levin, & Lincoln, 2000, and Chatters, 2000, for more detailed discussions of implications for practitioners).

Health and human service practitioners need to understand the place and status of churches in their communities. This might involve a systematic assessment of churches and other religious institutions residing in the service delivery area and surrounding communities. At the most fundamental level, this would involve an overall census of churches within the community that would include both larger churches that have an established history in the community as well as smaller storefront churches. On a more detailed level, it is important to understand the current programs and services that operate within an individual black church, the history of their development, and their existing (or potential) connections with similar programs organized by city, state, and federal agencies. These and other factors provide some indication of the resources and capacities inherent in churches and their possible orientation toward partnerships with health and human service practitioners.

In the effort to familiarize clergy and church members with the services that are provided by their agency, health and human service practitioners should also be involved in outreach activities to various religious institutions in their service delivery area. These outreach activities could include individual meetings with clergy and specific groups within the church (e.g., health boards), distribution of written materials, and informational presentations about the agency that take place during religious services and other events. Further, given clergy's pivotal role as gatekeepers for formal services, it would be particularly important to provide ministers with information about the specific referral procedures used at the agency. One or more agency staff could function as liaisons to area churches and would be responsible for establishing a point of contact and a channel of communication. Working in close partnership with the church's ministerial staff would provide access to the congregation and confer legitimacy to the church liaison and the agency itself.

A partnership model in which the needs and agenda of the church are given priority should guide the development of programs with religious institutions. These types of endeavors have been very successful in black churches. A variety of health programs (e.g., blood pressure screening, nutrition, stress reduction, smoking cessation, dental health screenings, exercise and health promotion, and general health awareness fairs) have been conducted in black churches in partnership with community health care agencies. Along similar lines, social service agencies and churches could capitalize on their unique and complementary resources to develop grant proposals for church-based programs. Working alliances of this sort may be particularly important in the current political atmosphere in which both federal and state governments are increasingly channeling funds for social service programs directly to churches.

Health and human service practitioners could function as resources for clergy and lay leaders who may be ill prepared to deal with some of the more serious problems confronting church members. In-service training programs for clergy may be particularly helpful for assessing whether a church member needs a referral for formal services (e.g., emergency referral for suicidal behavior, violent tendencies toward others). Conversely, clergy could provide in-service training to social workers on the history and dynamics of the congregation, the church's self-defined mission and purpose (e.g., social justice, individual salvation), and generally how church leadership interprets and applies religious beliefs and practices in relation to concrete life problems (e.g., marital and family difficulties). Collaborations of this sort might be particularly useful for clients who are facing especially difficult life problems (e.g., illness, disability, and death). For example, clergy could address issues of personal bereavement in relation to religious beliefs and discuss how individuals use religion to construct meaning in the face of devastating personal loss. Clergy frequently face issues of this sort, so their experiences may be useful to health and human service providers in understanding how to counsel clients and patients about spiritual concerns.

As this discussion suggests, there are a number of useful and exciting possibilities for linking clergy and health and human service practitioners. However, there are several obstacles that may limit the development of effective partnerships, such as conflicts in the perspectives and values held by professional human services and religious institutions. Health, social service, and religious institutions share many common goals and orientations regarding the provision of support and services to individuals, families, and communities. However, there are possible differences in how they define problematic personal behaviors (e.g., as illness or moral limitation), the appropriate measures used to ameliorate the condition, and the desired goals of intervention. Potential conflicts over basic beliefs, values, and the goals of programs represent a serious challenge to partnerships. Further, these partnerships involve a number of difficult ethical issues. Ministers may be reluctant to develop sexual education and AIDS prevention programs because they are inconsistent with their doctrinal beliefs. A religious response to these issues may focus on the development of abstinence-only programs, while health providers may see abstinence as one of several possible intervention aims. Finally, church and health and human service partnerships involve complicated issues of confidentiality and privileged communication between church members, ministers, and practitioners. Faced with these important issues, social service providers and clergy will have to find ways to resolve these differences, while at the same time preserving the integrity of the helping relationship and strengthening their partnership.

Turning to a consideration of church-based social support networks, the research literature indicates that these systems of aid and assistance are viable and useful conduits of tangible aid, emotional support, and spiritual comfort. However, there are a number of issues that bear attention. First, similar to the comments made regarding church attendance, individuals may not receive the church support that they need because of stigmatized personal and social statuses and circumstances. Research found that persons who were divorced were less likely to receive church support than their married counterparts. Although research is continuing, we have relatively little information about how characteristics of the individual or the problems that they face are associated with receiving different types and levels of church support. Second, a review of the caregiving literature for impaired adults suggests that black caregivers verify religious resources are important in coping with the stresses of caregiving. However, we also know that, on the whole, black caregivers are oftentimes involved in more intensive caregiving situations with higher needs for outside assistance. These findings call into question whether support resources from the church are adequate to meet the needs of caregivers or whether church networks are limited in their ability to recognize areas of unmet need for support. At the very least, these and other findings suggest that there is a need to investigate the nature of church support on particular issues and the interface between these supportive resources and other formally organized services. A related set of questions considers how religious social support networks are different and distinct from secular ones, how and when they interact, and whether there are certain groups of individuals for whom religious and secular support networks are essentially synonymous. Further, we need to determine if overlapping church and secular networks enhance or diminish the effectiveness of supportive efforts and the availability of a diverse group of informal helpers.

Although a relatively new area of inquiry, research on negative interaction within churches suggests that these dynamics are clearly evident, they impact individual perceptions of social relations within the church, and are of concern to church members. Negative interaction within churches is of interest for several reasons. First, current research evidence shows that negative interaction has significant adverse consequences for individuals, above and beyond the positive effects of social support. This suggests that, on balance, negative interaction does more to damage health than emotional support benefits health. There is a need to study the domains of negative interaction and the dynamics of their operation. Our focus group study suggested that gossip and feelings of being unwelcome might be important aspects of negative interaction among church members that bear additional examination. Finally, it would be important to consider whether negative interaction from church members is particularly potent because it comes from church members and potentially involves religious concerns that have high salience for individuals (e.g., negative assessments of others' beliefs and behaviors, attributions of sin). Comments from the focus group study indicated that ministers may attempt to address issues of negative interaction within the church and encourage individuals to reflect upon their own behavior and the impact of these interactions for the spiritual life of the church.

As discussed in Chapters 8 and 9, research findings on the relationship between religion and physical and mental health status suggests an overall beneficial effect. Health professionals (psychiatrists, clinical psychologists, social workers, physicians, and nurses) should recognize that, for many African American patients and clients, religion is a very powerful resource for protecting health, recuperating from illness, and staying well. Church participation, specific religious beliefs, congregational groups, ministers, and church officers can all be valuable allies to a therapist or provider because of both their salience as healthy influences on one's spiritual and emotional life and of their strong and historically recognized role as principal helping assets among African Americans, regardless of socioeconomic status or place of residence. Further, providers ought to be keen on assessing potential problems arising from religious or spiritual challenges in their patients' lives.

Health professionals must also try to become aware of discontinuities in patients' normative patterns of religious participation due to illness or other reasons. Involuntary separation from such a primary social, emotional, and spiritual resource could have serious consequences for general well-being and may even be etiologic for depression or other more severe psychiatric disorders. Useful suggestions and guidelines for sensitively assessing aspects of patients' religious lives and for treating religious patients, across a wide variety of faith traditions, can be found throughout the *Handbook of Religion and Mental Health* (Koenig, 1998). An important means to ensure that religious sources of distress are appropriately handled is through timely referral to clergy who are trained and credentialed in psychology or pastoral counseling.

Ministers are an important source of counseling and other health-related assistance for African American church congregants, and creative alliances among mental-health professionals, clergy, and medical and religious institutions can be an outstanding way to enhance primary and secondary prevention in relation to community mental health within African American communities (Levin, 1984, 1986). Finally, the vast collection of research findings regarding religion and physical and mental health and well-being verifies an overall beneficial influence on varied indicators of health (e.g., morbidity and mortality profiles) and health-related outcomes. However, the research findings also reveal that religion can have a negative impact on health and well-being status (Ellison & Levin, 1998) through a variety of pathways and mechanisms (e.g., negative religious coping and negative interaction within churches). Health professionals should be aware of this possibility in assessing the development, progression, and amelioration of health issues and problems.

In sum, religious organizations and their representatives are recognized as therapeutic communities and important resources for both the prevention and amelioration of mental and physical health problems. These resources function in a variety of health-related roles in primary, secondary, and tertiary prevention and as advocates and catalysts for health-related behavioral change. Churches and the health and human services professions (e.g., community mental health and public health) share distinctive values and orientations, such as a focus on promoting health and well-being, an emphasis on the impact of the social environment, individual and community empowerment, and a strong ethic for social responsibility and service to others. These principles are central to their roles in disease prevention and the promotion of health and well-being.

Finally, in discussing the implications of these research findings, we would be remiss if we did not acknowledge that there is considerable debate about whether and how research on religion should be used to inform practice in the fields of health and social welfare (Chatters, 2000). The findings reviewed here and the work of other researchers (e.g., Koenig et al., 2001; Pargament, 1997) clearly establish that religious and spiritual concerns are important to individuals and have a significant and potentially broad influence on health and social attitudes and behaviors. Given this, it is our responsibility as researchers and scholars not only to understand how and in what manner religion operates to influence health and social behaviors, but to determine how this information might be used to advance health and social welfare practice and positively affect relevant outcomes.

Current Research Projects

In this last section of the chapter, we briefly consider a number of current research projects that are focused, in part or whole, on religious involvement among African Americans. These efforts are noteworthy because they have addressed several of the limitations noted in previous research efforts on this topic. In particular, they have made important improvements in sample diversity, either by focusing exclusively on African Americans or by incorporating oversamples of black respondents. With respect to conceptualization and measurement issues, these studies frequently include diverse measures of religious involvement that reflect various dimensions of religiosity that are thought to have specific relevance for issues of health and health-related outcomes. These studies are guided by theoretical models (e.g., stress and coping) that specify particular linkages between religion and health and well-being outcomes and that propose alternative pathways of effects (e.g., preventive, moderator). Finally, current research efforts encompass sophisticated data analyses that provide an assessment of the independent influence of sociodemographic, religious, and other factors on outcomes of interest.

The 1998 General Social Survey has a special supplement of religion items that were developed by a National Institute on Aging Working Group on the Measurement of Religiousness/Spirituality for Use in Health Research (Fetzer Institute/National Institute on Aging, 1999). Percentages for several of these religion items have been reported here (see Chapter 2, section on the Interface Between Religiosity and Spirituality; Chapter 3, section on Research on Prayer Among Black Americans; Chapter 6, section on Profile of the Receipt of Support From Church Members; and Chapter 7, section on Survey Findings on Negative Interaction Among Church Members).

Neal Krause at the University of Michigan has undertaken a program of research focused on the measurement of religion among older adults (Krause, 2002b). This study began with focus groups of black and white elderly (Krause, Chatters, Meltzer, & Morgan, 2000b), which formed the basis for a series of in-depth cognitive interviews. The last stage of this project involved a nationwide study of older black and white respondents. The study sample consisted of 1,500 noninstitutionalized persons aged 66 years and older (752 blacks and 748 whites). Domains of religion assessed in the study include religious behaviors, church-based emotional and spiritual support, and perceptions of connection to God (Krause, 2002a). This is the first major survey in gerontology that has religion and its relation to health as its primary focus.

The National Survey of American Life: Coping with Stress in the 21st Century (NSAL) is a new data collection by the Program for Research on

Black Americans at the University of Michigan's Institute for Social Research. A few of the items from this study were presented in this volume. As of this writing, the study was recently out of the field, and data management and cleaning were being undertaken. Consequently only percentage distributions have been reported. This study includes face-to-face interviews with African Americans, non-Hispanic whites, and, for the first time in a national survey, blacks of Caribbean descent. In addition, there are interviews with adolescents (persons aged 13–17) using a similar questionnaire. The study's primary focus is on assessments of psychological distress and mental disorders. The NSAL expands upon a core group of religious involvement items that were included in the original National Survey of Black Americans (NSBA). The NSAL offers a unique opportunity to examine the role of religion in a sample of racially and ethnically diverse American adults and youth.

In closing, research on the role of religion in the lives of African Americans is experiencing unprecedented growth in the social, behavioral, and health sciences. Current research efforts are informed by recent theoretical, conceptual, methodological, and analytic refinements in understanding the nature and meaning of religious phenomena for individuals and groups and its relation to health and social behaviors. This work has great potential for contributing to knowledge about the role of religion in relation to these issues and in advancing health and social welfare practice. Emergent research demonstrates the potency of religious influences on health and social behaviors and validates the perspective that religious worldviews encompass more than simple lifestyle differences that can be reduced to discrete behaviors and attitudes. On the contrary, religious worldviews represent comprehensive and inclusive cultures and systems of life ways that imbue the world and events with meaning and significance. Finally, as this volume has demonstrated, research and scholarship on the role of religion in the lives of African Americans increasingly speak to fundamental issues of meaning, community, and human connection and their relation to the social well-being and health of individuals and groups.

Appendix A

Data Sources

This book represents an integration of research findings from studies involving both quantitative and qualitative data. The quantitative data are taken from eight (8) national surveys of the American population. The qualitative data are from a focus group study of African American men and women. Except for the *Monitoring the Future Survey*, which is based on high school seniors, all of the study samples consist of adults. Six of the national data sets and the qualitative data set were collected under the auspices of the same social science organization (the Institute for Social Research, University of Michigan). The Program for Research on Black Americans at the Institute for Social Research collected the majority of the data reported here (Drs. Taylor and Chatters have been members of PRBA for 25 years). Data from the General Social Surveys were collected by the National Opinion Research Center (the University of Chicago). These data sets are described below.

Quantitative Data

National Survey of Black Americans (NSBA)

The National Survey of Black Americans is based on a nationally representative cross-section sample of the adult (18 years and older) black population living in the continental United States. The NSBA was conducted by the Program for Research on Black Americans at the Institute for Social Research of the University of Michigan. The NSBA sample was drawn through a multistage, area-probability procedure that ensured that each black household had an equal likelihood of being selected. Seventy-six primary sampling units were selected for interviewing and, within these areas, smaller geographical clusters were then randomly selected. Professionally trained interviewers then visited each cluster in order to identify each habitable, occupied household, using special screening procedures developed to locate black homes. Within each selected black occupied household, one member was randomly chosen for interviewing. In all, 2,107 interviews were completed in 1979 and 1980, which represented a response rate of 69%. To date, the NSBA remains the most comprehensive survey on black American life, with more than 2,000 items covering a variety of issues. Of particular note is the special emphasis on the role of religion and the church in the lives of black Americans, church and family members as sources of informal social support, as well as numerous measures of health, well-being, and other psychosocial constructs.

Three Generation Family Study (TGFS)

In conjunction with the NSBA study, the Three Generation Family Study (TGFS), a national study of three-generational families, was conducted in 1979 and 1980. Respondents in the NSBA study were asked a series of questions to determine if they were members of three-generational families. If a respondent was a member of at least a three-generation family, then either the respondent's parent/child, grandparent/parent, or child/grandchild (depending upon the nature of the three-generation family) was interviewed. In addition, the original NSBA respondent was reinterviewed. In sum, a family member in each generation was interviewed in the TGFS. The original respondent received the reinterview questionnaire, while the respondent's two family members (parent/child, grandparent/parent, or child/grandchild) received the three-generation questionnaire. The TGFS yielded a total of 2,497 interviews. Of this total, there were 510 complete three-generation triads.

National Survey of Black Americans Panel Study

The original respondents of the NSBA were reinterviewed both in 1987–1988 and 1988–1989. Since the cost of locating the original 2,107 respondents and conducting face-to-face interviews was prohibitive, a telephone follow-up method was chosen. Tracking began in August 1987 and continued through the completion of interviewing in September 1988. Approximately 57% (1,210) of the original respondents were located and an interview attempted. Approximately 7% were thought to be deceased and another 34% either had no telephone and/or their whereabouts were unknown to relatives. Only 2% refused to be involved at the initial tracking stage. Out of the total of 1,210 respondents, 82% (951) agreed and participated in an interview. Only 77 (6.4%) refused to be interviewed. The remainder were hospitalized or otherwise physically or cognitively unable to be interviewed during the field period.

In 1988–1989 (Wave 3), interviews were attempted on all 951 respondents located and interviewed in 1987–1988. A total of 83.4% (793) of the respondents agreed to a re-interview. Only 6.1% (58) refused to be interviewed. Approximately 11 (1.2%) were deceased and 49 (4.2%) were physically or mentally unable to be interviewed. A total of 40 (4.2%) were lost to follow-up. Interviewing was completed in March 1989.

Overall, the results of the tracking and interviewing procedures were highly successful. After an 8-year period, only 34% of all 2,107 original respondents were lost to tracking. The remainder (66%) were located and accounted for. Once found, respondents were extremely cooperative, with an average of 83% participating over the two waves of re-interviewing. Finally, a fourth wave of the NSBA was collected in 1992. Of the 779 respondents recontacted, 659 were interviewed, which represents a response rate of 84%. While this is a study of noninstitutionalized African American adults, tracking information did not allow for the exclusion from the sampling frame of original respondents who had since entered an institution. This has led to an underestimated response rate.

A comparison of the respondents in Wave 1 with the nonrespondents in Waves 2, 3, and 4 reveals that respondents are more likely to own their own homes, be employed, be women, have more years of education, and to be slightly older. These differences are consistent with other panel studies in which renters, men, and younger respondents have higher rates of nonparticipation in later waves. In addition, nonrespondents in the later waves had lower levels of receiving church support than respondents (Taylor, Chatters, & Jackson, 1997). Although these differences were notable, they did not exceed 10%.

1984 National Black Election Survey

The 1984 *National Black Election Survey* (NBES) was conducted by the Program for Research on Black Americans at the Institute for Social Research. This survey follows the design of the National Election Survey, which is also collected at the Institute for Social Research. The NBES is based on a national probability sample. The sample was drawn using random digit dialing methods with a two-stage cluster design. Respondents were contacted both before and after the 1984 November presidential election. The questions used in this analysis are from the preelection survey, which had a sample size of 1,151 black adults of voting age (see Gurin, Hatchett, & Jackson, 1989, for a more detailed discussion of the sample).

National Survey of American Life

The National Survey of American Life: Coping with Stress in the 21st Century (NSAL) is a new data collection by the Program for Research on Black Americans at the University of Michigan's Institute for Social Research. The fieldwork for the study was done by the Institute for Social Research's Survey Research Center, in cooperation with the Program for Research on Black Americans. This study is sponsored by the National Institute of Mental Health. James S. Jackson is the Principal Investigator of this study, and Drs. Harold W. Neighbors, Robert Joseph Taylor, and David Williams are Co-Principal Investigators. The NSAL focuses on the physical, emotional, mental, structural, and economic conditions of African Americans, with a major emphasis on mental health and mental illness. As of this writing, the study has recently completed its field period, and data management and cleaning are currently underway. Consequently, only percentage distributions for variables are reported in this volume.

The sample of the NSAL consists of 64 primary sampling units (PSUs). Fifty-six of these primary areas overlap substantially with existing Survey Research Center's National Sample primary areas. The remaining eight primary areas were chosen from the South in order for the sample to represent African Americans in the proportion in which they are distributed nationally. Measures of size based on African American occupied housing units, rather than total occupied housing units, were used for sample selection of these 64 primary sampling units. From the 64 primary sampling units, 530 segments (blocks or block groups) were selected with probabilities proportional to the size of the African American population.

As of this writing, a total of 6,193 face-to-face interviews were conducted with persons aged 18 or older, including 3,583 African Americans, 1,006 non-Hispanic whites, and, for the first time in a national survey, 1,604 blacks of Caribbean descent. The interviews were all face to face and conducted within respondents' homes. The data collection was conducted from 2001 to 2003. Respondents were compensated for their time.

Americans' Changing Lives (ACL)

The Americans' Changing Lives (ACL) study is the result of the collaborative efforts of a group of investigators concerned with the nature and consequences of participation in productive activities in adulthood. Five separate studies, with similar foci and a shared data collection, were organized under the auspices of a National Institute on Aging Program Project, *Productive Activity, Stress, and Health in Middle and Later Life*. One of the five investigations was concerned with the influence of sociocultural factors on participation in productive activities among older Americans. Its specific focus was on investigating the manner in which sociocultural conditions influenced the participation of black adults in productive behaviors. James House was the PI of this study.

The data for this book were taken from the first wave of the ACL study, which had a sample of 3,617 adults, including 1,174 black adults 25 years of age and older. The ACL oversamples older blacks and black adults. The oversample for these groups provides for greater statistical power equivalent to that of a larger cross-section sample of the adult population.

NORC General Social Survey (GSS)

The National Data Program for the Social Sciences conducts the annual General Social Survey (GSS) for the National Opinion Research Center at the University of Chicago. The GSS is not a panel study, but rather a series of cross-sectional studies providing data on a wide spectrum of social indicators. The content of the GSS is fairly stable over time, although various items are added or deleted each year. Religiosity, defined in a broad sense, has historically been a central focus of GSS data collection efforts and, in particular years, numerous religion variables have been included. More important, several key indicators of religiosity (e.g., denomination, religious attendance) are available in every GSS since 1972. Assessments of common non-organizational religious activities, subjective indicators of religiosity and religious belief scales, often appear in the GSS. The 1998 General Social Survey contains a major section on religious participation that was written by a National Institute on Aging workgroup (Fetzer Institute/National Institute on Aging, 1999). The number of respondents who completed the 1998 NIA/Fetzer module on religious participation was 1,445.

Unfortunately, one of the limitations of the GSS is that only about 150 black respondents are typically included in each year of the study. Prior experience in conducting research on the black population has demonstrated that it is extremely expensive to reach some segments of this group, particularly respondents who reside in inner-city neighborhoods in large urban areas and large-scale housing projects. Typically, surveys of the general population fail to spend the necessary resources to obtain interviews from this group. As a result, the black respondents who participate in the GSS (and most surveys of the general population) are those who are more accessible and easier to interview. This is somewhat understandable given that the costs associated with interviewing a black respondent in larger urban areas (e.g., New York, Chicago) are 3 to 10 times more than an interview with a white middle-class respondent. GSS data from several years can be pooled to create a combined data set with larger numbers of black respondents. However, this does not correct the aforementioned problems with respect to sample representativeness. Bearing these limitations in mind, however, the GSS remains an important source of data for examining religious participation.

1996 Monitoring the Future (MTF)

The Monitoring the Future Survey has been conducted annually with high school seniors since 1975. It is a nationally representative survey that explores changes in attitudes and behaviors of high school seniors. Although the major focus of MTF is adolescent drug use, other topics are examined as well, including academic achievement and parental involvement. Three questions are included on religion. After 1996, MTF does not collect data on religion in the state of California. Consequently, we utilized the 1996 MTF data for this book. The sample size of the 1996 survey is 14,823, with 2,221 black respondents (see Smith, Denton, Faris, & Regnerus, 2002, and Wallace & Forman, 1998, for a detailed discussion of this sample).

Qualitative Data

Appraisals of Religiosity, Coping and Church Support

The qualitative analysis is based on the results of a focus group study of religion and mental health among African Americans ("Appraisals of Religiosity, Coping and Church Support"). This study was conducted by the Program for Research on Black Americans, University of Michigan. Robert Joseph Taylor was the Principal Investigator and Linda Chatters, Jacqueline S. Mattis, and Harold W. Neighbors were Co-Principal Investigators. The study was conducted in 1999 and participants were recruited from Southeastern Michigan.

A total of 13 focus groups were conducted; 10 groups consisted of persons in the age range of 18 to 54 years (five of which were women and the other five men). The three remaining groups consisted of individuals who were at least 55 years of age: two groups of older women and one group of older men. In total, 78 people participated in the focus group study, evenly split between women and men.

Selection criteria for the study required that participants self-identified as Christian and indicated a minimum level of religious sentiment. The decision to focus on only adherents of the Christian faith was based on several considerations. First, the vast majority of African Americans identify as Christians as reflected in the research and writing on religious affiliation in this group. Second, there was a compelling need to establish a common religious background and a baseline level of religious sentiment within the group. It was thought that a shared religious framework would facilitate the overall group process and avoid potential distractions arising from major differences of opinion concerning religious faith and belief (e.g., Christian vs. Muslim) and the relevance of religion (persons who are very religious vs. those who are agnostic or atheist) for group members. Finally, pastors, ministers, and their spouses were excluded from the study so that focus group members could feel free to express their opinions among a group of peers without the potential for bias due to the presence of a religious authority figure.

The study investigators acted as the focus group facilitators for all of the groups. Doctoral-level staff who had extensive experience in conducting focus groups trained the facilitators. Facilitators participated in several practice focus groups and pretests of the focus group protocol in order to ensure a high level of consistency in procedures across each of the focus groups. Facilitators were gender-matched to appropriate focus groups; all facilitators were African American. Focus groups lasted between 1½ and 2 hours, and focus group members were compensated $35 for their participation.

The main focus of this study was to explore the relationship between religion and mental health among African Americans. The protocol covered the following content areas: religious activities (including church attendance, reading religious materials, and watching/listening to religious programming), prayer, the use of prayer as a form of coping with serious life problems, the use of church members as a source of informal social support, negative social interactions among church members, and the use of pastors and ministers for help when dealing with a serious personal problem.

This study possesses the usual limitations found in many qualitative investigations. First, since the study is not based on a probability sample, the results cannot be generalized to the broader population. Second, some level of bias occurs in the recruitment and selection of the focus group participants. That is, people who are religious are more likely to volunteer to take part in a study on religious participation. These limitations are less of a concern in the present volume because the focus group study is not the sole source of data on these topics, but one of several sources of information that are used. Further, the stated purposes in using the focus group information were to assist in the interpretation of extant survey findings and to suggest new areas and topics for inquiry. Finally, we recognize that because the focus group format involves a group process, there are undetermined social influences in operation that may affect the views and opinions expressed by individual participants.

It is important to note that, in some cases, statements made by the focus group participants and presented here in the book have been altered slightly for greater ease of understanding. None of the substance and meaning of participants' remarks, however, have been changed. Phrases that are used repeatedly in conversational speech, such as "you know," "um," and "ah," were either reduced in number or deleted from the passages. Sometimes phrases were omitted because the speaker changed thoughts in mid-sentence. The following quote is an example of the changes that were made. The first quote is taken verbatim from the transcripts, while the second, edited version shows how it was altered slightly.

Original response:

> They really did and they, you know, the church, you know, I don't have a fear about going when I have a problem, because when I don't have a problem I go and when I don't have a problem I pay my tithes and my offering and when I try to do the things that I know that is, you know, right to do and, you know. Not to say that, okay I feel like they owe me because I have been doing, you know, doing what I'm supposed to be, you know. But if I, you know, if I'm a good member in standing there and they, you know, do something for me, certainly I would accept it if I'm in need, you know. A lot of people probably say, I wouldn't take from the church, I wouldn't, you know, accept that or whatever, but you know, if you're in need then you need to be able to, you know, like I said earlier, you know, you can miss your blessing because you don't know when God is actually speaking. God is saying, you know, learn to receive, you know. Especially for people who are givers, they have a hard time receiving and I'm certainly a giver, you know, and and for me receiving has really never been a real problem. You know, a lot of people say well, I'm a giver and I don't like to receive or I have a problem receiving.

Abbreviated response:

> I don't have a fear about going when I have a problem, because when I don't have a problem I pay my tithes and my offering and I try to do

the things that I know is right to do. Not to say that I feel like they owe me because I have been doing what I'm supposed to be. But if I'm a good member in standing there and they do something for me, certainly I would accept it if I'm in need. A lot of people probably say, I wouldn't take from the church, I wouldn't accept that or whatever, but if you're in need you can miss your blessing because you don't know when God is actually speaking. God is saying learn to receive. Especially for people who are givers, they have a hard time receiving and I'm certainly a giver and for me receiving has really never been a real problem. A lot of people say well, I'm a giver and I don't like to receive or I have a problem receiving.

Although the second version is condensed, the substance of the response is unchanged. The major difference is that the 17 instances in which the respondent said "you know" were removed.

Appendix B

Multivariate Tables

Table B.1   Logistic Regression of Demographic Variables on Religious Artifacts in the Home (NSBA)[a]

Predictors	Religious Artifacts B
Constant	1.5*
Age	.034***
Gender	
Male	−.403***
Income	−.018
Education	−.018
Marital status	
Divorced	−.469**
Separated	−.503**
Widowed	−.200
Never married	−.140**
Urbanicity	−.274*
Region	
Northeast	−.332*
North Central	−.243[b]
West	−.698**

$X^2 = 210.25$
N 2,082

NOTES: a. Several of the predictors in this analysis are represented by dummy variables; Gender, 0 = female, 1 = male; Marital status, married and common-law is the excluded category; Urbanicity, 0 = rural, 1 = urban; Region, South is the excluded category.
b. $.05 < p < .10$
* $p < .05$; ** $p < .01$; *** $p < .001$.

Table B.2   Regression of Demographic Variables on Closeness to Religious Blacks (NSBA)[a]

	Closeness to Religious Blacks	
Predictors	b	B
Constant	4.06***	—
Age	.008***	.843***
Gender		
Male	−.087*	−.054*
Income	.003	.019
Education	−.108***	−.136***
Marital status		
Divorced	−.155**	−.064**
Separated	−.074	−.029
Widowed	−.012	−.005
Never married	−.122**	−.066**
Urbanicity	−.115**	−.061**
Region		
Northeast	−.276***	−.139***
North Central	−.252***	−.136***
West	−.364***	−.115***

$R^2 = 0.148$
Adjusted $R^2 = 0.143$
N 2,052

NOTES: a. Several of the predictors in this analysis are represented by dummy variables; Gender, 0 = female, 1 = male; Marital status, married and common-law is the excluded category; Urbanicity, 0 = rural, 1 = urban; Region, South is the excluded category.
b. $.05 < p < .10$.
* $p < .05$; ** $p < .01$; *** $p < .001$.

Table B.3   Regression Analysis of Demographic Variables on Frequency of Prayer (NSBA[a])

Predictors	Prayer	
	b	*B*
Constant	6.32	—
Age	.001***	.218***
Gender		
Male	−.449***	−.216***
Income	−.000	−.009
Education	.000	.004
Marital Status		
Divorced	−.009	−.03
Separated	−.111	−.032
Widowed	−.149[b]	−.05[b]
Never married	−.283***	−.116***
Urbanicity	−.006	−.027
Region		
Northeast	−.232***	−.089***
North Central	−.145*	−.059*
West	−.367***	−.086***

$R^2 = .136$
Adjusted $R^2 = .130$
N 1,816

NOTES: a. Several of the predictors in this analysis are represented by dummy variables; Gender, 0 = female, 1 = male; Marital status, married and common-law is the excluded category; Urbanicity, 0 = rural, 1 = urban; Region, South is the excluded category.
b. $.05 < p < .10$

* $p < .05$; ** $p < .01$; *** $p < .001$.

Recommended Reading
and Resource Guide

Research and writing on the topic of religion and African American life has seen tremendous expansion over the past several years. The following "Recommended Reading and Resource Guide" is a compilation of articles, books, and reports that are considered pivotal to this body of literature. For the most part, items listed in the Guide are focused on the religious life of African Americans as reflected in empirical survey research investigations. However, we also cite readings and resources on the general population that provide relevant background information or are considered to be particularly critical explorations of an issue. In addition, a number of authoritative compilations and encyclopedias on these topics are reviewed. The Guide is organized around the book's chapters and provides either a narrative description of key research findings or a brief synopsis of individual works. A list of works cited follows each section.

Chapter 2: Religious Participation

There are a number of excellent social historical analyses of African American religious traditions. We cite Lincoln and Mamiya's (1990) classic work for its thorough review of existing models of black religious participation and its contextual analysis (e.g., historical, political, economic) of the African American church. Coupled with this is a description and report from their survey of black clergy and black churches of the seven major historical black denominations. Topics within the book include discussions of the historical development of black Baptist, Methodist, and Pentecostal denominations and critical analyses of several prominent issues facing the

Black Church (e.g., the role of women, economics and the Black Church, urban churches, the civil rights movement). The reader is also referred to other prior works by C. Eric Lincoln, which are considered classics in the field. In addition, readers are referred to the seminal works of James Cone on black theology (e.g., 1997), other historical accounts of black churches (e.g., Raboteau, 2001; Wilmore, 1998), and womanist/feminist analyses of the role of women in the Black Church (Dodson, 2002; Gilkes, 2000).

Billingsley's (1999) recent volume provides in-depth case studies and historical accounts of a number of black churches that were initially established in the antebellum South (located primarily in Savannah, Georgia and Richmond, Virginia). The book also presents findings from a survey of black churches, with particular attention to issues of how churches come to define their distinctive mission (e.g., activism, social justice, personal salvation) and the means by which "activist" churches enact their role within the church and surrounding communities.

The Fetzer Institute/National Institute on Aging Report, *Multidimensional Measurement of Religiousness/Spirituality for Use in Health Research,* is a collaboration between the Fetzer Institute (Kalamazoo, Michigan) and the National Institute on Aging. This volume reflects the contributions of a working group of leading scholars and researchers (among whom Levin is included) on religious involvement and its association with health. Twelve papers addressing various aspects of religious involvement are provided that describe background literature, conceptual and methodological issues, measurement approaches, proposed theoretical linkages to health outcomes, and recommended items for use in research on religion-health associations. The domains of religiousness/spirituality that are assessed include organizational religiousness, private religious practices, religious/ spiritual coping, religious support, religious preference, and forgiveness, among others. Given the range of topics represented in the Fetzer/NIA report, it is a valuable resource for several other chapters in this book (e.g., religious participation, support from church members).

Finally, the *Encyclopedia of African American Religions* (Murphy, Melton, & Ward, 1993) is an indispensable resource for information concerning the development of the historical black denominations and churches, as well as the full spectrum of religious traditions within United States (e.g., Muslim, Nation of Islam, Vodou). Entries include brief biographies of both famous and lesser-known religious figures and church officials, as well as accounts of the development and growth of individual churches (e.g., Abyssinian Baptist Church, Harlem, New York). The volume is meticulously referenced and authoritative in its coverage.

Selected References

Billingsley, A. (1999). *Mighty like a river: The Black Church and social reform.* New York: Oxford University Press.

Cone, J. H. (1997). *God of the oppressed.* Maryknoll, NY: Orbis Books.

Dodson, J. E. (2002). *Engendering church.* Lanham, MD: Rowman & Littlefield.

Fetzer Institute/NIA. (1999). *Multidimensional measurement of religiousness/spirituality for use in health research.* Kalamazoo, MI: John E. Fetzer.

Gilkes, C. T. (2000). *If it wasn't for the women . . . : Black women's experience and womanist culture in church and community.* Maryknoll, NY: Orbis Books.

Lincoln, C. E., & Mamiya, L. H. (1990). *The Black Church in the African American experience.* Durham, NC: Duke University Press.

Murphy, L. G., Melton, J. G., & Ward, G. L. (1993). *Encyclopedia of African American religions.* New York: Garland.

Raboteau, A. J. (2001). *Canaan land: A religious history of African Americans.* New York: Oxford University Press.

Wilmore, G. S. (1998). *Black religion and black radicalism: An interpretation of the religious history of African Americans* (3rd ed.). Maryknoll, NY: Orbis Books.

Chapter 3: Prayer

The volume by Poloma and Gallup (1991) is the most thorough social science investigation of prayer to date. The book is based on results of a 1988 Gallup Poll that asked a series of detailed questions on prayer. This is particularly noteworthy because very few surveys contain any items on religious participation and, of those that do, typically only two or three questions address the issue of prayer. The book examines the demographic correlates of prayer and the relationship between prayer and forgiveness, life satisfaction, and political activism. One limitation of the book is that insufficient attention is paid to racial differences and to prayer among minority groups.

Research focusing on the topics of prayer and religious coping, health effects of prayer, clinical applications of prayer, and prayer and its relation to physical and mental health outcomes are discussed throughout Koenig, McCullough, and Larson's *Handbook of Religion and Health.* Finally, Krause et al.'s (2000) article on use of the focus group methodology to study prayer among older adults highlights several important ideas regarding the nature, timing, and operation of prayer and distinctions between individual and group prayer. Further, findings from the focus group study dispute the seeming passivity of prayer as a means of coping with life problems.

Selected References

Koenig, H. G., Larson, D. B., & McCullough, M. E. (2001). *Handbook of religion and health*. New York: Oxford University Press.

Krause, N., Chatters, L. M., Meltzer, T., & Morgan, D. L. (2000). Using focus groups to explore the nature of prayer in late life. *Journal of Aging Studies, 14*(2), 191–212.

Poloma, M. M., & Gallup, G. H. (1991). *Varieties of prayer*. Philadelphia: Trinity Press International.

Chapter 4: Prayer as Coping

Pargament's (1997) is the definitive book on religious coping. It begins by developing and elaborating working definitions of the constructs of religion and coping and then goes on to demonstrate how these two constructs are integrated. The book presents a detailed overview of Pargament's own program of research on how religion helps people cope with problems and in what situations that religious coping may be harmful to physical and mental health. In addition, the book provides a thorough review of research and perspectives on religion and coping, as well as thoughtful discussions of the clinical applications of this body of research.

Ellison and Taylor's (1996) article on religious coping explores the social and situational antecedents of the use of prayer as a coping behavior within a national sample of African Americans. The article provides a useful review of theoretical arguments and empirical evidence for the use of prayer as coping across different categories of personal problems and social location factors, as well as varying levels of religiosity and social and psychological resources. Theoretical arguments linking these factors with religious coping are developed and tested. The findings of this paper are discussed in Chapter 3.

Krause (1998) investigated the relationships among stress, religious coping and mortality using data from a national survey of older adults. He finds that religious coping offsets the effects of stress in highly valued roles on mortality. The impact of religious coping, however, is only significant for those adults with less educational attainment. This paper provides an excellent discussion of why religious coping may assist some people in dealing with adversity.

Selected References

Ellison, C. G., & Taylor, R. J., (1996). Turning to prayer: Religious coping among black Americans. *Review of Religious Research, 38,* 111–131.

Krause, N. (1998). Stressors in highly valued roles, religious coping, and mortality. *Psychology and Aging, 13,* 242–255.

Pargament, K. I. (1997). *The psychology of religion and coping: Theory, research and practice.* New York: Guilford.

Chapter 5: Use of Ministers

Neighbors and Jackson's (1996) edited book on mental health issues within the African American population provides an excellent overview of many issues of concern to blacks and mental health (e.g., coping with personal problems, help-seeking behaviors, mental health service use). Although the book does not address religion and mental health, it does address issues of stress, coping and formal and informal help seeking. The article by Neighbors, Musick, and Williams (1998) is one of a handful of studies that specifically examines reports of soliciting assistance from the clergy in response to serious personal problems. The article provides a useful review of related background work addressing the use of help-seeking in a religious context and poses several important questions about how and under what circumstances assistance from clergy might serve to facilitate the use of formal mental health services.

Selected References

Neighbors, H. W., & Jackson, J. S. (1996). *Mental health in black America.* Thousand Oaks, CA: Sage.

Neighbors, H. W., Musick, M. A., & Williams, D. R. (1998). The African American minister: Bridge or barrier to mental health care? *Health Education and Behavior, 25,* 759–777.

Chapter 6: Social Support

Chatters et al. (2002) investigates sociodemographic and family and church factors as correlates of support from family and church members among a representative sample of African Americans. Overall, patterns of family and church support indicate that slightly more than half of respondents receive assistance from both family and church networks, one quarter receive assistance from family only, and roughly equal percentages (9%) either receive help from church members only or do not receive help from either group. Findings from multinomial logistic regression analysis indicated significant age, gender, marital, and parental status differences in patterns of support from family and church. Perceptions of family closeness, degree of interaction with family, and overall levels of participation in church activities were associated with distinctive patterns of assistance.

Taylor et al. (1997) examined change, over time, in selected characteristics of the family, friend, and church support networks of 17- to 102-year-old black Americans. Data from Waves 1 and 2 and Waves 1 and 4 from the Panel Study of the National Survey of Black Americans were compared. In addition to examining change in network involvement, the analysis also assesses the degree to which support network involvement remains stable over time. Two independent variables (i.e., gender, age) and seven dependent variables (i.e., family interaction, family support, family closeness, family satisfaction, friendship interaction, presence of a best friend, church support) are examined. Overall findings indicate that family, church, and friend network involvement among black Americans is consistent and viable. Despite important changes in black family structure that have occurred over the past 30 years, black adults are well integrated within important social networks. Black adults' involvement in church-based support networks was not as widespread as noted previously, although fully half of all respondents reported consistent use of these networks over time.

Krause's (2002) recent analysis and test of a conceptual model of church-based social support among older adults addresses a number of important questions regarding the presence and nature of race differences in the associations between support and health outcomes. In addition to demonstrating that older blacks have higher levels of religious involvement and are more likely to experience the health benefits of religious involvement than are older whites, these findings describe the pathways through which social support impacts health. This study advances the literature on religion-health connections by testing a theoretically derived model of religion's impact on health, with an explicit investigation of the potential influence of race on these associations.

Selected References

Chatters, L. M., Taylor, R. J., Lincoln, K. D., & Schroepfer, T. (2002). Patterns of informal support from family and church members among African Americans. *Journal of Black Studies, 33*(1), 66–85.

Krause, N. (2002). Church-based social support and health in old age: Variations by race. *Journal of Gerontology: Social Sciences, 57B,* S332-S347.

Taylor, R. J., Chatters, L. M., & Jackson, J. S. (1997). Changes over time in support network involvement among black Americans. In R. J. Taylor, J. S. Jackson, & L. M. Chatters (Eds.), *Family life in black America* (pp. 293–316). Thousand Oaks, CA: Sage.

Chapter 7: Negative Interaction

Rook's (1984) pioneering work is the foundation of a growing body of literature on the negative side of social relationships. This particular study examined the influence of positive (e.g., social support) and negative (e.g., conflict) interaction on psychological well-being. Findings that negative interactions were better predictors of well-being compared to positive interactions was important for shifting the focus of the social support literature to include the negative side of social relations. Since this work, the literature on the role of social support in promoting health has taken a more balanced approach to include the costs and benefits of social relationships.

Using focus group data from older black and white adults, Krause et al. (2000) provides an excellent overview of various sources of interpersonal conflict that may arise within church settings. The article reviews current theory and research concerning the linkages between the experience of negative interaction and its impact on health. Comments from several focus groups of older black and white adults explore interpersonal conflict among church members, conflict between church members and their pastors, and conflict over church doctrine. In addition, focus group comments explore how respondents cope with negative interactions involving church members.

Lincoln (2000) provides an excellent in-depth review of research investigating the impact of negative interaction on psychological well-being. In particular, the article critically reviews 28 studies that investigate the relationship between social support, negative social interaction, and their simultaneous effects on psychological well-being. The studies are grouped according to three conceptual models of the effects of social interaction: the additive effects model, the moderator model, and the domain specific model.

Selected References

Krause, N., Chatters, L. M., Meltzer, T., & Morgan, D. L. (2000). Negative interaction in the church: Insights from focus groups with older adults. *Review of Religious Research, 41*(4), 510–533.

Lincoln, K. D. (2000). Social support, negative social interactions, and psychological well-being. *Social Service Review, 74*(2), 231–252.

Rook, K. S. (1984). The negative side of social interaction: Impact on psychological well-being. *Journal of Personality and Social Psychology, 46,* 1097–1108.

Chapter 8: Physical Health

Several published reviews have appeared in recent years that attempt to summarize the impact of religion, broadly defined, on health-related outcomes. Most of these reviews include studies of African Americans or of black-white differences in religion-health associations, although not all of them explicitly discuss racial identity or its influence on how religion affects health.

The most thorough review articles on this topic were produced by the authors of this book. A recent summary by Chatters (2000) appeared in the authoritative *Annual Review of Public Health*. In this chapter-length overview, which includes 185 references, detailed information is provided that (a) summarizes how religion has been conceptualized and assessed in health-related research; (b) reviews studies of the impact of religion on health outcomes; (c) reviews additional scientific studies of religious effects on well-being, lifestyle behaviors, and health care use, and of religious coping; (d) discusses a variety of theoretical models of religion and health, including several proposed mediating factors; (e) lists both positive and negative aspects of religious participation; (f) offers reflection on measurement, methodological, ethical, and practice-related issues; and (g) critiques the role that race and ethnicity have played in this literature. An earlier and briefer review (Levin, Chatters, Ellison, & Taylor, 1996) covered similar ground but with more attention to summarizing findings from existing literature reviews and to detailing the potential importance of religious congregations for large-scale public-health programming.

Over the past decade, a couple dozen books have appeared that cover the topic of religion, spirituality, and health. Most purport to offer some kind of overview of research, but they vary in how well they cover the field. It is apparent that the authors of many of the books on the market, both academic and popular, are not entirely familiar with the scope and breadth of research and theory that exists, nor do they possess the requisite methodological background to interpret empirical findings properly. In contrast, three books provide reliable summary overviews of existing research and accurately discuss the meaning and implications of study findings.

The *Handbook of Religion and Health* (Koenig, McCullough, & Larson, 2001) is an encyclopedic, 700-page summary of existing research on religious factors in physical and mental health and health services use. Approximately 1,600 scholarly sources are referenced, including citation of about 1,200 empirical studies of religion's impact on a couple dozen or so categories of health- or quality-of-life-related outcomes. These include separate chapters on heart disease, hypertension, cerebrovascular disease, immune system functioning, cancer, mortality, disability, pain and somatic symptoms, and health behaviors. Implications for both health and religious professionals are discussed. The book is capped off by a 75-page table that provides details on religion and health studies, listed chronologically and by the outcome under investigation.

The same team was involved in writing and editing a monograph sponsored by the John Templeton Foundation (Larson, Swyers, & McCullough, 1998). This document provides summary reports prepared by respective panels of experts convened over the course of three meetings in the middle 1990s. More than 70 individuals were invited to participate, and they produced reviews and recommendations related to physical and mental health, addictions, neuroscience, and intervention research. The list of participants did not include any of the authors of the present book nor Brown and Gary or their associates. This monograph, and the *Handbook,* thus have little to say about African Americans or about race or ethnicity, in general. Still, both books provide useful summaries of existing work in this field.

The best introduction and summary of the religion and health field is the popular book *God, Faith, and Health* (Levin, 2001). Written for a general audience, but including nearly 25 pages of scholarly references, this book summarizes evidence linking dimensions of religiousness to physical and mental health. Each chapter examines a respective type of spiritual expression (religious affiliation, fellowship, worship and prayer, beliefs, faith, mystical states of consciousness), and, after summarizing results of prominent studies, focuses on psychosocial factors that help to explain that chapter's religion-health association (healthy behavior, social support, positive emotions, healthy beliefs, salutary thoughts, psychophysiology). Each chapter also contains a case report, personal reflections, and a list of questions for readers to ponder. *God, Faith, and Health* emphasizes studies by members of the research team that wrote the present book, nearly all of which make use of samples of African-American or other minority-group respondents or emphasize racial differences.

Selected References

Chatters, L. M. (2000). Religion and health: Public health research and practice. *Annual Review of Public Health, 21,* 335–367.

Koenig, H. G., McCullough, M. E., & Larson, D. B. (2001). *Handbook of religion and health.* New York: Oxford University Press.

Larson, D. B., Swyers, J. P., & McCullough, M. E. (1998). *Scientific research on spirituality and health: A consensus report.* Sponsored by the John M. Templeton Foundation. Rockville, MD: National Institute for Healthcare Research.

Levin, J. (2001). *God, faith, and health: Exploring the spirituality-healing connection.* New York: John Wiley.

Levin, J. S., Chatters, L. M., Ellison, C. G., & Taylor, R. J. (1996). Religious involvement, health outcomes, and public health practice. *Current Issues in Public Health, 2,* 220–225.

Chapter 9: Mental Health and Well-Being

As with physical health, the past decade has seen an increase in scholarly interest in the influence of religion on mental health and well-being. Published literature reviews and academic books exist but not as much popular writing as for physical health. Much of this work does not focus on summarizing results of empirical research studies but rather on discussing theoretical or conceptual issues of interest to psychiatrists, clinical psychologists, or pastoral counselors. Good reviews of published research can be found, however, including overviews of work involving African Americans.

A fine resource is Koenig's (1998) *Handbook of Religion and Mental Health.* This is an edited volume of reviews by prominent scientists and clinicians and covers outcomes such as personality, neuropsychology, coping, depression, anxiety, psychosis, and addiction. Notable, too, are chapters that provide reflections on the relationship between religion and mental health from the perspectives of several major faith traditions (Protestant, Catholic, Mormon, Unity, Jewish, Buddhist, Hindu, Muslim). A key chapter in the *Handbook* is a review of empirical studies of religion and mental health, written by two of the authors of the present book (Levin & Chatters, 1998). This chapter also explores in great detail a variety of proposed salutogenic mechanisms for a positive religion–mental-health relationship. Another important contribution is an extensive theoretical section that includes (a) a review of theoretical perspectives on religion and mental health; (b) an outline of theoretical frameworks from sociology, psychiatry, and theology that help to interpret the impact of religion on mental health; and (c) proposal of five theoretical models positing precisely how religion, health, mental illness, and mediating factors might impact on each other.

Two other reviews, both by authors of the present book, provide reviews of academic writing on religion and dimensions of psychological well-being. In the first edition of the authoritative *Aging, Spirituality, and Religion: A Handbook,* the chapter on religion and well-being (Levin & Tobin, 1995) prefaced its discussion of religion with detailed discussions of the conceptual boundaries of the psychological well-being construct as well as its major determinants. Foremost among those described were race, age, socioeconomic status, and health. In Levin's (1994) edited book, *Religion in Aging and Health: Theoretical Foundations and Methodological Frontiers,* Chatters and Taylor (1994) provide a comprehensive overview of all existing empirical research on religious involvement in older African Americans. This chapter highlights the work of the present research team, including studies of social and health correlates and outcomes. Since that chapter was written, about a decade ago, much more work has been done, especially by our team. The present book is, in a sense, an update and expansion of this early chapter.

Selected References

Chatters, L. M., & Taylor, R. J. (1994). Religious involvement among older African Americans. In J. S. Levin (Ed.), *Religion in aging and health: Theoretical foundations and methodological frontiers* (pp. 196–230). Thousand Oaks, CA: Sage.

Koenig, H. G. (Ed.). (1998). *Handbook of religion and mental health.* San Diego, CA: Academic Press.

Levin, J. S. (Ed.). (1994). *Religion in aging and health: Theoretical foundations and methodological frontiers.* Thousand Oaks, CA: Sage.

Levin, J. S., & Chatters, L. M. (1998). Research on religion and mental health: An overview of empirical findings and theoretical issues. In H. G. Koenig (Ed.), *Handbook of religion and mental health* (pp. 33–50). San Diego, CA: Academic Press.

Levin, J. S., & Tobin, S. S. (1995). Religion and psychological well-being. In M. A. Kimble, S. H. McFadden, J. W. Ellor, & J. J. Seeber (Eds.), *Aging, spirituality, and religion: A handbook* (pp. 30–46). Minneapolis, MN: Fortress Press.

References

Academy of Religion and Mental Health. (1959). *Religion, science, and mental health: Proceedings of the First Academy Symposium on Inter-discipline Responsibility for Mental Health—a Religious and Scientific Concern, 1957.* New York: New York University Press.

Ai, A. L., Dunkle, R. E., Peterson, C., & Bolling, S. F. (1998). The role of private prayer in psychological recovery among midlife and aged patients following cardiac surgery. *The Gerontologist, 38*(5), 591–601.

Ai, A. L., Peterson, C., Bolling, S. F., & Koenig, H. (2002). Private prayer and optimism in middle-aged and older patients awaiting cardiac surgery. *The Gerontologist, 42*(1), 70–81.

Ainlay, S. C., & Smith, D. R. (1984). Aging and religious participation. *Journal of Gerontology, 39*(3), 357–363.

Antonucci, T. C. (1985). Personal characteristics, social support, and social behavior. In R. H. Binstock & E. Shanas (Eds.), *Handbook of aging and the social sciences* (2nd ed., pp. 94–128). New York: Van Nostrand Reinhold.

Appiah-Kubi, K. (1989). Religion and healing in an African community: The Akan of Ghana. In L. E. Sullivan (Ed.), *Healing and restoring: Health and medicine in the world's religious traditions* (pp. 203–224). New York: Macmillan.

Aranda, M. P., & Knight, B. G. (1997). The influences of ethnicity and culture on the caregiver stress and coping process: A sociocultural review and analysis. *The Gerontologist, 37,* 342–354.

Arcury, T. A., Quandt, S. A., McDonald, J., & Bell, R. A. (2000). Faith and health self-management of rural older adults. *Journal of Cross-Cultural Gerontology, 15,* 55–74.

Argyle, M., & Beit-Hallahmi, B. (1975). *The social psychology of religion.* Boston: Rutledge & Kegan Paul.

Armstrong, T. D., & Crowther, M. R. (2002). Spirituality among older African Americans. *Journal of Adult Development, 9*(1), 3–12.

Bearon, L. B., & Koenig, H. G. (1990). Religious cognitions and use of prayer in health and illness. *Gerontologist, 30*(2), 249–253.

Becker, R. J. (1971). Religion and psychological health. In M. P. Strommen (Ed.), *Research on religious development: A comprehensive handbook* (pp. 391–421). New York: Hawthorn.

Beeghley, L., Van Velsor, E., & Bock, E. W. (1981). The correlates of religiosity among black and white Americans. *The Sociological Quarterly, 22,* 403–412.

Beit-Hallahmi, B. (1989). *Prolegomena to the psychological study of religion.* Lewisburg, PA: Bucknell University Press.

Bentz, W. K. (1970). The clergyman's role in community mental health. *Journal of Religion and Health, 9,* 7–15.

Berardo, F. M. (1967). *Social adaptation to widowhood among a rural-urban aged population.* Washington Agricultural Experiment Station Bulletin 689, College of Agriculture, Washington State University.

Bergin, A. E. (1983). Religiosity and mental health: A critical reevaluation and meta-analysis. *Professional Psychology: Research and Practice, 14,* 170–184.

Berry, M., & Blassigame, J. (1982). *Long memory: The black experience in America.* New York: Oxford University Press.

Billingsley, A. (1992). *Climbing Jacob's ladder.* New York: Simon & Schuster.

Billingsley, A. (1999). *Mighty like a river: The Black Church and social reform.* New York: Oxford University Press.

Billingsley, A., & Caldwell, C. H. (1991). The church, the family, and the school in the African American community. *Journal of Negro Education, 60,* 427–440.

Blaine, B., & Crocker, J. (1995). Religiousness, race, and psychological well-being: Exploring social psychological mediators. *Personality and Social Psychology Bulletin, 21,* 1031–1041.

Blazer, D. & Palmore, E. (1976). Religion and aging in a longitudinal panel. *The Gerontologist, 16*(1), 82–85.

Braithwaite, R. L., & Taylor, S. E. (Eds.). (1992). *Health issues in the black community.* San Francisco: Jossey-Bass.

Brown, D. R., Ahmed, F., Gary, L. E., & Milburn, N. G. (1995). Major depression in a community sample of African Americans. *American Journal of Psychiatry, 152,* 373–378.

Brown, D. R., & Gary, L. E. (1987). Stressful life events, social support networks, and physical and mental health of urban black adults. *Journal of Human Stress, 13,* 165–174.

Brown, D. R., & Gary, L. E. (1994). Religious involvement and health status among African-American males. *Journal of the National Medical Association, 86,* 825–831.

Brown, D. R., Ndubuisi, S. C., & Gary, L. E. (1990). Religiosity and psychological distress among blacks. *Journal of Religion and Health, 29,* 55–68.

Brown, K. M. (1989). Afro-Caribbean spirituality: A Haitian case study. In L. E. Sullivan (Ed.), *Healing and restoring: Health and medicine in the world's religious traditions* (pp. 255–285). New York: Macmillan.

Brown, R. K. (2003). The Black Church and charitable choice. *African American Research Perspectives, 9*(1), 79–90.

Bryant, J. R. (1980). The Black Church as a unifier of the black community. In L. S. Yearwood (Ed.), *Black organizations: Issues on survival techniques* (pp. 5–8). Washington, DC: University Press of America.

Bryant, S., & Rakowski, W. (1992). Predictors of mortality among elderly African-Americans. *Research on Aging, 14,* 50–67.

Bulman, R. J., & Wortman, C. B. (1977). Attributions of blame and coping in the "real world": Severe accident victims react to their lot. *Journal of Personality and Social Psychology, 35,* 351–361.

Caldwell, C. H., Chatters, L. M., Billingsley, A., & Taylor, R. J. (1995). Church-based support programs for elderly black adults: Congregational and clergy characteristics. In M. A. Kimble, S. H. McFadden, J. W. Ellor, & J. J. Seeber (Eds.), *Aging, spirituality, and religion: A handbook* (pp. 306–324). Minneapolis, MN: Fortress Press.

Castelli, J. (1994). *How I pray.* New York: Ballantine Books.

Chalfant, H., Roberts, P. A., Heller, P. L., Biones, D., Aguirre-Hochbaum, S., & Farr, W. (1990). The clergy as a resource for those encountering psychological distress. *Review of Religious Research, 31,* 305–313.

Chatters, L. M. (2000). Religion and health: Public health research and practice. *Annual Review of Public Health, 21,* 335–367.

Chatters, L. M., Levin, J. S., & Taylor, R. J. (1992). Antecedents and dimensions of religious involvement among older black adults. *Journal of Gerontology: Social Sciences, 47,* S269–S278.

Chatters, L. M., & Taylor, R. J. (1989a). Age differences in religious participation among black adults. *Journal of Gerontology: Social Science, 44,* S183–S189.

Chatters, L. M., & Taylor, R. J. (1989b). Life problems and coping strategies of older black adults. *Social Work, 34,* 313–319.

Chatters, L. M., & Taylor, R. J. (1994). Religious involvement among older African Americans. In J. S. Levin (Ed.), *Religion in aging and health: Theoretical foundations and methodological frontiers* (pp. 196–230). Thousand Oaks, CA: Sage.

Chatters, L. M., Taylor, R. J., & Lincoln, K. D. (1999). African American religious participation: A multi-sample comparison. *Journal for the Scientific Study of Religion, 38,* 132–145.

Chatters, L. M., Taylor, R. J., Lincoln, K. D., & Schroepfer, T. (2002). Patterns of informal support from family and church members among African Americans. *Journal of Black Studies, 33*(1), 66–85.

Chaves, M., & Higgins, L. H. (1992). Comparing the community involvement of black and white congregations. *Journal for the Scientific Study of Religion, 31,* 425–440.

Clemente, F., & Sauer, W. J. (1976). Life satisfaction in the United States. *Social Forces, 54,* 621–631.

Clipp, E. C., Pavalko, E. K., & Elder, G. H., Jr. (1992). Trajectories of health: In concept and empirical pattern. *Behavior, Health, and Aging, 2,* 159–179.

Cohen, S., & Rodriguez, M. S. (1995). Pathways linking affective disturbances and physical disorders. *Health Psychology, 14,* 374–380.

Coke, M. M. (1992). Correlates of life satisfaction among elderly African Americans. *Journal of Gerontology, 47,* 316–320.

Cone, J. (1985). Black theology in American religion. *Journal of the American Academy of Religion, 53*, 755–771.

Connell, C. M., & Gibson, G. D. (1997). Racial, ethnic, and cultural differences in dementia caregiving: Review and analysis. *The Gerontologist, 37*, 355–364.

Conway, K. (1985-1986). Coping with the stress of medical problems among black and white elderly. *International Journal of Aging and Human Development, 21*, 39–48.

Cornwall, M. (1989). The determinants of religious behavior: A theoretical model and empirical test. *Social Forces, 68*, 572–592.

Cross, W. (1991). *Shades of black: Diversity in African American identity.* Philadelphia: Temple University Press.

Davis, A. A., & Rhodes, J. E. (1994). African American teenage mothers and their mothers: An analysis of supportive and problematic interactions. *Journal of Community Psychology, 22*, 12–20.

Davis, A. A., Rhodes, J. E., & Hamilton-Leaks, J. (1997). When both parents may be a source of support and problems: An analysis of pregnant and parenting female African American adolescents' relationships with their mothers and fathers. *Journal of Research on Adolescence, 7*(3), 331–348.

de Vaus, D., & McAllister, I. (1987). Gender differences in religion: A test of the structural location theory. *American Sociological Review, 52*, 472–481.

Demo, D., & Hughes, M. (1990). Socialization and racial identity among black Americans. *Social Psychology Quarterly, 43*, 364–374.

Dilworth-Anderson, P., & Burton, L. M. (1996). Rethinking family development. *Journal of Social & Personal Relationships, 13*(3), 325–334.

Dilworth-Anderson, P., Williams, S. W., & Cooper, T. (1999). The contexts of experiencing emotional distress among family caregivers to elderly African Americans. In Interventions for family caregivers [Special issue]. *Family Relations: Interdisciplinary Journal of Applied Family Studies, 48*(4), 391–396.

Dilworth-Anderson, P., Williams, I. C., & Gibson, B. E. (2002). Issues of race, ethnicity, and culture in caregiving research: A 20-year review (1980–2000). *The Gerontologist, 42*(2), 237–272.

Domino, G., & Servain, B. J. (1985–1986). Recognition of suicide lethality and attitudes toward suicide in mental health professionals. *Omega: Journal of Death and Dying, 16*, 3010–3018.

Dressler, W. W. (1993). Health in the African American community: Accounting for health inequalities. *Medical Anthropology Quarterly, 7*, 325–345.

Drevenstedt, G. L. (1998). Race and ethnic differences in the effects of religious attendance on subjective health. *Review of Religious Research, 39*, 245–263.

Du Bois, W. E. B. (1903). *The Negro church in America.* Atlanta, GA: Atlanta University Press.

Ellison, C. G. (1991a). Identification and separatism: Religious involvement and racial orientations among black Americans. *Sociological Quarterly, 32*, 477–494.

Ellison, C. G. (1991b). Religious involvement and subjective well-being. *Journal of Health and Social Behavior, 32*, 80–99.

Ellison, C. G. (1994). Religion, the life-stress paradigm, and the study of depression. In J. S. Levin (Ed.), *Religion in aging and health: Theoretical foundations and methodological frontiers* (pp. 78–121). Thousand Oaks, CA: Sage.

Ellison, C. G. (1995). Race, religious involvement and depressive symptomatology in a southeastern U.S. community. *Social Science and Medicine, 40,* 1561–1572.

Ellison, C. G. (1998). Religion, health and well-being among African Americans. *African American Research Perspectives, 4,* 94–103.

Ellison, C. G. (1999). Religious preference. In Fetzer Institute/National Institute on Aging report. *Multidimensional measurement of religiousness/spirituality for use in health research* (pp. 81–84). Kalamazoo, MI: John E. Fetzer Publications.

Ellison, C. G., & Gay, D. A. (1990). Region, religious commitment, and life satisfaction among black Americans. *Sociological Quarterly, 31,* 123–147.

Ellison, C. G., Gay, D. A., & Glass, T. A. (1989). Does religious commitment contribute to individual life satisfaction? *Social Forces, 68,* 100–123.

Ellison, C. G., Hummer, R. A., Cormier, S., & Rogers, R. G. (2000). Religious involvement and mortality risk among African American adults. *Research on Aging, 22,* 630–667.

Ellison, C. G., & Levin, J. S. (1998). The religion-health connection: Evidence, theory and future directions. *Health Education and Behavior, 25,* 700–720.

Ellison, C. G., & Sherkat, D. E. (1990). Patterns of religious mobility among black Americans. *The Sociological Quarterly, 31,* 551–568.

Ellison, C. G., & Sherkat, D. E. (1995). The "semi-involuntary institution" revisited: Regional variations in church participation among black Americans. *Social Forces, 73,* 1415–1437.

Ellison, C. G., & Sherkat, D. E. (1999). Identifying the semi-involuntary institution: A clarification. *Social Forces, 78*(2), 793–802.

Ellison, C. G., & Taylor, R. J. (1996). Turning to prayer: Religious coping among black Americans. *Review of Religious Research, 38,* 111–131.

Eng, E., & Hatch, J. (1991). Networking between agencies and black churches: The lay health advisor model. *Prevention in Human Services, 10*(1), 123–146.

Eng, E., Hatch, J., & Callan, A. (1985). Institutionalizing social support through the church and into the community. *Health Education Quarterly, 12,* 81–92.

Enright, R. D., Freedman, S., & Rique, J. (1998). The psychology of interpersonal forgiveness. In R. D. Enright & J. North (Eds.), *Exploring forgiveness* (pp. 46–62). Madison: University of Wisconsin Press.

Ferraro, K. F., & Koch, J. R. (1994). Religion and health among black and white adults: Examining social support and consolation. *Journal for the Scientific Study of Religion, 33,* 362–375.

Fetzer Institute/National Institute on Aging. (1999). *Multidimensional measurement of religiousness/spirituality for use in health research.* Kalamazoo, MI: John E. Fetzer Publications.

Fichter, J. H., & Maddox, G. L. (1965). Religion in the South, old and new. In J. C. McKinney & E. T. Thompson (Eds.), *The South in continuity and change* (pp. 359–383). Durham, NC: Duke University Press.

Frank, J. D. (1975). The faith that heals. *Johns Hopkins Medical Journal, 137,* 127–131.

Frazier, E. F. (1974). *The Negro church in America.* New York: Schocken.

Furnham, A. (1990). The Protestant work ethic and Type A behaviour: A pilot study. *Psychological Reports, 66,* 323–328.

Gant, L. M., & Ostrow, D. G. (1995). Perceptions of social support and psychological adaptation to sexually acquired HIV among white and African American men. *Social Work, 40*(2), 215–224.

Gartner, J., Larson, D. B., & Allen, G. D. (1991). Religious commitment and mental health: A review of the empirical literature. *Journal of Psychology and Theology, 19,* 6–25.

Gary, L. E. (1985). Correlates of depressive symptoms among a select population of black men. *American Journal of Public Health, 75,* 1220–1222.

Gilkes, C. T. (1980). The Black Church as a therapeutic community: Suggested area for research into the black religious experience. *Journal of the Interdenominational Theological Center, 8,* 29–44.

Glenn, N. D., Gotard, E., & Simmons, J. L. (1977). Are regional cultural differences diminishing? *Public Opinion Quarterly, 31,* 176–193.

Glock, C. Y., Ringer, B. R., & Babbie, E. E. (1967). *To comfort and to challenge.* Berkeley: University of California Press.

Gottlieb, J. F., & Olfson, M. (1987). Current referral practices of mental health care providers. *Hospital and Community Psychiatry, 38,* 1171–1181.

Grant, J. (1989). *White women's Christ and black women's Jesus: Feminist Christology and womanist response.* Atlanta, GA: Scholars Press.

Griffith, E. E. H. (1982). The impact of culture and religion on psychiatric care. *Journal of the National Medical Association, 74,* 1175–1179.

Griffith, E. E. H., Young, J. L., & Smith, D. L. (1984). An analysis of the therapeutic elements in a black church service. *Hospital and Community Psychiatry, 35,* 464–469.

Gunnoe, M. L., & Moore, K. A. (2002). Predictors of religiosity among youth aged 17–22: A longitudinal study of the National Survey of Children. *Journal for the Scientific Study of Religion, 41*(4), 613–622.

Gurin, P., Hatchett, S., & Jackson, J. S. (1989). *Hope and independence: Blacks' response to electoral and party politics.* New York: Russell Sage.

Haber, D. J. (1984). Church-based programs for black caregivers of non-institutionalized elders. *Journal of Gerontological Social Work, 7,* 43–56.

Hays, J. C., Landerman, L. R., Blazer, D. G., Koenig, H. G., Carroll, J. W., & Musick, M. A. (1998). Aging, health and the "Electronic church." *Journal of Aging and Health, 10*(4), 458–482.

Heisel, M. A., & Faulkner, A. O. (1982). Religiosity in an older black population. *The Gerontologist, 22,* 354–358.

Hill, R. B. (1999). *The strengths of African American families: Twenty-five years later* (2nd ed.). Thousand Oaks, CA: Sage.

Hong, B. A., & Wiehe, V. R. (1974). Referral patterns of the clergy. *Journal of Psychology and Theology, 2,* 291–297.

House, J. S., Landis, K. R., & Umberson, D. (1988). Social relationships and health. *Science, 241,* 540–545.

Hummer, R. A., Rogers, R. G., Nam, C. B., & Ellison, C. G. (1999). Religious involvement and U.S. adult mortality. *Demography, 36,* 273–285.

Hunsberger, B. (1985). Religion, age, life satisfaction, and perceived sources of religiousness: A study of older persons. *Journal of Gerontology, 40(5),* 615–620.

Hunt, L. L. (1998). Religious affiliation among blacks in the United States: Black Catholic status advantages revisited. *Social Science Quarterly, 79(1),* 170–192.

Hunt, L. L., & Hunt, M. O. (1999). Regional patterns of African American church attendance: Revisiting the Semi-Involuntary Thesis. *Social Forces, 78(2),* 779–791.

Hunt, L. L., & Hunt, M. O. (2001). Race, region, and religious involvement: A comparative study of whites and African Americans. *Social Forces, 80(2),* 605–631.

Idler, E. L. (1987). Religious involvement and the health of the elderly: Some hypotheses and an initial test. *Social Forces, 66,* 226–228.

Idler, E. L., & George, L. M. (1998). What sociology can help us understand about religion and mental health. In H. G. Koenig (Ed.), *Handbook of religion and mental health* (pp. 51–62). San Diego, CA: Academic Press.

Idler, E. L., & Kasl, S. V. (1992). Religion, disability, depression, and the timing of death. *American Journal of Sociology, 97,* 1052–1079.

Idler, E. L., & Kasl, S. V. (1997). Religion among disabled and nondisabled persons. I: Cross-sectional patterns in health practices, social activities, and well-being. *Journal of Gerontology: Social Sciences, 52B,* S294–S305.

Idler, E. L., Musick, M. A., Ellison, C. G., George, L. K., Krause, N., Levin, J. S., Ory, M., Pargament, K. I., Powell, L. H., Williams, D. R., & Underwood-Gordon, L. (2000). *NIA/Fetzer Measure of Religiousness and Spirituality: Conceptual background and findings from the 1998 General Social Survey.* Unpublished manuscript.

Jackson, J. J. (1983). Contemporary relationships between black families and black churches in the United States: A speculative inquiry. In W. V. D'Antonio & J. Aldous (Eds.), *Families and religion: Conflict and change in modern society* (pp. 191–220). Beverly Hills, CA: Sage.

Jackson, J. S. (1991). *Life in black America.* Newbury Park, CA: Sage.

Jackson, J. S., Chatters, L. M., & Taylor, R. J. (1993). *Aging in black America.* Newbury Park, CA: Sage.

Jackson, J. S., Tucker, M. B., & Bowman, P. J. (1982). Conceptual and methodological problems in survey research on black Americans. In W. T. Liu (Ed.), *Methodological problems in minority research.* Chicago: Pacific/Asian American Mental Health Research Center.

Jacobson, C. K., Heaton, T. B., &. Dennis, R. M. (1990). Black-white differences in religiosity: Item analysis and a formal structural test. *Sociological Analysis, 51,* 257–270.

James, S. A., Hartnett, S. A., & Kalsbeek, W. D. (1983). John Henryism and blood pressure differences among black men. *Journal of Behavioral Medicine, 6,* 259–278.

James, S. A., & Thomas, P. E. (2000). John Henryism and blood pressure in black populations: A review of the evidence. *African American Research Perspectives, 6,* 1–10.

Janevic, M. R., & Connell, C. M. (2001). Racial, ethnic, and cultural differences in the dementia caregiving experience: Recent findings. *The Gerontologist, 41*(3), 334–347.

Janzen, J. M. (1989). Health, religion, and medicine in Central and Southern African traditions. In L. E. Sullivan (Ed.), *Healing and restoring: Health and medicine in the world's religious traditions* (pp. 225–254). New York: Macmillan.

Jarvis, G. K., & Northcutt, H. C. (1987). Religion and differences in morbidity and mortality. *Social Science and Medicine, 25,* 813–824.

Kennedy, G. J., Kelman, H. R., Thomas, C., & Chen, J. (1996). The relation of religious preference and practice to depressive symptoms among 1,855 older adults. *Journal of Gerontology: Psychological Sciences, 51,* P301–308.

Kiev, A. (Ed.). (1964). *Magic, faith, and healing: Studies in primitive psychiatry today.* New York: Free Press.

King, M. B., & Hunt, R. A. (1969). Measuring the religious variable: Amended findings. *Journal for the Scientific Study of Religion, 8,* 321–323.

King, M. B., & Hunt, R. A. (1972). Measuring the religious variable: Replication. *Journal for the Scientific Study of Religion, 11,* 240–251.

Koenig, H. G. (1990). Research on religion and mental health in later life: A review and commentary. *Journal of Geriatric Psychiatry, 23,* 23–53.

Koenig, H. G. (1994). Religion and hope for the disabled elder. In J. S. Levin (Ed.), *Religion in aging and health: Theoretical foundations and methodological frontiers* (pp. 18–51). Thousand Oaks, CA: Sage.

Koenig, H. G. (1995). *Research on religion and aging: An annotated bibliography.* Westport, CT: Greenwood.

Koenig, H. G. (Ed.). (1998). *Handbook of religion and mental health.* San Diego, CA: Academic Press.

Koenig, H. G. (1999). *The healing power of faith: Science explores medicine's last great frontier.* New York: Simon & Schuster.

Koenig, H. G., Cohen, H. J., Blazer, D. G., Pieper, C., Meador, K. G., Shelp, F., Goli, V., & DiPasquale, B. (1992). Religious coping and depression among elderly, hospitalized medically ill men. *American Journal of Psychiatry, 149,* 1693–1700.

Koenig, H. G., Hays, J. C., Larson, D. B., George, L. K., Cohen, H. J., McCullough, M. E., Meador, K. G., & Blazer, D. G. (1999). Does religious attendance prolong survival?: A six-year follow-up study of 3,968 older adults. *Journal of Gerontology: Medical Sciences, 54A,* M370–M376.

Koenig, H. G., Kvale, J. N., & Ferrel, C. (1988). Religion and well-being in later life. *The Gerontologist, 28,* 18–28.

Koenig, H. G., McCullough, M. E., & Larson, D. B. (2001). *Handbook of religion and health*. New York: Oxford University Press.

Kotarba, J. A. (1983). Perceptions of death, belief systems, and the process of coping with chronic pain. *Social Science and Medicine, 17*, 683–691.

Krause, N. (1992). Stress, religiosity, and psychological well-being among older blacks. *Journal of Aging and Health, 4*, 412–439.

Krause, N. (1993). Measuring religiosity in later life. *Research on Aging, 15*, 170–197.

Krause, N. (2002a). Church-based social support and health in old age: Variations by race. *Journal of Gerontology: Social Sciences, 57B*, S332–S347.

Krause, N. (2002b). A comprehensive strategy for developing closed-ended survey items for use in studies of older adults. *Journal of Gerontology: Social Sciences, 57B*, S263–S274.

Krause, N., Chatters, L. M., Meltzer, T., & Morgan, D. L. (2000a). Negative interaction in the church: Insights from focus groups with older adults. *Review of Religious Research, 41*(4), 510–533.

Krause, N., Chatters, L. M., Meltzer, T., & Morgan, D. L. (2000b). Using focus groups to explore the nature of prayer in late life. *Journal of Aging Studies, 14*(2), 191–212.

Krause, N., & Ellison, C. G. (2003). Forgiveness by God, forgiveness of others, and psychological well-being in late life. *Journal for the Scientific Study of Religion, 42*(1), 77–93.

Krause, N., Ellison, C. G., & Wulff, K., (1998). Emotional support, negative interaction, and psychological well-being in the church. *Journal for the Scientific Study of Religion, 37*, 726–742.

Krause, N., & Tran, T. V. (1989). Stress and religious involvement among older blacks. *Journal of Gerontology: Social Sciences, 44*, S4–S13.

Kumanyika, S. K., & Charleston, J. B. (1992). Lose weight and win: A church-based weight loss program for blood pressure control among black women. *Patient Education and Counseling, 19*, 19–32.

Lannin, D. R., Matthews, H. F., Mitchell, J., Swanson, M. S., Swanson, F. H., & Edwards, M. S. (1998). Influences of socioeconomic and cultural factors on racial differences in late-stage presentation of breast cancer. *Journal of the American Medical Association, 279*, 1801–1807.

Larson, D. B., Hohmann, A. A., Kessler, L. G., Meador, K. G., Boyd, J. H., & McSherry, E. (1988). The couch and the cloth: The need for linkage. *Hospital and Community Psychiatry, 39*, 1064–1069.

Larson, D. B., Pattison, E. M., Blazer, D. G., Omran, A. R., & Kaplan, B. H. (1986). Systematic analysis of research on religion variables in four major psychiatric journals, 1978–1982. *American Journal of Psychiatry, 143*, 329–334.

Larson, D. B., Sherrill, K. A., Lyons, J. S., Craigie, F. C., Jr., Thielman, S. B., Greenwold, M. A., & Larson, S. S. (1992). Associations between dimensions of religious commitment and mental health reported in the *American Journal of Psychiatry* and *Archives of General Psychiatry*: 1978–1989. *American Journal of Psychiatry, 149*, 557–559.

Larson, R. F. (1968). The clergyman's role in the therapeutic process: Disagreement between clergymen and psychiatrists. *Psychiatry, 31,* 250–260.

LaVeist, T. A. (1994). Beyond dummy variables and sample selection: What health services researchers ought to know about race as a variable. *Health Services Research, 29,* 1–16.

Lawton, M. P., Rajagopal, D., Brody, E., & Kleban, M. H. (1992). The dynamics of caregiving for a demented elder among black and white families. *Journal of Gerontology: Social Sciences, 47,* S156–S164.

Lenski, G. (1961). *The religious factor: A sociological study of religion's impact on politics, economics, and family life.* Garden City, NY: Doubleday.

Levin, J. (2001). *God, faith, and health: Exploring the spirituality-healing connection.* New York: John Wiley.

Levin, J. (2002). Religion. In D. J. Ekerdt (Ed.), *Encyclopedia of aging.* New York: Macmillan Reference USA.

Levin, J. (in press-a). Prayer, love, and transcendence: An epidemiologic perspective. In K. W. Schaie & N. Krause (Eds.), *Religious influences on health and well-being in the elderly.* New York: Springer.

Levin, J. (in press-b). Spiritual determinants of health and healing: An epidemiologic perspective on salutogenic mechanisms. *Alternative Therapies in Health and Medicine.*

Levin, J. S. (1984). The role of the Black Church in community medicine. *Journal of the National Medical Association, 76,* 477–483.

Levin, J. S. (1986). Roles for the black pastor in preventive medicine. *Pastoral Psychology, 35,* 94–103.

Levin, J. S. (1989). Religious factors in aging, adjustment, and health: A theoretical overview. In W. M. Clements (Ed.), *Religion, aging and health: A global perspective* (pp. 133–146). Compiled by the World Health Organization. New York: Haworth.

Levin, J. S. (1994a). Investigating the epidemiologic effects of religious experience: Findings, explanations, and barriers. In J. S. Levin (Ed.), *Religion in aging and health: Theoretical foundations and methodological frontiers* (pp. 3–17). Thousand Oaks, CA: Sage.

Levin, J. S. (1994b). Religion and health: Is there an association, is it valid, and is it causal? *Social Science and Medicine, 38,* 1475–1482.

Levin, J. S. (Ed.). (1994c). *Religion in aging and health: Theoretical foundations and methodological frontiers.* Thousand Oaks, CA: Sage.

Levin, J. S. (1995). Religion. In G. L. Maddox (Ed.), *The encyclopedia of aging: A comprehensive resource in gerontology and geriatrics* (2nd ed., pp. 799–802). New York: Springer.

Levin, J. S. (1996). How religion influences morbidity and health: Reflections on natural history, salutogenesis and host resistance. *Social Science and Medicine, 43,* 849–864.

Levin, J. S. (1997). Religious research in gerontology, 1980–1994: A systematic review. *Journal of Religious Gerontology, 10*(3), 3–31.

Levin, J. S., & Chatters, L. M. (1998a). Religion, health, and psychological well-being in older adults: Findings from three national surveys. *Journal of Aging and Health, 10,* 504–531.

Levin, J. S., & Chatters, L. M. (1998b). Research on religion and mental health: An overview of empirical findings and theoretical issues. In H. G. Koenig (Ed.), *Handbook of religion and mental health* (pp. 33–50). San Diego, CA: Academic Press.

Levin, J. S., Chatters, L. M., Ellison, C. G., & Taylor, R. J. (1996). Religious involvement, health outcomes, and public health practice. *Current Issues in Public Health, 2,* 220–225.

Levin, J. S., Chatters, L. M., & Taylor, R. J. (1995). Religious effects on health status and life satisfaction among black Americans. *Journal of Gerontology: Social Sciences, 50B,* S154–S163.

Levin, J. S., Jenkins, C. D., & Rose, R. M. (1988). Religion, Type A behavior, and health. *Journal of Religion and Health, 27,* 267–278.

Levin, J. S., & Schiller, P. L. (1987). Is there a religious factor in health? *Journal of Religion and Health, 26,* 9–36.

Levin, J. S., & Taylor, R. J. (1993). Gender and age differences in religiosity among black Americans. *The Gerontologist, 33,* 16–23.

Levin, J. S., & Taylor, R. J. (1997). Age differences in patterns and correlates of the frequency of prayer. *The Gerontologist, 37*(1), 75–88.

Levin, J. S., & Taylor, R. J. (1998). Panel analyses of religious involvement in African Americans: Contemporaneous vs. longitudinal effects. *Journal for the Scientific Study of Religion, 37,* 695–709.

Levin, J. S., Taylor, R. J., & Chatters, L. M. (1994). Race and gender differences in religiosity among older adults: Findings from four national surveys. *Journal of Gerontology: Social Sciences, 49,* S137–S145.

Levin, J. S., Taylor, R. J., & Chatters, L. M. (1995). A multidimensional measure of religious involvement for African Americans. *The Sociological Quarterly, 36,* 157–173.

Levin, J. S., & Tobin, S. S. (1995). Religion and psychological well-being. In M. A. Kimble, S. H. McFadden, J. W. Ellor, & J. J. Seeber (Eds.), *Aging, spirituality, and religion: A handbook* (pp. 30–46). Minneapolis, MN: Fortress Press.

Levin, J. S., & Vanderpool, H. Y. (1987). Is frequent religious attendance *really* conducive to better health?: Toward an epidemiology of religion. *Social Science and Medicine, 24,* 589–600.

Levin, J. S., & Vanderpool, H. Y. (1989). Is religion therapeutically significant for hypertension? *Social Science and Medicine, 29,* 69–78.

Levin, J. S., & Vanderpool, H. Y. (1992). Religious factors in physical health and the prevention of illness. In K. I. Pargament, K. I. Maton, & R. E. Hess (Eds.), *Religion and prevention in mental health: Research, vision, and action* (pp. 83–103). New York: Haworth.

Lincoln, C. E. (1974a). *The Black Church since Frazier.* NY: Schocken.

Lincoln, C. E. (Ed.). (1974b). *The black experience in religion.* Garden City, NY: Anchor.

Lincoln, C. E., & Mamiya, L. H. (1990). *The Black Church in the African American experience.* Durham, NC: Duke University Press.

Lincoln, K. D. (2000). Social support, negative social interactions, and psychological well-being. *Social Service Review, 74*(2), 231–252.

Lincoln, K. D., Chatters, L. M., & Taylor, R. J. (in press). Psychological distress among black and white Americans: Differential effects of social support, negative interaction and personal control. *Journal of Health and Social Behavior.*

Lincoln, K. D., Taylor, R. J., & Chatters, L. M. (in press). Correlates of emotional support and negative interaction among older black Americans. *Journal of Gerontology: Social Sciences.*

Maier, S. F., Watkins, L. R., & Fleshner, M. (1994). Psychoneuroimmunology: The interface between behavior, brain, and immunity. *American Psychologist, 49,* 1004–1017.

Mansfield, C. J., Mitchell, J., & King, D. E. (2002). The doctor as God's mechanic? Beliefs in the southeastern United States. *Social Science and Medicine, 54,* 339–409.

Markides, K. S. (1983a). Aging, religiosity, and adjustment: A longitudinal analysis. *Journal of Gerontology, 38,* 621–625.

Markides, K. S. (1983b). Minority aging. In M. W. Riley, B. B. Hess, & K. Bond (Eds.), *Aging in society: Selected reviews of recent research* (pp. 115–137). Hillsdale, NJ: Lawrence Erlbaum.

Markides, K. S., & Machalek, R. (1984). Selective survival, aging, and society. *Archives of Gerontology and Geriatrics, 3,* 207–222.

Martin, P. P., Younge, S., & Smith, A. (2003). Searching for a balm in Gilead: The HIV/AIDS epidemic and the African-American church. *African American Research Perspectives, 9*(1), 70–78.

Marx, G. (1967). Religion: Opiate or inspiration of civil rights militancy among Negroes. *American Sociological Review, 32,* 64–72.

Maton, K. I. (1989). Community settings as buffers of life stress? Highly supportive churches, mutual help groups, and senior centers. *American Journal of Community Psychology, 17*(2), 203–232.

Maton, K. I., & Pargament, K. I. (1987). The roles of religion in prevention and promotion. *Prevention in Human Services, 6,* 161–205.

Matthews, D. A., McCullough, M. E., Larson, D. B., Koenig, H. G., Swyers, J. P., & Milano, M. G. (1998). Religious commitment and health status. *Archives of Family Medicine, 7,* 118–124.

Mattis, J. S. (2000). African American women's definitions of spirituality and religiosity. In African American culture and identity: Research directions for the new millennium [Special issue]. *Journal of Black Psychology, 26*(1), 101–122.

Mattis, J. S. (2002). The role of religion and spirituality in the coping experience of African American women: A qualitative analysis. *Psychology of Women Quarterly, 26,* 308–320.

Mattis, J. S., Beckham, W., Saunders, B., Williams, J., McAllister, D., Myers, V., Knight, D., Rencher, D., & Dixon, C. (in press). Who will volunteer? Religiosity, everyday racism and social participation among African American men. *Journal of Adult Development*.

Mattis, J. S., Eubanks, S., Zapata, A., Belkin, M., Grayman, N., Mitchell, N., & Cooper, S. (in press). Factors influencing religious non-involvement among African American men. *Review of Religious Research*.

Mattis, J. S., Jagers, R., Hatcher, C., Lawhon, G., Murphy, E., & Murray, Y. (2000). Religiosity, communalism and volunteerism among African American men: An exploratory analysis. *Journal of Community Psychology, 28,* 391–406.

Mattis, J. S., Murray, Y. F., Hatcher, C. A., Hearn, K. D., Lawhon, G. D., Murphy, E. J., & Washington, T. A. (2001). Religiosity, spirituality, and the subjective quality of African American men's friendships: An exploratory study. *Journal of Adult Development, 8*(4), 221–230.

Mattis, J. S., Taylor, R. J., & Chatters, L. M. (2001). Are they truly not religious? A multi-method analysis of the attitudes of religiously noninvolved African American women. *African American Research Perspectives, 7*(1), 90–103.

Mattlin, J. A., Wethington, E., & Kessler, R. C. (1990). Situational determinants of coping and coping effectiveness. *Journal of Health and Social Behavior, 31,* 103–122.

Maugans, T. A., & Wadland, W. C. (1991). Religion and family medicine. A survey of physicians and patients. *Journal of Family Practice, 32,* 210–213.

McAdoo, H. P. (1981). *Black families.* Beverly Hills, CA: Sage.

McAdoo, H., & Crawford, V. (1990). The Black Church and family support programs. *Prevention and Human Services, 9,* 193–203.

McAuley, W. J., Pecchioni, L., & Grant, J. A. (2000). Personal accounts of the role of God in health and illness among older rural African American and White residents. *Journal of Cross-Cultural Gerontology, 15,* 13–35.

McCullough, M. E., Hoyt, W. T., Larson, D. B., Koenig, H. G., & Thoresen, C. (2000). Religious involvement and mortality: A meta-analytic review. *Health Psychology, 19,* 211–222.

McCullough, M. E., Pargament, K. I., & Thoresen, C. E. (2000). *Forgiveness.* New York: Guilford.

McFadden, S. H. (1996a). Religion and spirituality. In J. E. Birren (Ed.), *Encyclopedia of gerontology: Age, aging, and the aged* (Vol. 2, pp. 387–397). San Diego, CA: Academic Press.

McFadden, S. H. (1996b). Religion, spirituality, and aging. In J. E. Birren & K. W. Schaie (Eds.), *Handbook of the psychology of aging* (4th ed., pp. 162–177). San Diego, CA: Academic Press.

McIntosh, D., & Spilka, B. (1990). Religion and physical health: The role of personal faith and control beliefs. *Research in the Social Scientific Study of Religion, 2,* 167–194.

McKay, N. Y. (1989). Nineteenth-century black women's spiritual autobiographies: Religious faith and self-empowerment. In Personal Narratives Group (Eds.),

Interpreting women's lives: Feminist theory and personal narrative (pp. 139–154). Bloomington: Indiana University Press.

McRae, M. B., Carey, P. M., & Anderson-Scott, R. (1998). Black churches as therapeutic systems: A group process perspective. *Health Education and Behavior, 25*(6), 778–789.

Meylink, W. D., & Gorsuch, R. L. (1988). Relationship between clergy and psychologists: The empirical data. *Journal of Psychology and Christianity, 7,* 56–72.

Miltiades, H. B., & Pruchno, R. (2002). The effect of religious coping on caregiving appraisals of mothers of adults with developmental disabilities. *The Gerontologist, 42*(1), 82–91.

Mindel, C. H., & Vaughan, E. (1978). A multidimensional approach to religiosity and disengagement. *Journal of Gerontology, 33,* 103–108.

Moberg, D. O. (1965). Religiosity in old age. *The Gerontologist, 5*(2), 78–87.

Moberg, D. O. (Ed.). (1971). *Spiritual well-being: Background and issues.* Washington, DC: White House Conference on Aging.

Moberg, D. O. (1990). Religion and aging. In K. F. Ferraro (Ed.), *Gerontology: Perspectives and issues* (pp. 179–205). New York: Springer.

Mobley, M. F., Katz, E. K., & Elkins, R. L. (1985). Academic psychiatry and the clergy: An analysis of ministerial referrals. *Hospital and Community Psychiatry, 36,* 79–81.

Mollica, R. R., Streets, F. J., Boscarino, J., & Redlich, F. C. (1986). A community study of formal pastoral counseling activities of the clergy. *American Journal of Psychiatry, 14,* 323–328.

Mueller, C. W., & Johnson, W. T. (1975). Socioeconomic status and religious participation. *American Sociological Review, 40,* 785–800.

Musick, M., Wilson, J., & Bynum, W. (2000). Race and formal volunteering: The differential effects of class and religion. *Social Forces, 78,* 1539–1571.

Musick, M. A. (1996). Religion and subjective health among black and white elders. *Journal of Health and Social Behavior, 37,* 221–237.

Musick, M. A., Koenig, H. G., Hays, J. C., & Cohen, H. J. (1998). Religious activity and depression among community-dwelling elderly persons with cancer: The moderating effect of race. *Journal of Gerontology: Social Sciences, 53B,* S218–S227.

Myers, L. J. (1987). The deep structure of culture: The relevance of traditional African culture in contemporary times. *Journal of Black Studies, 18,* 72–85.

Myers, S. S., & Benson, H. (1992). Psychological factors in healing: A new perspective on an old debate. *Behavioral Medicine, 18,* 5–11.

Navaie-Waliser, M., Feldman, P. H., Gould, D. A., Levine, C., Kuerbis, A. N., & Donelan, K. (2001). The experiences and challenges of informal caregivers: Common themes and differences among whites, blacks and Hispanics. *The Gerontologist, 41*(6), 733–741.

Neighbors, H. W. (1985). Seeking professional help for personal problems: Black Americans' use of health and mental health services. *Community Mental Health Journal, 21,* 156–166.

Neighbors, H. W. (1991). Mental health. In J. S. Jackson (Ed.), *Life in black America* (pp. 221–237). Newbury Park, CA: Sage.

Neighbors, H. W., Jackson, J. S., Bowman, P. J., & Gurin, G. (1983). Stress, coping, and black mental health: Preliminary findings from a national study. *Prevention in Human Services, 2,* 5–29.

Neighbors, H. W., Musick, M. A., & Williams, D. R. (1998). The African American minister: Bridge or barrier to mental health care? *Health Education and Behavior, 25,* 759–777.

Nelsen, H. M. (1988). Unchurched black Americans: Patterns of religiosity and affiliation. *Review of Religious Research, 29*(4), 398–412.

Nelsen, H. M., & Nelsen, A. K. (1975). *Black Church in the sixties.* Lexington: University Press of Kentucky.

Nelsen, H. M., Yokley, R. L., & Nelsen, A. K. (1971). *The Black Church in America.* New York: Basic Books.

Nobles, W. (1991). African philosophy: Foundations of black psychology. In R. L. Jones (Ed.), *Black psychology* (3rd ed., pp. 47–63). Berkeley, CA: Cobb and Henry.

Nooney, J., & Woodrum, E. (2002). Religious coping and church-based social support as predictors of mental health outcomes: Testing a conceptual model. *Journal for the Scientific Study of Religion, 41,* 359–368.

Olson, L. M., Reis, J., Murphy, L., & Gem, J. H. (1988). The religious community as a partner in health care. *Journal of Community Health, 13,* 249–257.

Ormel, J., Stewart, R., & Sanderman, R. (1989). Personality as modifier of the life change–distress relationship: A longitudinal modeling approach. *Social Psychiatry and Psychiatric Epidemiology, 24,* 187–195.

Osler, W. (1910, June 18). The faith that heals. *British Medical Journal,* 1470–1472.

Oyama, O., & Koenig, H. G. (1998). Religious beliefs and practices in family medicine. *Archives of Family Medicine, 7,* 431–435.

Packer, S. (1997). Letter to the editor. *Journal of Gerontology: Psychological Sciences, 52B,* P156.

Pargament, K. I. (1997). *The psychology of religion and coping: Theory, research, practice.* New York: Guilford.

Pargament, K. I., & Hahn, J. (1986). God and the just world: Causal and coping attributions to God in health situations. *Journal for the Scientific Study of Religion, 25,* 193–207.

Pargament, K. I., Silverman, W. H., Johnson, S., Echemendia, R., & Snyder, S. (1983). The psychosocial climate of religious congregations. *American Journal of Community Psychology, 11,* 351–381.

Patillo-McCoy, M. (1998). Church culture as a strategy of action in the black community. *American Sociological Review, 63,* 767–784.

Pattison, E. M. (1978). Psychiatry and religion circa 1978: Analysis of a decade, Part II. *Pastoral Psychology, 27,* 119–141.

Perry, E. J. (1981). The Memphis church-based high blood pressure program. *Urban Health, 1,* 69–70.

Petersen, L. R., & Roy, A. (1985). Religiosity, anxiety, and meaning and purpose: Religion's consequences for psychological well-being. *Review of Religious Research, 27,* 49–62.

Picot, S. J., Debanne, S. M., Namazi, K. H., & Wykle, M. L. (1997). Religiosity and perceived rewards of black and white caregivers. *The Gerontologist, 37,* 89–101.

Pollner, M. (1989). Divine relations, social relations, and well-being. *Journal of Health and Social Behavior, 30,* 92–104.

Poloma, M. M., & Gallup, G. H. (1991). *Varieties of prayer.* Philadelphia: Trinity Press International.

Poloma, M. M., & Pendleton, B. F. (1990). Religious domains and general well-being. *Social Indicators Research, 22,* 255–276.

Potts, R. (1991). Spirits in the bottle: Spirituality and alcoholism treatment in African American communities. *Journal of Training and Practice in Professional Psychology, 5*(1), 53–64.

Quarles, B. (1964). *The Negro in the making of America.* New York: Collier Books.

Raboteau, A. J. (1986). The Afro-American traditions. In R. L. Numbers & D. W. Amundsen (Eds.), *Caring and curing: Healing and medicine in the Western religious traditions* (pp. 539–562). New York: Macmillan.

Reichlin, S. (1993). Neuroendocrine-immune interactions. *New England Journal of Medicine, 329,* 1246–1253.

Report to the President's Commission on Mental Health (Vol. 1). (1978). Washington, DC: Government Printing Office.

Rhodes, J. E., Ebert, L., & Meyers, A. B. (1994). Social support, relationship problems and the psychological functioning of young African American mothers. *Journal of Social and Personal Relationships, 11,* 587–599.

Roof, W. C. (1978). Social correlates of religious involvement. *Annual Review of the Social Sciences of Religion, 2,* 53–70.

Ross, C. E. (1990). Religion and psychological distress. *Journal for the Scientific Study of Religion, 29,* 236–245.

Sanua, V. D. (1969). Religion, mental health, and personality: A review of empirical studies. *American Journal of Psychiatry, 125,* 1203–1213.

Schiller, P. L., & Levin, J. S. (1988). Is there a religious factor in health care utilization?: A review. *Social Science and Medicine, 27,* 1369–1379.

Scobie, E. D., & Scobie, G. E. (1998). Damaging events: The perceived need for forgiveness. *Journal for the Theory of Social Behavior, 28,* 373–401.

Segall, M., & Wykle, M. (1988–1989). The black family's experience with dementia. *Journal of Applied Social Sciences, 13,* 170–191.

Sellers, R. M., Smith, M. A., Shelton, J. N., Rowley, S. A. J., & Chavous, T. M. (1998). Multidimensional model of racial identity: A reconceptualization of African American racial identity. *Personality & Social Psychology Review, 2*(1), 18–39.

Shahabi, L., Powell, L. H., Musick, M. A., Pargament, K. I., Thoresen, C. E., Williams, D., Underwood, L., & Ory, M. A. (2002). Correlates of self-perceptions of spirituality in American adults. *Annuals of Behavioral Medicine, 24*(1), 59–68.

Sherkat, D. E. (1998). Extending the semi-involuntary institution: Regional differences and social constraints on private religious consumption among African Americans. *Journal for the Scientific Study of Religion, 37*(3), 383–396.

Sherkat, D. E. (2002). African-American religious affiliation in the late 20th century: Cohort variations and patterns of switching, 1973–1998. *Journal for the Scientific Study of Religion, 41*(3), 485–493.

Sherkat, D. E., & Ellison, C. G. (1991). The politics of black religious change: Disaffiliation from black mainline denominations. *Social Forces, 70*(2), 431–454.

Sherrill, K. A., Larson, D. B., & Greenwold, M. (1993). Is religion taboo in gerontology?: Systematic review of research on religion in three major gerontology journals, 1985–1991. *American Journal of Geriatric Psychiatry, 1,* 109–117.

Smith, A. (1981). Religion and mental health among blacks. *Journal of Religion and Health, 20,* 264–287.

Smith, C., Denton, M., Faris, R., & Regnerus, M. (2002). Mapping American adolescent religious participation. *Journal for the Scientific Study of Religion, 41,* 597–612.

Snyder, C. R. (2000). The past and possible futures of hope. *Journal of Social and Clinical Psychology, 19,* 11–28.

Spector, R. E. (1979). *Cultural diversity in health and illness.* New York: Appleton-Century-Crofts.

Srole, L., & Langner, T. (1962). Religious origin. In L. Srole, T. S. Langner, S. T. Michael, M. K. Opler, & T. A. C. Rennie (Eds.), *Mental health in the metropolis: The Midtown Manhattan Study* (pp. 300–324). New York: McGraw-Hill.

St. George, A., & McNamara, P. H. (1984). Religion, race and psychological well-being. *Journal for the Scientific Study of Religion, 23,* 351–363.

Stack, C. (1974). *All our kin.* New York: Harper & Row.

Staples, R., & Johnson, L. B. (1993). *Black families at the crossroads: Challenges and prospects.* San Francisco: Jossey-Bass.

Stark, R. (1971). Psychopathology and religious commitment. *Review of Religious Research, 12,* 165–176.

Steffen, P. R., Hinderliter, A. L., Blumenthal, J. A., & Sherwood, A. (2001). Religious coping, ethnicity, and ambulatory blood pressure. *Psychosomatic Medicine* [Special issue], *63*(4), 523–530.

Steinitz, L. Y. (1980). Religiosity, well-being, and Weltanschauung among the elderly. *Journal for the Scientific Study of Religion, 19,* 60–67.

Sternberg, E. M. (2000). *The balance within: The science connecting health and emotions.* New York: Freeman.

Sterritt, P., & Pokorny, M. (1998). African American caregiving for a relative with Alzheimer's disease. *Geriatric Nursing, 19,* 127–134.

Strawbridge, W. J., Cohen, R. D., Shema, S. J., & Kaplan, G. A. (1997). Frequent attendance at religious services and mortality over 28 years. *American Journal of Public Health, 87,* 957–961.

Strawbridge, W. J., Shema, S. J., Cohen, R. D., Roberts, R. E., & Kaplan, G. A. (1998). Religiosity buffers effects of some stressors on depression but exacerbates others. *Journal of Gerontology: Social Sciences, 53B,* S118–S126.

Stump, R. W. (1987). Regional contrasts within black Protestantism: A research note. *Social Forces, 66,* 143–151.

Summerlin, F. A. (Compiler). (1980). *Religion and mental health: A bibliography* (National Institute of Mental Health; DHHS Publication No. [ADM] 80–964). Washington, DC: Government Printing Office.

Taylor, R. J. (1986). Religious participation among elderly blacks. *The Gerontologist, 26,* 630–636.

Taylor, R. J. (1988a). Correlates of religious non-involvement among black Americans. *Review of Religious Research, 30,* 126–139.

Taylor, R. J. (1988b). Structural determinants of religious participation among black Americans. *Review of Religious Research, 30,*114–125.

Taylor, R. J. (1993). Religion and religious observances. In J. S. Jackson, L. M. Chatters, & R. J. Taylor (Eds.), *Aging in black America* (pp. 101–123). Newbury Park, CA: Sage.

Taylor, R. J., & Chatters, L. M. (1986a). Church-based informal support among elderly blacks. *The Gerontologist, 26,* 637–642.

Taylor, R. J., & Chatters, L. M. (1986b). Patterns of informal support to elderly black adults: Family, friends, and church members. *Social Work, 31,* 432–438.

Taylor, R. J., & Chatters, L. M. (1988). Church members as a source of informal social support. *Review of Religious Research, 30,* 193–203.

Taylor, R. J., & Chatters, L. M. (1991a). Nonorganizational religious participation among elderly black adults. *Journal of Gerontology: Social Sciences, 46,* S103–S111.

Taylor, R. J., & Chatters, L. M. (1991b). Religious life of black Americans. In J. S. Jackson (Ed.), *Life in black America* (pp. 105–123). Newbury Park, CA: Sage.

Taylor, R. J., Chatters, L. M., & Celious, A. K. (2003). Extended family households among black Americans. *African American Research Perspectives, 9*(1), 133–151.

Taylor, R. J., Chatters, L. M., & Jackson, J. S. (1997). Changes over time in support network involvement among black Americans. In R. J. Taylor, J. S. Jackson, & L. M. Chatters (Eds.), *Family life in black America* (pp. 293–316). Thousand Oaks, CA: Sage.

Taylor, R. J., Chatters, L. M., Jayakody, R., & Levin, J. S. (1996). Black and white differences in religious participation: A multi-sample comparison. *Journal for the Scientific Study of Religion, 35,* 403–410.

Taylor, R. J., Ellison, C. G., Chatters, L. M., Levin, J. S., & Lincoln, K. D. (2000). Mental health services in faith communities: The role of clergy in black churches. *Social Work, 45*(1), 73–87.

Taylor, R. J., Jackson, J. S., & Chatters, L. M. (1997). *Family life in black America.* Thousand Oaks, CA: Sage.

Taylor, R. J., Luckey, I., & Smith, J. M. (1990). Delivering services in black churches. In D. S. Richmond Garland & D. L. Pancoast (Eds.), *The church's ministry with families: A practical guide* (pp. 194–209). Dallas: Word Publishing.

Taylor, R. J., Mattis, J. S., & Chatters, L. M. (1999). Subjective religiosity among African Americans: A synthesis of findings from five national samples. *Journal of Black Psychology, 25*(4), 524–543.

Taylor, R. J., & Sellers, S. L. (1997). Informal ties and employment among black Americans. In R. J. Taylor, J. S. Jackson, & L. M. Chatters (Eds.), *Family life in black America* (pp. 146–156). Thousand Oaks, CA: Sage.

Taylor, R. J., Thornton, M. C., & Chatters, L. M. (1987). Black Americans' perceptions of the socio-historical role of the church. *Journal of Black Studies, 18,* 123–138.

Thomas, S. B., Quinn, S. C., Billingsley, A., & Caldwell, C. H. (1994). The characteristics of northern black churches with community health outreach programs. *American Journal of Public Health, 84,* 575–579.

Thornton, M., Chatters, L. M., Taylor, R. J., & Allen, W. (1990). Sociodemographic and environmental correlates of racial socialization by black parents. *Child Development, 61,* 401–409.

Thornton, M., & Taylor, R. J. (1988). Intergroup attitudes: Black American perceptions of Asian Americans. *Ethnic and Racial Studies, 11,* 474–488.

Thornton, M., Taylor, R. J., & Brown, T. N. (1999). Correlates of racial label use among Americans of African descent: Colored, Negro, black and African American. *Race and Society, 2*(2), 149–164.

Thornton, M. C., Tran, T. V., & Taylor, R. J. (1997). Multiple dimensions of racial group identification among adult black Americans. *Journal of Black Psychology, 23*(3), 293–309.

Turner, R. P., Lukoff, D., Barnhouse, R. T., & Lu, F. G. (1995). Religious or spiritual problem: A culturally sensitive diagnostic category in the *DSM-IV. Journal of Nervous and Mental Disease, 183,* 435–444.

Van Ness, P. H., & Kasl, S. V. (2003). Religion and cognitive dysfunction in an elderly cohort. *Journal of Gerontology: Social Sciences, 58B,* S21–S29.

Veroff, J., Douvan, E., & Kulka, R. (1981). *The inner American.* New York: Basic Books.

Virkler, H. A. (1979). Counseling demands, procedures, and preparation of parish ministers: A descriptive study. *Journal of Psychology & Theology, 7*(4), 271–280.

Wach, J. (1944). *Sociology of religion.* Chicago: University of Chicago Press.

Wallace, J. M., & Forman, T. A. (1998). Religion's role in promoting health and reducing risk among American youth. In Public health and health education in faith communities [Special issue]. *Health Education and Behavior, 25*(6), 721–741.

Wallace, J. M., Jr., & Williams, D. R. (1998). Religion and adolescent health-compromising behavior. In J. Schulenberg, J. L. Maggs, & K. Hurrelmann (Eds.),

Health risks and developmental transitions during adolescence (pp. 444–468). Cambridge, UK: Cambridge University Press.

Walls, C. T., & Zarit, S. H. (1991). Informal support from black churches and the well-being of elderly blacks. *The Gerontologist, 31,* 490–495.

Welch, M. R. (1978). The unchurched: Blacks' religious non-affiliates. *Journal for the Scientific Study of Religion, 17,* 289–293.

Wheeler, E. A., Ampadu, L. M., & Wangari, E. (2002). Lifespan development revisited: African-centered spirituality throughout the life cycle. *Journal of Adult Development, 9*(1), 71–78.

White, T. M., Townsend, A. L., & Stephens, M. A. (2000). Comparisons of African American and white women in the parent care role. *The Gerontologist, 40,* 718–728.

Williams, D. R. (1994). The measurement of religion in epidemiologic studies: Problems and prospects. In J. S. Levin (Ed.), *Religion in aging and health: Theoretical foundations and methodological frontiers* (pp. 125–148). Thousand Oaks, CA: Sage.

Winett, R. A., Major, J. S., & Stewart, G. (1979). Mental health treatment and referral practices of clergy and physician caregivers. *Journal of Community Psychology, 7,* 318–323.

Witter, R. A., Stock, W. A., Okun, M. A., & Haring, M. J. (1985). Religion and subjective well-being in adulthood: A quantitative synthesis. *Review of Religious Research, 26,* 332–342.

Wood, J. B., & Parham, I. A. (1990). Coping with perceived burden: Ethnic and cultural issues in Alzheimer's family caregiving. *Journal of Applied Gerontology, 9,* 325–329.

Woodberry, R. D., & Smith, C. S. (1998). Fundamentalism et al: Conservative Protestants in America. *Annual Review of Sociology, 24,* 25–56.

Wuthnow, R., Christiano, K., & Kuzlowski, J. (1980). Religion and bereavement: A conceptual framework. *Journal for the Scientific Study of Religion, 19,* 408–422.

Young, G., & Dowling, W. (1987). Dimensions of religiosity in old age: Accounting for variation in types of participation. *Journal of Gerontology, 42,* 376–380.

Zinnbauer, B. I., Pargament, K. I., Cowell, B., Rye, M., & Scott, A. B. (1997). Religion and spirituality: Unfuzzying the fuzzy. *Journal for the Scientific Study of Religion, 36,* 549–564.

Author Index

Subject Index

About the Authors

Robert Joseph Taylor, PhD, MSW, is the Sheila Feld Collegiate Professor of Social Work and the Associate Dean for Social Work Research at the University of Michigan. He is a Faculty Associate with the Program for Research on Black Americans at the Institute for Social Research. He is also a Faculty Associate with the Center for Afro-American and African Studies and affiliated with the Center for Research on Race, Religion and Health at the Institute for Social Research. He is currently on the editorial board of the *Journal of Marriage and the Family*. Professor Taylor has published extensively in two major areas (informal social support networks and religious participation). His work on informal networks investigates the role of family, friends, and church members as sources of social support to adult and elderly black Americans. His work in the Sociology of Religion investigates the demographic correlates of religious participation among black adults and black elderly. He has been Principal Investigator on several grants from the National Institute on Aging that examine the role of religion in the lives of black and white elderly adults. He has been Co-Principal Investigator with James Jackson on several grants from the National Institute of Mental Health on the correlates of mental health and mental illness among black Americans. He is Co-Principal Investigator for the National Institute on Aging grant, "Church-based Assistance and Older Blacks." He has edited two books, *Family Life in Black America* (1997) and *Aging in Black America* (1993), with James S. Jackson and Linda M. Chatters.

Linda M. Chatters, PhD, holds a joint position as Associate Professor in the Department of Health Behavior & Health Education at the School of Public Health and the School of Social Work. She is also a Faculty Associate with the Program for Research on Black Americans, Institute for Social Research at the University of Michigan. The major focus of Dr. Chatters' research is the study of adult development and aging as it relates to the mental and physical health status and social functioning of older persons in a variety of social contexts (i.e., the family, church, and community). A particular emphasis of this work has been the investigation of various dimensions of religious involvement among the African American population. She is also interested in assessing the independent contributions of relevant religious, personal, and social status factors on well-being among elderly and non-elderly populations. She is Principal Investigator for the National Institute on Aging grant, "Church-based Assistance and Older Blacks." Dr. Chatters is the author of "Religion and health: Public health research and practice" which appeared in the *Annual Review of Public Health* (2000).

Jeff Levin, PhD, MPH, an epidemiologist and former medical school professor, is the pioneering scientist whose research beginning in the 1980s helped to create the field of religion and health. He left a successful academic career in 1997 to devote his full-time efforts to writing, research, and consulting. He was the first scientist to systematically review and critique the empirical literature on the health effects of religious involvement. His research has been funded by several NIH grants, and he also has received funding from private sources, including the American Medical Association and the Institute of Noetic Sciences.

Dr. Levin has served as chairman of the NIH Working Group on Quantitative Methods in Alternative Medicine, as president of the International Society for the Study of Subtle Energies and Energy Medicine, and as an editorial board member of several peer-reviewed journals, including the *Journal of Gerontology: Social Sciences, The Gerontologist, Journal of Religious Gerontology,* and *Alternative Therapies in Health and Medicine.* He has authored more than 130 scholarly publications and given more than 120 conference presentations and invited lectures and addresses, mostly on the role of religion in physical and mental health and aging. He has published four other books: *God, Faith, and Health: Exploring the Spirituality–Healing Connection; Religion in Aging and Health: Theoretical Foundations and Methodological Frontiers; Faith Matters: A Festschrift in Honor of Dr. David B. Larson;* and *Essentials of Complementary and Alternative Medicine.* He is a Fellow of the Gerontological Society of America and lives in rural Kansas.